Czechoslovakia Behind the Curtain

Janet –

I hope that you enjoy this romp through the past!

I very much enjoyed my years in CZ.

Let me know what you think!

Regards,

Tom

Czechoslovakia Behind the Curtain

Life, Work and Culture in the Communist Era

THOMAS K. MURPHY

McFarland & Company, Inc., Publishers
Jefferson, North Carolina

LIBRARY OF CONGRESS CATALOGUING-IN-PUBLICATION DATA

Names: Murphy, Thomas K., 1961– author.
Title: Czechoslovakia behind the curtain : life, work and culture in the Communist Era / Thomas K. Murphy.
Description: Jefferson, North Carolina : McFarland & Company, Inc., Publishers, 2018 | Includes bibliographical references and index.
Identifiers: LCCN 2018023803 | ISBN 9781476672809 (softcover : acid free paper) ♾
Subjects: LCSH: Czechoslovakia—Civilization—20th century. | Czechoslovakia—Social conditions—1945–1992. | Czechoslovakia—Politics and government—1945–1992. | Czechoslovaks—Attitudes.
Classification: LCC DB2218 .M87 2018 | DDC 943.704—dc23
LC record available at https://lccn.loc.gov/2018023803

BRITISH LIBRARY CATALOGUING DATA ARE AVAILABLE

ISBN (print) 978-1-4766-7280-9
ISBN (ebook) 978-1-4766-3177-6

Printed in the United States of America

McFarland & Company, Inc., Publishers
Box 611, Jefferson, North Carolina 28640
www.mcfarlandpub.com

To Eileen

Acknowledgments

I owe a debt of gratitude to many people who helped me see this project through many years of research. In particular, I thank Ivana Takáčová, Gae Holladay, Petra Jordan, Elizabeth Ryan, Tomáš Koziak, David Reichardt, Jana Kunická, and Zora Vidovencová for their invaluable assistance and support.

Contents

Preface

The goal of this project was to get beneath the ideology of the Cold War and to understand the day-to-day life that ordinary people experienced in Communist Czechoslovakia. That is important because the reality of the mundane often differed considerably from the pronouncements of the party and from the general popular understanding of communism in the West. To get at this data, I performed about 100 interviews, mostly with Czechs and Slovaks, on subjects ranging from religion, travel and the events of the Prague Spring to shopping and entertainment.

Interviews were conducted face to face throughout Europe as well as over the phone. Secondary source research was performed at the Library of Congress in Washington, D.C., and at the library of the University of Maryland.

This project joins a considerable body of contemporary research that examines the Czech and Slovak lands during the communist period, including Paula Bren's *The Green Grocer and His TV*, Mary Heimann's *Czechoslovakia: The State That Failed*, Miroslav Vaněk's *Velvet Revolutions: An Oral History of Czech Society*, Kevin McDermott's *Communist Czechoslovakia, 1945–89: A Political and Social History*, James Krapfl's *Revolution with a Human Face*, Padraic Kenney's *A Carnival of Revolution: Central Europe 1989*, Bradley Adams' *The Struggle for the Soul of the Nation*, and the pioneering examinations of popular culture under East German and Yugoslav variations of communism by Anna Funder's *Stasiland*, Jan Hensel's *Zonenkinder*, Slavenka Drakulić's *Café Europa: Life After Communism* and *How We Survived Communism and Even Laughed.*

While previous research has tended to focus on events such as the

Prague Spring of 1968, the Velvet Revolution, consumerism, media, and life since 1989, my research is intended to concentrate on the lacunae of every day events *within* the communist period over time. Politics and ideology are secondary to the business of ordinary life, adaptation and survival.

Introduction

In the fall of 1997, several months after defending my doctoral dissertation in history, I left the United States to teach at Prešov University, Slovakia, as a scholar sponsored by the Civic Education Project. CEP was a program of the Open Society Foundation, one of many organizations founded by well known philanthropist George Soros. Czechoslovakia no longer existed in 1997, having broken in half during the Velvet Revolution of 1993. The new Slovakia still bore deep evidence of four decades of communist rule by the time I arrived. Housing and infrastructure were often worse for wear, and the political class was sorting itself out—not least of which was Vladimír Mečiar, who had used nationalist rhetoric and appeals to villagers and pensioners to bolster his increasingly authoritarian regime.

Politics has always interested me. I grew up in Washington, D.C., and worked during and after college on numerous state and national campaigns as well as done staff and intern work for several members of the House of Representatives and a U.S. senator. Having grown up during the latter part of the Cold War, I was exposed to a steady diet of American imagery about the nature of the singular communist adversary and the character and values that comprised The Other. In the Cold War views of such influential persons as George Kennan, Henry Kissinger, and Aleksandr Solzhenitsyn, and despite occasional shades of emphasis and intent, *Communism* as such was presented as a monolithic phenomenon, inspired by Marxist–Leninist ideology, and presented in a more or less uniform manner throughout the disparate areas of the world where it proliferated. Doctrines of *political realism* created an amoral mindset by which religious, ideological, or cultural differences—even leaders—mattered little in understanding world order. Thus, Soviet Communism, Cuban Communism, Chinese Communism, and the regimes of the various Warsaw Pact members were, implicitly, more or less the same in operation and effect. This interpretation of uniformity of behavior, leaving no room for regional, cultural, political, or historical difference, made little sense to me as a student. My fundamental political assumption was that most American conceptions of communism (or, rather, anti-communism) were designed for domestic consumption, serving the interests of the American political class and interparty competition in domestic and foreign affairs.

A monolithic Cold War image of communism made good political sense: it contrasted good (us) with evil (them), was not overly nuanced and therefore easy to understand, and could, when necessary, be used against both *domestic* and foreign political enemies. Domestic use of anti-communism was amply demonstrated during the McCarthy Red Scare years, the Civil Rights Era and Vietnam. Anti-communism was both a means for politicians to establish legitimacy and a weapon to wield against opponents and programs that failed the anti-communist litmus tests. At one time or another during (and before) the Cold War, promotion of race rights, women's rights, social security, and social welfare programs (to name but a few) were all termed "communistic" by some element of the American political establishment, often with considerable success.[1]

I taught in Slovakia for two years, from 1997 to 1999, while traveling widely in the Czech Republic, where many of my Open Society colleagues were based. I gradually began to see that many of the traditional conceptions of communism and the Cold War, with which I had been indoctrinated through American politics or academia, were, for lack of a better term, a bit off the mark. The role of the United States in bringing the Cold War to a close was considerably mitigated in the minds of Czechs and Slovaks. While credit was given to the Voice of America and the BBC as a vital means of alternative news, the internal contradictions, corruption, and illegitimacy of the Soviet and Czech Communist systems were generally perceived as determining factors in the stagnation and ultimate demise of those regimes. American military escalation tended to be viewed with either indifference or skepticism. Populations in Eastern Europe had already witnessed American, European, and, later, NATO inaction with regard to the Munich Accords of 1939; the communist ascendancy (or coup, depending on your reading of history) in 1948 Czechoslovakia; the Soviet invasion of Hungary in 1956; and the subsequent invasion of Czechoslovakia in 1968.

Over time, I began to see that Western Cold War stereotypes and

Marxist–Leninist ideology aside, the Czechoslovak Socialist society had a character and identity both unique and rich in its organization, goals and execution. This is not to say that the system was just, efficient, or even fully legitimate. But it possessed an inner logic that could not be accessed through the limited perspective of traditional Western Cold War rhetoric. I grew to understand that life in Communist Czechoslovakia was better understood if taken on its own terms. A more personal, nuanced and culturally specific approach made more sense of life there during the post–World War II period. For example, how satisfied were people with their government over time? What was the standard of living, and did it improve? Did large numbers of people wish to leave the country? How represented and empowered did the people feel?

A Few Words on Literature and Methodology

Traditional literature on Eastern European communist regimes tends to focus either on (1) ideological issues, human rights, or (2) comparative aspects of formal political structures or post–1989 developments concerning capitalist elements and market transformation. The literature about communism as a strategic or ideological phenomenon is vast, as is Cold War historiography; both reflect the tenor of different eras in U.S.–Russia relations. Each of these fields is politically loaded. But many new works—some popular and some academic—have emerged in recent decades, asking new questions and providing fresh perspectives.

Several path-breaking, popular works on communist culture appeared shortly after the events of 1989. They are, mostly, personal recollections of individuals. Slavenka Drakulić's *Café Europa* and *How We Survived Communism and Even Laughed*[2] provide insightful perspectives of life and popular culture inside of Communist Yugoslavia after 1989. For example, Drakulić treats the issue of money in the communist world in a particularly familiar manner—I remember this well from my time in Slovakia. Money was spent without hesitation as it had little value in itself. Inflation devalued it even further, so saving strategies were futile. Furthermore, most people could survive in the local economy with little or no money in pocket (prices being controlled and quite low). Money was not only monetarily but also *culturally* devalued. Many of the interviewees with whom I spoke recalled that, as children, they never had any money—but also that they didn't need any.

More recently, there have been several works dedicated to the events of the 1989 Velvet Revolution. James Krapfl, in *Revolution with a Human Face*, employs cultural and social history to depict the actions of ordinary individuals during the 1989–1992 transition, as an old order was overthrown and a new, democratic culture established. Krapfl argues that "socialism," per se, was not the reason for change and revolution, but rather that the old regime was arbitrary and unresponsive to the needs of the population. The revolution represented a return to a more humanistic form of politics that rejected the banality of the administrative state.[3]

A broad interpretation of events in central and Eastern Europe is provided in Padraic Kenney's *A Carnival of Revolution: Central Europe 1989*. Kenney examines the power behind the news: homegrown efforts in several central European countries to recalibrate the political order, including underground artists, musicians and theatrical efforts, to depict new possibilities. His method is oral history, employing several hundred interviews in a dozen countries.[4]

Several more general histories of Czechoslovakia have also appeared in recent years. One, Mary Heimann's *Czechoslovakia: The State That Failed*, examines the entire life of the Czechoslovak state, from an outgrowth of Austria-Hungary and the negotiations following World War I to the eventual "Velvet Divorce" between Czechs and Slovaks in 1993.[5] Kevin McDermott's *Communist Czechoslovakia, 1945–89: A Political and Social History* represents a more concentrated overview of the entire regime in Czechoslovakia. McDermott looks at elites during the admittedly complex rule as well as ordinary citizens and their various motivations to join or abstain from joining the Party. His account is both socially and politically historical, concluding that Communist Czechoslovakia is too easily explained away as a Soviet creation. Instead, indigenous cultural and social forces provided their own inner logic for the establishment and perpetuation of the regime for more than 40 years.[6]

Other regional histories have appeared as well, some written for general audiences. German writer Jana Hensel provides a trenchant look inside East Germany in her 2002 book *Zonenkinder*, which was eventually translated as *After the Wall*. This reflection from a young adult offers insight into familial relations—secrets that succeeding generations held from each other often for the best of reasons. Hensel describes a cardinal rule in the German Democratic Republic: always know in advance what others want you to be, and, by playing that role, avoid attracting attention. One stayed under the radar—in school, in taste, and in most private interactions. Talk was the enemy: "The key was to remain invisible and average."[7]

I encountered this same mentality when teaching in Slovakia. No student was to fail, and none were expected to excel. Poor students were to be "helped" by the better ones (leading to some very interesting attitudes towards assisted learning—what Westerners might call "cheating").

Anna Funder, examining East Berlin during the Cold War, created a seminal piece of non-fiction in 2004 with her *Stasiland: Stories from Behind the Berlin Wall.* What is most rewarding in Funder's account is the focus on lost culture—the discovery (or *re*-discovery) of the reality of East German culture and life, in the midst of social, political and psychological dislocation during the communist period. Such discoveries are also important in my own research.

Many of the newer accounts of the old regimes of central Eastern Europe rely upon storytelling, the gleaning of information from nontraditional sources. Traditional Cold War history, insofar as it addresses issues in the Warsaw Pact nations, tended in the past to focus almost exclusively on elite structures and players. Examining popular culture during the late communist period, I have chosen to employ, in the main, an oral historical approach. Listening to the stories of ordinary or exceptional individuals allows the unearthing of otherwise unarticulated historical phenomena—data that is not protected by documents or other tangible media. The oral histories, in fact, *belong* to the storytellers. Noted oral historian Staughton Lynd observes, "It is their story, not our story: they not we are those who do oral history."[8] The great Chicago oral historian Studs Terkel said in a 1992 interview that doing oral history "is like prospecting. The transcripts are the ore. I've got to get to the gold dust. It's got to be the person's truth, highlighted. It's not just putting down what people say."[9] The portrayal of information gleaned from an interview is complex. There is an element of anthropology involved, insofar as the oral historian is trying to unearth motive and meaning from individual narratives. At the same time, the oral historian is, of course, a historian, attempting to construct and convey a meta-narrative and to make sense of the story. Finally, an oral historical account is an effort towards fusing individual narrative and meta-narrative into a synthesis that creates clarity about a topic.

As described previously, scholarly and non-scholarly research on the both the communist and post-communist periods in Czechoslovakia has expanded in recent decades. A new historiography has emerged, delving into issues such as consumerism, entertainment, and the transition from the upheavals of 1989. Old political and cultural stereotypes have been moderated and new perspectives created. Most important, individual national histories and experiences have emerged in literature. Some examples include Bradley Adams' *The Struggle for the Soul of a Nation*, which examines the intellectual and moral debates that predominated post-war Czechoslovakia, as well as the support structures that the communists employed to take control of the country.[10] These structures include the Roman Catholic Church, various Protestant sects, and elements of the non-communist left.

More recently, Czechoslovak media and social culture have been assessed by Paula Bren's examination of post–1968 media and consumer culture in her work *The Green Grocer and His TV*. Bren, along with Mary Neuberger, examines Czech consumerism in *Communism Unwrapped*. John Connelly has documented contrasting experiences in Eastern European higher education through the Stalinist era with *The Sovietization of East German, Czech, and Polish Higher Education*.[11]

Miroslav Vaněk's 2016 work on Czechoslovak history under communism utilizes an oral historical approach similar to my own, albeit for a somewhat different but overlapping time frame. His *Velvet Revolutions: An Oral History of Czech Society* recounts the turbulent late communist period, from the Prague Spring of 1968 to present day recollections of what the communist period represented. He grants great authority to his interviewees, who recount their own remembrances, often at odds with official narratives presented in the West. What emerges is a very complex and convoluted image of both the past and present. There are few clear conclusions. Does freedom trump security? Is desire for peace a generational issue, understood only by the survivors of the dark years of World War II?[12]

Some would argue that communism was an ideology at odds with capitalism and traditional liberalism.[13] The conflict between capitalism and communism played out during the Cold War was, in this view, a moral crusade. The crusade could be dictated by historical determinism (the orthodox Marxist view), expediency of Western geopolitical market needs (the revisionist New Left perspective), domestic political considerations, or combinations of these and other reasons.[14] The broad, traditionally held assumption was that communism was a monolithic phenomenon, centrally driven and essentially uniform.[15] Contemporary research undercuts this traditional rendering of communism, as it neglects nationalism, culture, technological advancement, diplomacy with neighbors, and history, to name but a few factors.

New perspectives on non-elites, consumer culture, and everyday experiences breathe new life into a subject area previously treated as static and one dimensional. While the West assumed that life was uniformly dreary in an imagined "bloc" of identical Eastern regimes, the truth is far more subtle—and interesting. In the first place, individual communist governments differed—sometimes significantly—in their priorities and methods, not to mention their alliance to Moscow: this difference reached far beyond the non–Warsaw Pact regime of Tito's Yugoslavia or Enver Hoxha's Albania.[16]

It is often said that, during the Cold War, the Soviets and Americans had one mission in common: to distort the meaning of "socialism." Until not so long ago, the literature on the so-called "communist era" tended to focus on geopolitical strategy, Soviet hegemony in Eastern Europe, U.S. security concerns, and the post–1989 "liberation" period. Previous neglect of communist social structure may say more about historians, the nature of historical memory and realpolitik than it does about the people within the communist systems. Despite new research, old ideas and prejudices persist in assessing the communist period. A salient example of this is found in the Museum of Communism in Prague, a panoply of Western Cold War stereotypes, displaying only images of Stalin and Russia, with scarcely a Czech or Slovak in sight. (As an added curiosity, the museum is American sponsored.) It appears that, to many non-academics, the monolithic character of communism remains an unchallenged fact.

The Role of Memory

Should unpleasant past realities be revisited—and to what end? Some have argued that the phenomenon of "collective post-communist amnesia" can affect an entire nation, blotting out both crimes and mundane memories.[17] In an era of "post-national" politics in Europe, for example, the concern that old nationalist prejudices might be reawakened and create a destabilizing effect (for instance, the Yugoslav example of the 1990s) has proven very real. In both the West and in the former Eastern Bloc, one cannot help but sense that communism represented a discredited historical error that should simply be eliminated from human memory.

But a society that willfully keeps skeletons in its closet is not a secure society. Indeed, the goal of the "truth and reconciliation" movement in South Africa was an attempt to exorcize those historical demons—and to preempt future cultural conflict—through honest confrontation and understanding.[18] Given how rapidly the cultural iconography of the communist period has disappeared, one might ask if a collective sweeping of the past under the rug is such a good idea. Prague's Museum of Communism, housed next door to a McDonalds, tells the "official" story of the Cold War. In Budapest, at least, one may still visit old communist-era monuments in a designated city park. But elsewhere, streets have been renamed, monuments torn down (including many dedicated to the USSR for liberating Eastern Europe from Nazi rule), and memory has been lost.

Less obvious (but perhaps more insidiously harmful) has been the limited available literature describing the individual socialist systems of the East, especially in their everyday operation. Systems differed, sometimes radically, ranging from the influence wielded by the Catholic Church in Poland; the liberal proclivities of many in the reformist Czechoslovak government under Alexander Dubček in 1968; the centralized dictatorship of Nicolae Ceaușescu in Romania, or the Hungarian reformer Imre Nagy in the 1955-56 period—not to mention the isolationist and paranoid Enver Hoxha regime in Albania, or Tito's "middle way" of non-aligned communism in Yugoslavia. But the mundane and ordinary are often lost when ideology or governmental policy are focused upon. The good news is that, in recent years, a new scholarship has emerged, scholarship that looks more critically at both individual regimes and at the political and consumer cultures within those systems.

This book attempts to distinguish communist ideology from the day-to-day existence that formed the *experience* of communism—and to make some sense of how to move beyond the rhetoric—of both the Cold War and the present day—in which the system actually operated in the past and is remembered today. The voices of those who lived, thrived, suffered and endured the communist experience of Eastern Europe tell their own tales and perhaps recover realities previously relegated to the historically unknowable.

Methodologically, the book is an oral history supplemented with secondary literature. I performed approximately 100 interviews for this book, in six countries. Other interviews appear as well, using contemporary literature on the topic and region. As my connection to the region—through the Open Society Foundation—was academic, many of those interviewed were, in some way, connected to teaching and academia, either as professors, activists, or relatives of such persons. Most of those interviewed had university educations, and all were old enough to remember firsthand the pre–1989 regime, although some were just children at the time.

Interviewees came from both rural and urban areas; in all, they are likely skewed a bit in favor of the urban. More interviewees are Slovak than Czech, although both have significant representation. With some exceptions, interviewees have lived continuously in the Czech and Slovak republics. Perhaps a quarter of interviewees are émigrés. Interviews were sometimes conducted in English, on other occasions in Slovak (with which I have a working familiarity), and at other times in both languages. Translators were used when needed. Although my connection to Czechoslovakia is an academic one, I intend that the interviews and work be accessible to a general adult reading audience. Thus, this book is not intended as a strictly academic work, but rather as a popular work, by an academic.

Understanding day-to-day experience in Communist Czechoslovakia is undergoing a significant transformation since the Cold War. How did the system *actually* function for those who lived under it? As the Cold War came to a close, the West stood in triumph but rarely bothered to ask this "seemingly" geopolitically question. Addressing this neglect of lives lived under communism is the goal of this book. I will concentrate on the period from approximately 1960 to 1990 in Czechoslovakia—after the communist purges of the 1950s and consolidation of power in Czechoslovakia, through the prosperous 1960s and 1970s and the stagnation of the 1980s, to the period of collapse in 1989. Although I consider secondary literature and recent research in popular culture, my principal source of data on popular culture in Communist Czechoslovakia is interviews with people who lived through these transitions. Most of the interviews are with Czechs and Slovaks although several Polish, Hungarian, Romanian, and Albanian interviews helped to provide a comparative perspective. What emerges is a diffuse, contradictory, and interesting picture of an orthodox communist society, the complete legacy of which is still largely unexamined.

While the book concentrates on the recollections and stories of those who lived in Communist Czechoslovakia, the chapters are organized to provide also a glimpse of the power *behind* the popular experience of culture. The first two chapters concern work and school, two fundamental functions of any modern society. Chapters Three and Four focus on leisure time, consumerism, and travel. In Chapter Five, I look at the social function of the Communist Party, including recruitment, rhetoric, and impact on day-to-day living. Chapters Six and Seven deal with the important events of the Prague Spring, the subsequent Soviet invasion of 1968, and the traumatized "normalization" period that followed. Chapter Eight examines the role of religion in Czechoslovakia and how religious belief intersected with politics. In Chapter Nine, the cultural history of Roma people under the old regime is examined—along with diverse efforts at assimilation, social exclusion and control. Chapter Ten examines the role of historical and cultural *memory* both generally and in the specific context of Communist Czechoslovakia. Here, I examine the evolving memories of the former Communist Czechoslovakia from 1991 to the present.

The book makes no definitive pretense as a definitive interpretation of the communist period in Czechoslovakia. Instead, I prefer to allow the historical subjects room to speak for themselves. Narratives and images create a composite reality that reflects and coaxes out the manifold interests, politics, social needs and reform impulses of a dynamic period in central Eastern European history. Narratives unravel a popular and cultural understanding of life under a regime once seen only as political and geopolitical.

Chapter One

Work

"In Czechoslovakia, everybody holds a job."

In the Czechoslovakia of the communist period, work was a highly valued activity. Unemployment was almost unknown, because work was required of everyone. Typically, one was not permitted to be unemployed. Official doctrine tended to reward certain kinds of work over others. For example, skilled manual labor was valued over analytical work, such as teaching. This hierarchy of work reflected both the orthodoxy of Marxism–Leninism on the superiority of physical, working class labor, and the commensurate distrust of those whose work involved the use of analytical data.

By 1960, the Czechoslovak economy had been subjected to a strong dose of Stalinist revision in both Party membership and salary structure. Communists who came into power in 1948 inherited an expanding Czech economy. The regime attempted to create new avenues of social mobility to those who would pledge political loyalty, as a means to allow individuals from humble backgrounds an opportunity to lead burgeoning industries. Accordingly, by 1949 the Communist Party of Czechoslovakia had 2.5 million members and candidate members—the highest number of members in proportion to population (one in five) in any country. Besides creating these new opportunities, the communists kept open the doors of upward mobility that were already forced ajar under the impact of industrialization. The blurring of distinctions between the manual and professional occupations which had commenced with the war boom accelerated.[1]

The leveling off of income differences between manual and non-manual work is another way by which the regime attempted to discourage mobility. Officially, by the 1960s "the differential rewards for work which made the statuses of individual occupations quite pronounced at the outset of the Czechoslovak command economy [the Stalinist period] have been reduced so that the average earning capacity of the entire labor force is about equal." The three major wage categories of industrial occupations ranked as follows: engineers and technological workers, earning about 20 percent more than workers; skilled and semi-skilled workers; and white-collar administrative staff (clerical), who earned about 20 percent less than workers. This gap of monetary rewards constricted continually, providing few incentives for workers to leave manual occupations.[2] Meanwhile, the country's labor codes were modernized and unified in the 1960s, as a means of "promoting socialism."[3]

Environmental Issues and Work

From the early days of the communist regime, economic policy emphasized ecological exploitation and growth over concern for the environment. By the early 1980s, degradation of the environment had become so advanced that certain areas of the country were in danger of becoming "uninhabitable," according to one Czech interviewed by the West German media in 1983.[4] Complicating the state's difficulties was the onset of an economic depression and general economic stagnation. Care for the environment was written into the Czechoslovak constitution, and, over the years, various environmental measures were passed.[5]

By 1983, the overriding question was whether these pieces of progressive legislation were actually being observed by state agencies and industries. Enforcement officials, known as "procurators," concluded in a 1979 report that "the responsible agencies do not protect the interests of society in environmental matters adequately, and that they make little use of the legal instruments that enable the punishment of those infracting their legal obligations in the field of ecological care."[6]

Two years later, in 1981, the state of affairs was charged with having little positive impact. The failure to utilize pollution protection technology and the preference for economic and technical progress had continued to hamper efforts to improve environmental conditions in Czechoslovakia. Law #20 was described as having been fundamentally ignored by planners: "The state of the environment does not constitute a plan target; the economic plan forces the enterprises to produce a certain volume and assortment of goods, with no regard for environmental concerns."[7] Clearly, then, even after the passage of pro-environmental legislation over the course of nearly two decades, central planners focused instead on increasing production, distribution, and consumption.

Czech lands were particularly vulnerable to environmental despoliation and ranked consistently among the highest polluting areas in all of Europe. An estimated 6,000 square kilometers of the Czech lands (particularly northern Bohemia) were permanently exposed to excessive concentrations of severe pollutants. Nearly three million people lived in this region—almost 40 percent of Czechs. The problems accelerated in the 1960s; first, the airspace was contaminated with sulfur dioxide, estimated at three million tons by 1980. Slovakia suffered significantly less during this period. The 1983 study depicts the Slovak lands as standing a good chance at reducing significantly "solid emission of dust and cinders," while the Czech lands are expected to climb 25 percent or more in pollutants. The reason for the discrepancy was a decision in the early 1960s to reorient the country's economy towards heavy manufacturing, based on low quality domestic coal as the main source of fuel. Iron and steel were emphasized. (The development of the new and massive VSŽ Steelworks in eastern Košice, as a means of stimulating the productive capacity of the Slovak lands in the early 1960s, is illustrative.) In the end, sulfur dioxide pollution more or less doubled between the mid–1950s and mid–1960s. It was said that Czechoslovakia released more sulfur dioxide than (much larger) West Germany, by 1983.[8]

Since the late 1950s, at least, water pollution constituted a problem in Czechoslovakia. By 1960, 5 percent of all rivers were polluted beyond acceptable standards, and by the early 1980s, more than 7 percent of all rivers had been classified as "worst polluted categories III and IV," meaning that large areas of flowing water could no longer support fish. In 1981, a sample of drinking water in Slovakia showed that 21 percent of tap water was contaminated. Well water in both the Czech and Slovak sectors fared even worse: 70–80 percent of all wells in Slovakia were contaminated, producing diseases such as dysentery, jaundice and virus-based hepatitis. Additional problems included non-chronic pollutants, such as one-time dumps of contaminants, particularly oil derivatives. In the Czech lands, large quantities of airplane fuel were found to have leaked into the ground from underground storage areas at Ruzyně Airport in Prague. While a market-based economy might find fault with private interests or companies polluting, in Czechoslovakia the state was, in the end, the only responsible party.[9]

Both public health and morale were affected by government environmental policies from the 1960s into the 1980s. By 1983, nearly 30 percent of the country's rivers were seriously polluted, along with the water table. Rising incidences of cancer, tuberculosis and other diseases were becoming evident. Northern and western Bohemia suffered the worst, with the highest death rates in the country. There, 50 percent of all births were considered at risk. In Bohemia, it became annual policy to send children away once or twice per year to shield them from the effects of environmental contamination. The wearing of handkerchiefs over the mouth while outdoors became standard practice in some regions, and homeowners were instructed to keep their windows shut. Social problems also grew; from the late 1960s until the 1980s, northern Bohemia experienced rising alcoholism and increased crime and juvenile delinquency. Birthrates declined, obesity and work absenteeism rose, and emigration began to climb.[10] In the end, the economic and social problems that led to the reformist movement of 1968 remained unaddressed, festering beneath the surface.

Factory Work and Culture

As Czechoslovakia was a highly industrialized state, the factory was a fact of life for many. The Czech lands had been industrialized earlier, but by the 1960s, various schemes to bring heavy industry to Slovakia were put into play, in order to bring it into parity with the western territories. Many endured the realities of factory life throughout the 1960s and 1970s, and a distinct work and production ethic developed during this period. As described by a former factory manager from Košice, in eastern Slovakia:

> Our plant had about 1700 overall employees. Overseeing everyone was the Head of the Economic Section, whose job was to coordinate workers and overall production that would come from them. The central issue for management at the time was *planning*. All good managers understood that one always asked for more than one needed. The trick was to ask for an *exact* amount, broken down into the smallest increments possible. This gave the appearance of credibility and exactitude. If you asked for money in this fashion, more often than not you would receive it. Once you received state funds for your factory operations, the key action was to spend that money in its entirety. Well, not exactly in its entirety. One tried to spend as close to the granted budget as was possible. The closer that a manager came to spending the originally allotted sum for his franchise, the more respect was bestowed upon that employee. A "perfect" planner spent nearly what was allocated to him.[11]

The work ethic in Czechoslovakia was, indeed, remarkably different from Western work ethics—and often in self-conscious ways. The work culture of the West was seen as stressful, demoralizing and unproductive in its demands on the individual worker. Czech and Slovak workers were well aware of the need by American workers to hold two or more jobs, work long hours, and live lives of chronic insecurity. The rationale for opposing such a corrosive ethic was that, in Czechoslovakia, all basic needs were met, standards of health and prosperity were roughly uniform, and Western-inspired "drives towards material acquisition" were simply not worth the toll that they would ultimately exact.[12]

Providing gainful employment was itself a major goal of the Czechoslovak government. Efficiency and productivity within the workplace, while purportedly important (if one is to judge by official pronouncements), often took a back seat to full employment. Janka, a lumber worker from Banská Bystrica, a mining city in the central Slovak mountains, described a workplace as inefficient as it was potentially deadly. Refused entry to university—possibly for black marks on her official record, reflecting an earlier conflict with local authorities—she obtained work at a lumber mill. Of the 45 or so employees at the mill, 40 or so were women. The rest—the management—were all male.

At the lumber mill, women had all of the heavy lifting jobs and started the day by six in the morning. By ten o'clock, she says, the assigned work for the day was usually completed, but most of the staff was already drunk.[13] While intoxication in the workplace was unofficially tolerated, conditions often deteriorated under tipsy workers. Janka's boss, a true Communist believer, would often lapse into fits of depression, crying that the ideals of communism had been "betrayed" by the current government. Other employees would clear the floor, watching for wayward forklifts manned by intoxicated employees: "It was common to have intoxicated workers in the yard. Some were operating heavy machinery. One woman, a forklift driver, was a notorious drunk, who occasionally dropped loads of lumber in the lift area. We would always steer clear of the areas in which she was working. New employees would be counseled not to walk around or near those areas."[14] It was assumed (and usually widely known) that some cells of Party members existed within the workforce. Janka belonged to the Young Socialists but often clashed with her manager. Some contentious issues included inefficiency in the workplace, "lying" about goals, quotas, work performance, safety, and policies in general. Among the major sticking points were complaints about the "lack of real work" and the "fakery" of management and employees alike, to legitimize corrupt and do-nothing work forces.[15]

A story of managerial misconduct is told by Tomáš regarding a pharmaceutical factory in eastern Czechoslovakia, in the vicinity of the Ruthenian central city, Prešov. The factory, ostensibly a producer of medicines for everyday use, was widely rumored (an "open secret," as it was called locally) to be a chemical weapons facility. It was said to owe its location, in the remote east, to the fears of an American invasion. In fact, Tomáš explained, the entire network of factories in Czechoslovakia was decentralized to resist any possible U.S. invasion.[16]

In a specialized operation such as pharmaceutical research and production, management in the 1960s and 1970s tended to be in the hands of Czechs, who possessed superior and more specialized training than Slovaks. The work environment consisted of a constant barrage of positive and remonstrative slogans and phrases, repeated *ad nauseam*. On occasion, competitions were held with nationalistic themes. For example, Tomáš entered into a "millionaires" inventors competition that was promoted as a means to "help enrich the country" with a million crowns (the Czechoslovak currency) worth of prosperity. In fact, he won the competition, having developed microbiological items for the expansion of beef production. As meat was a luxury in Czechoslovakia, his invention was a meat substitute (soya being rare, as the climate was too cold for cultivation). With his prize of 15,000 CZ crowns, Tomáš was able to purchase two red leather chairs, while the director of his division at the factory was given *50,000* crowns in appreciation for Tomáš' work.[17]

When Tomáš attempted to approach other governments to sell his idea, his director threatened him, warning that "your children will not study" (i.e., will be banned from attending gymnasium and university) if he were to continue. One letter of inquiry sent to a private firm was blocked by his director. In the end, the Czech government decided that it was better to sell the idea abroad than to put it to use in-country. The product was subsequently sold to the West for a multi-million-dollar profit, much of which was skimmed by Party officials. Eventually, Tomáš was "promoted" to an administrative position and banned from the laboratory. He still owns the two chairs that he bought with his winnings from the competition and keeps them stored safely, in perfect condition, as one would protect a curious set of museum pieces.[18]

Such stories are consistent with Czechoslovak economic policy during and after the post–1968 "normalization" period. In an effort to ease the pain of newly enforced political oppression, the regime sought to focus on *consumption*—to create a society of benign consumers engaged in politically passive, individualistic material indulgence. Part of the state strategy of easing citizens into acceptance of political normalization was a conscious easing of workplace standards: productivity demands were lowered, the work ethic deliberately slackened, and job security enhanced without tying it to job performance or productivity. In fact, the government was attempting, in the early 1970s, to buy the cooperation of its populace through work policy and material comfort. This worked for a time, until the oil crisis of 1974 brought it all to a screeching halt.[19]

Location of one's work could be a determining factor in salary and comparative advantage. For example, in southeastern Czechoslovakia, the city of Komárno was designated as a "center of state interest," as much heavy industry was located there. The decentralization of Czech industry may have had as its initial impulse protection against Western invasion, but the industrialization of the central and eastern regions of the country also played a significant role in economic development. As a result, the period from the late 1950s onward saw the rapid expansion of heavy industry into Bratislava, Žilina, Košice, Martin, and other previously provincial eastern towns. Komárno was located on the Danube, and thus its strategic location to the shipyards made it an important place. Factories deemed essential to national security were often placed remotely. In cities such as Martin and Dubnica, some weapons factories were located 100 feet underground. Light weaponry tended to be produced in the Czech lands, while heavier products were churned out in Slovakia.[20] As local resident Pavol recollects, Komárno was a city "looked after" by the authorities, not least because it was a major producer of tank wheels. Certain consumer luxuries, such as bananas, seemed to find their way to Komárno more often than other, less vital cities.[21]

The *type* of work that someone performed was also a determiner of salary and status. Engineers in Komárno tended to be Czechs, and workers Slovak. A skilled industrial worker might earn 5,000 crowns per month—or more, if they produced high-end items like automobiles. (To place the salaries in perspective, a liter of milk in the 1970s was 2–3 crowns, and 250 grams of butter was about 10 crowns.) Miners made even more, perhaps 8,000 crowns per month, in some regions. Teachers and university professors, however, tended to take in lower salaries. The reasoning behind this discrepancy was, in part, a fulfillment of the ideological elevation of manual, proletariat labor over the traditionally middle class or "bourgeois" professions. However, other motives were present to depress academic and other professional salaries, which sometimes ranged in the vicinity of 1,000–1,500 crowns per month. The "literate" professions were held suspect, as they were capable of conveying information to others—information that the state might not deem appropriate. Anyone engaged in the *idea* culture was watched very carefully.[22]

Although necessity often dictated that highly trained Czechs would handle engineering and other specialty functions in industry, a different logic often applied to management. People were "classed," in terms of their training, work and education, in categories such as "farmer," "worker," or "intelligentsia." Of these, the "worker" designation carried the greatest cachet in the Marxist–Leninist regime; as a result, many workers were placed into administrative positions, performing functions for which they had little training, and overseeing businesses of which they had little knowledge. In this sense, they were said to be "fulfilling the historical role of the worker." As a rule, these well-placed workers could be counted on as committed Party members.[23]

Workers were told routinely, through official workplace propaganda, that "capitalists are not just; they exploit workers and all others around them." But in a city such as Martin, a large tank producer for Czechoslovakia, finished tanks were routinely sold outside of Czechoslovakia for world market prices. Workers did not benefit from the international largesse, as the government (and party) retained the profits for their own purposes. A local resident explains: "Many workers would ask why a German doing the same kind of labor could make twenty times the salary of a Czech. In the end, the system survived from the robbing of its own people."[24]

Women and Work

The role of women during the communist regime is a controversial topic. On the one hand, the official stance of the government was that women were effectively equal to men in the workplace. In fact, the official line did not always fit the reality of the day, according to Lucia: "There was very nice propaganda about the equality of women with men, as in 'we love their contribution' and so forth. That is true. The problem was that many jobs were praised and overstated in their importance, when in fact they were rather ordinary or lousy jobs."[25]

By a bit of contrast, Jakub commented on the role of women in the workplace: "Although my mother was quite anti-communist, I think that equality in the work place was one thing that the communists got right. The regime succeeded here—there was no glass ceiling. More managers were men and more teachers were women, but it was 'normal' for a woman to work, and they were not looked down upon."[26]

Anecdotal stories about the role of women in Czechoslovakia often follow a consistent narrative; women traditionally played a significant (if not officially acknowledged) role in the social and economic spheres of society. Generally speaking, Czech and Slovak women have often been depicted as relatively liberated, autonomous actors. Further, common wisdom has suggested that, after the trauma of the events of 1968, women assumed an even more important role in Czechoslovakia: the political "emasculation" of men by the Soviet invasion resulted in increased alcoholism and general escapism. Women then filled the roles of responsibility, redoubling their efforts to maintain domestic order.

Some, however, do not look upon the communist period as a particularly "liberating" time for women; Alena Valterová, for example, after forming a feminist political party, the Political Party of Women and Mothers, in 1990, argued that the communist period spoke well of women's rights, but did not provide the substance to match the rhetoric:

> Our main emphasis is on changing the legislation and the customs through which women's discrimination has been perpetuated. We will not organize knitting or cooking classes. That belongs to a sphere of social initiatives. However important these may be, we want to move on. The old Women's Union was a social club that was comparable to a club of stamp collectors. Most of their representatives were members of the Communist Party and, if they wanted to defend women's rights more vigorously, they ran the risk of cadre screening. Our program starts from the heritage of the past—too many broken, what we call incomplete families, with women's needs and interests unmet and undefended.[27]

The interview with Ms. Valterová continues to describe how women require more information about their rights as citizens. Further, she stresses that the prevalent passivity among women needed to be addressed. She notes that every fifth woman in Czechoslovakia is a single mother and sole provider for her family. In 1988, official sources indicate that roughly 650,000 people lived below the poverty line, with this figure swelling to 900,000 by 1989.[28] Alena is not sentimental about the communist period, and she expresses some disdain towards the reformist agenda that gripped Czechoslovakia shortly after the collapse of the Soviet Union:

> Civic Forum has a rather negative attitude towards the women's movement. We stated as long ago as last January [1990], that we have little in common with Civic Forum and with the old official Communist Women's Union. That position still stands. Our relationship with the trade unions is more hopeful, since we share a similar position with them. We didn't have and still don't have access to decision-making, to legislative plans and the new proposals that are now being made. If the trade unions defend the rights of working people, we shall have something to share with them. In Czechoslovakia at present, about 50 per cent of women work because of financial necessity.

> They will become economically dependent on their partners. Their entitlements to pensions and loss of qualification will be in doubt. They will be socially isolated because of the lack of provision of services. Others will have to make a choice not to have any children. At the same time, most of our women have been brought up not as mothers but with a view that a person is valued according to his/her economic activity.[29]

Unpaid Labor: Brigáda Work

Much of the labor performed in Czechoslovakia was both compulsory and unpaid. This was the Brigáda work—a social obligation fulfilled typically by students. Brigáda work was based on the socialist idea that manual labor was important, possessed dignity, and should be experienced by all people. As a rule, young people did not work while attending primary or secondary school; thus, Brigáda work was, for most, an introduction into the world of work. There were two types of work: technical and agricultural. If assigned to the agricultural track, in the first year of secondary education one would be assigned to perform manual labor at one of a number of agricultural collectives. This could include myriad tasks, such as the picking of hops, potatoes, or grapes. Other students engaged technical trades, such as bricklaying, considered a "natural" form of work. Excursions were organized by the schools and were unpaid.[30]

Brigáda workers were subject to a steady stream of socialist themes as they departed for their work assignments. Much of the propaganda was accepted with tongue-in-cheek acquiescence by young people, many of whom welcomed the opportunity for time away from home with peers. Dano, from the eastern region of Trebišov, described a lengthy trip with his fellow students to an area near Prague (a nearly 12-hour train trip) for the purpose of producing conserves: "We were bombarded with rhetoric and slogans about the ideal socialist worker and the need for 'humility' and appreciation for manual labor. Brigáda work was intended to build up society and allow for all citizens to appreciate all kinds of work. We joked about the slogans, as most young people were quite cynical about official pronouncements. One might say that we developed this cynicism 'stop by stop' during the communist period. However, in the end, Brigáda work was a very positive thing—great food, companionship, and an overall party atmosphere."[31]

As white collar work was considered suspect and elitist, salaries of "producers" tended to be higher than salaries of those who performed non-manual labor, and one year of "labor" was typically required for the producer. The rationale was clear; one needed to "understand" manual work, and those who performed it.[32] Brigáda work was welcomed by most students as an adventure, but it was, nonetheless, tightly controlled. Failure to participate in Brigáda work could result in a mark on one's record, which could seriously affect a student's ability to enter university or to find a preferred job in the future.

Other Eastern Bloc countries had similar work schemes for young people. Neighboring Poland, for example, demanded a "zero year practicum" of labor for aspiring university students, before matriculation. Officially, the unpaid labor functioned as a "protection against arrogance" among the elite citizenry. Zuzka, an aspiring university student in Krakow, worked at a cucumber pickling factory before commencing her university studies. This *práce społečná*, or "social work," was considered obligatory for the sake of the general betterment of society, an idea dating from the Second World War. Students would pick potatoes, clean windows, repair old buildings. The tasks were all part of a relaxed and festive experience. Schools were let out for Brigáda, and students enjoyed a vacation while learning a greater societal value of respect for physical work.[33]

Students took Brigáda work with a grain of salt. Janka from Prešov explains:

> Assignments were usually local; they would try to get you work as close to your home as possible. I was assigned to work in a fruit canning factory in Sabinov [eastern Slovakia]. The assignment was for three weeks, but I doubt if we performed more than three days of actual labor. Most of the time, we just needed to *pretend* to work. At harvest time, large numbers of students were recruited to pick potatoes, and for this work we sometimes received a small compensation. The work was mandatory, but we didn't mind, as it was done during what would have been school time. At other times, we were asked to pick potato bugs, by hand, off of the plants. We were told that the United States had dropped the pests from planes to destroy our crops.[34]

Brigáda Work and Youth Policy

Brigáda work could serve two positive purposes, inculcating work and class values to young people and keeping kids off of the streets and out of trouble. In fact, youth delinquency was sometimes a major social problem for the state. A conference report from a group of educational workers, meeting at the ski town of Tatranská Lomnica in 1960, stated that children were "rampant in the streets." The conference had, as its principal goal, the formation and implementation of "school associations" designed to provide meaningful outlets of talents and energy for youth after school hours. The conference noted, however, that, thus far, only about 5 percent of eligible school children had taken advantage of such programs.[35]

Among reasons put forth for the increased delinquency of youth were longer work hours for parents, including the introduction of second shifts..... Youth clubs were to provide better surveillance of school-aged youths, develop hobbies and combat boredom. Clubs were a means of substituting parental attention at critical times of the day. Youth clubs had a long tradition in Czechoslovakia, dating back to the First Republic period of 1918–1938. The clubs were revived shortly after the Second World War but were subsequently banned by the communist regime in 1948. Later, as authorities saw the potential economic, social and ideological utility of the clubs, they were gradually reintroduced.[36]

The greatest threats posed by restless youth were violence, rowdiness, and hooliganism. Communist authorities typically associated such deviance only with Western capitalist countries; the rise of hooliganism in Czechoslovakia was of great concern. For example, in November 1960, state radio announced that 14 youths in Prague had been arrested on charges of "theft, rowdy behavior, self inflicted injuries, and various moral crimes." Three of the alleged culprits were girls. Perhaps most significantly, the gang was characterized as a "non-class" group, meaning that their offences could not be understood in Marxist economic terms. While some of the youths were from working-class families, others came from the intelligentsia. (Also noteworthy: one of the boys apprehended had injured himself to avoid Brigáda work.) Thus, by the beginning of the 1960s, the goals of economic expansion in Czechoslovakia had to contend with various social obstacles, requiring new policies and programs.[37]

Professional Work: Mental Health

The field of mental health was influenced heavily by ideological and political considerations. Nowhere was this influence more evident than in psychiatry. One practitioner writes that therapists "were actually very free" in the last decade or so of the communist period. But, she adds, "by 1990, the new government decided that psychiatry had been misused for political and other reasons during the old regime."[38] She cites the example of a Jewish patient who was (wrongly, in her mind) transported to a hospital unit for treatment of schizophrenia, when in fact he suffered only from routine dementia. Doctors, she says, were often pressured into supporting presumed "diagnoses."[39]

On other occasions, "patients" were brought to the hospital by police, sometimes after having been detained at demonstrations or even mere celebrations. Doctors were under heavy pressure not to release such individuals, especially if they had been deemed "disturbance makers." In one case, a protester was detained after being accused of urinating on an official delegate (in fact, he had urinated on the delegate's car). When the psychiatrist refused to treat him, opining that he was not sick, she was threatened with arrest.[40] Nevertheless, she maintains that ethics in the field of mental health actually maintained a *higher* standard than today; "there was a stronger sense of what was right and wrong, what was good and bad, and what was accurate and inaccurate; today, the level is not so high—and it has been compromised.... There is more interference today between doctor and patient, perhaps due to market considerations, along with more 'fakery,' regarding conditions and diagnoses."[41]

Special Hospitals

Concerning mental health, not all Czechs and Slovaks were treated equally. High officials and other VIPs had their own system of hospitals, or *Štátne sanatórium* (also called *Štátny domov s opatrovateľskou službou*), where they could go for treatment. Treatment at such facilities was, as might be imagined, anonymous, gentle, and discreet. The facilities better resembled spas than hospitals, and patients attended for a variety of reasons—often exhaustion, alcoholism and delirium tremens. Patients were often the wives, husbands, or children of notables, and most checked in using code (assumed) names. "It was quite fashionable for a person to enroll at one of the *Štátne nemocnici* [state hospitals], as it conferred some prestige. Typically, men would sign in as Jan Novák [the Czech equivalent of "John Doe"] and women as Jana Nováková ["Jane Doe"]. Privacy was always assured."[42] Štátne hospitals were staffed solely with Party members, and the employment benefits were good. Vierka, a psychotherapist, for example, was offered a raise in salary, shorter hours and a free apartment for working there. For her, the experience confirmed several of the "miracles of socialism"; everyone was employed, but nobody worked; the shops and pharmacies were empty, but you could always get everything you needed from someone.[43]

Work culture in Czechoslovakia developed into both a patriotic activity under the communist regime, as evidenced by the nationalist-inspired Brigáda corps, and a multilayered, ideologically-driven phenomenon that served the interests of the political classes. At the same time, despite corruption and favoritism, the policy of full employment provided a standard that helped to level class and gender hierarchies but also provided a sense of purpose, autonomy and self-respect to the better part of the working population—often, however, at the expense of shortsighted economic policies that led to environmental degradation and health problems. The equality of women in the workplace might have been settled policy under law and ideology, but the disparity between official pronouncements and the reality of the workplace was often profound.

Chapter Two

School and Education

"In Czechoslovakia, there was complete freedom of speech. The problems started after one spoke!"

The Czechoslovak educational system under the communist regime was comprised of preschool, primary education, secondary instruction (further separated into vocational and grammar schools), and a university system comprised of technical, professional, and liberal arts studies. Education was free of charge to all, and students competed on the basis of competitive exams for admission. Certain built-in preferences prevailed however, as working-class students received preference over prospective students from more affluent families. Vocational school served to supply about 12 percent of agricultural workers and more than 45 percent of industrial laborers by 1990. Schools in Czechoslovakia were controlled by two separate bodies: the Ministry of Education and the Communist Party Central Committee. Both of these units provided input into both curriculum and admissions.[1] Public as well as school and university libraries were controlled from above, and books deemed to "retard or impair (our) journey towards socialism" were banned. Lists of banned books were circulated throughout the library system.[2] Sometimes, only objectionable *sections* of books were deemed offensive and banned. (In Slovakia, I came across a book on the history of Yugoslavia, from the early 1950s. The book was available at the university library, but one chapter had been sealed shut with tape—the chapter on Tito's split with Stalin, in 1948. All four corners of the pages for the chapter were sealed with tape, and a lengthwise piece of tape was affixed to the sides. As a measure towards discouraging tampering, a bright red, official seal had been placed on each of the four corners of the first and last pages of the chapter. No tampering was evident, but such a seemingly minor offense could result in a major disciplinary action at school. In another case, an interviewee explained how a single missing tile in the boy's bathroom in a Banská Bystrica primary school set off an investigation of the entire school population.) Materials that celebrated Marxist–Leninist values comprised the standard, having been selected by both the Ministry of Education and the Party.[3]

Primary School and Secondary School

Primary school encompassed grades 1 through 5, and middle school grades 6 through 9. Early education was highly structured, and tended to be dominated by female instructors. One exception to this rule was often the physical education teacher. As a rule, corporal punishment did not exist in the primary schools, although it was sometimes found in the secondary school system. Careful records were kept of student behavior, however, and both *red (good)* and *black (bad)* marks for behavior were doled out, sometimes liberally.

All students were grouped together in class, regardless of ability. During period breaks during the school day, students were often required to walk together in uniform circles, as a means of preserving order. Students who did not behave were often asked to stand in the corner of the classroom. No pledge was recited at the start of the school day. (A daily pledge had in fact been common for decades in the United States when students placed their hands over their hearts and pledged allegiance to the United States). During my two years teaching in eastern Slovakia, my students never ceased to show shocked indignation to the fact that American children were required to "pledge" their loyalty to the American state. "This," some of them said, "seemed an even more advanced form of control than the communist system."[4] In the classroom, photographs of Czech and Slovak leaders, particularly Gustáv Husák and General Ludvík Svoboda, were omnipresent. Lunchtime breaks might be occupied by hopscotch and various running and jumping games.

Many students brought toys to school, such as miniature cars and dolls. Although the Barbie doll did not find her way to Czechoslovakia, a crying, unnamed local brand rubber doll was popular with girls in the 1970s. One interviewee noted that a "walking doll" of nearly two feet in height (imported from the Soviet Union) created quite stir in Czechoslovakia. The doll would accompany the owner and appear to "walk" alongside her.[5]

Student appearance and behavior were among the top concerns of administrators throughout the 1960s and into the 1980s. Boys were required to maintain short hair. Long hair could result in a refusal of admittance to class. Shorts, worn by either males or females, were prohibited from school. Makeup on women was considered suspect; a small, discreet amount was tolerated, but makeup deemed "excessive" was prohibited and could result in summary dismissal. Of course, exceptions were made, based on the status of the student in question. For example, in Bratislava, during the 1970s, the son of the Soviet ambassador was permitted to have long hair.[6] By the 1970s, jeans were considered *de rigeur* fashion, as were sporting "warm up" suits. In fact, these "modern"-style sports suits were said to have been so popular in the Soviet Union that they were often worn proudly to formal functions, such as state academic exams.[7]

School Admissions

The admissions process in the university system was widely suspected of being corrupt and ideologically driven, and admissions to high school could be equally so. The story of Vierka S. is illustrative. The child of a doctor and "regular Stalinist," one would think that Vierka would have had an easy time being accepted into the high school of her choice. However, her father was so upset with the reforms of the 1968 Dubček reform period that he began to doubt the orthodoxy of the Communist Party. When he was called in for an "examination" (a formal procedure during the period of "normalization," which consisted of an interview—and often the expulsion of the Party member), he refused, citing the flaws of the "revisionist" regime of Gustáv Husák. Later, he quit the Party altogether.[8]

For Vierka, however, her father's "crimes" towards the Party placed formidable obstacles in her way when she applied to high school. Although a straight "A" student, Vierka was rejected at every school to which she applied. Finally, in desperation, the family hired a (so-called) "French woman," who was sent with a bottle of cognac to the office of an admissions official with the instructions that she was "not to leave until Vierka had been approved for admission." In the end, Vierka was admitted for study. Later on, her father decided that the hardship to his family was not worth the trouble and decided once again to join the Communist Party. His application, however, was refused.[9]

On the other hand, some recent research has suggested that ideological favoritism in secondary school admissions may have been a bit of a myth: "A lifelong professor at one university testified that the admission committees never received any written order to deprive 'politically unreliable' applicants of the possibility to study, nor did they receive a detailed specification of what exactly was meant by political loyalty. The official ideology was contained only in very abstract declarations made by the Central Committee of the Communist Party. It was probably never set out in detailed rules, definitions, and prescriptions."[10] Instead, one's family class background appears to have been connected more closely to politics in the Stalinist 1950s and the post–1968 "normalization" period of 1970–1974, than in the late 1950s, and the 1960s, which represented a relatively unregulated period in education.[11]

High School Social and Academic Culture

School dances were popular for students aged 13 and up and were carefully supervised. Drugs were largely unknown, and little knowledge existed on substances such as marijuana and hashish, though alcohol may have been present, and was generally tolerated by authorities. Music was important. In Bratislava, for example, students routinely listened to Austrian radio (Austria was just across the Danube) and recorded songs onto their cassette tape players. In the 1970s, popular music at Bratislava dances included albums and cassettes by many Western bands, such as Pink Floyd, Slade, Beatles, Led Zeppelin and Sweet.[12]

The grading system in Czechoslovakia was a holdover from the pre-communist period. Grades were usually evaluated based on a scale of numbers 1 through 4, with a lower number representing a higher achievement. Grades were considered a reflection of a student's ability, but the social mores that governed success were born of a dual ethic, encouraged (however implicitly) by socialist values; no student should excel, or draw attention to individual achievement (that was elitist), and no student should fail (that represented a lack of social solidarity). Within the classroom, this egalitarian ethic led to some rather interesting social dynamics. What the Western world might term "cheating," that is, assisting another with information, Czechoslovak students often saw as "assisted education," or helping a fellow student to succeed. Clearly, it was more important to ensure camaraderie among students than to stand out as exceptional—and no one in the system was expected to fail.[13] The notion of helping a fellow student in the classroom environment was often considered a perfectly legitimate act of social solidarity, as opposed to Western, individualistic concepts of "cheating" and "plagiarism."[14] Abstract morality was a subservient consideration to social cohesion and cooperation. Regarding "assisted learning," or "cheating," as many in the West would term it, schemes utilized by students in the classroom were both ingenious and effective. Some techniques (pre-mobile phone) included "bombs," tightly-packed, narrow, accordion-shaped cheat sheets—four to 12 inches long, but tiny in circumference, which provided summary notes and could be held in the palm and turned with the right thumb while commensurately holding a pen. Also employed were "flap sheets," where paper was taped to a woman's leg under a ripped jeans flap, or secured to the leg under a miniskirt, and would appear as the student sat down and the miniskirt rose. A "bomb" might take six to eight hours to produce and was often considered a minor work of both art and study.[15]

Nor was politics removed from the classroom—students were often asked if their parents were Party members or not.[16] Jaro from Trebišov recalls that his father was the director of a primary school and a Party member. Work rules at the time dictated that those who supervised eight or more people needed to be candidates for Party membership. Jaro's father was, in fact, a true believer. Nevertheless, because the grandfather, a landowner, refused to join the Party, Jaro's father was denied access to his own school by authorities for more than three months. Jaro describes the "true believer" in his father this way: "Like many true believers, he did not ask analytical questions, and reality seemed to him to be composed of a single system. He had a positive impression of the United States, and, in fact, some of his friends and neighbors emigrated to New Jersey. He did not see the world through a pluralistic or ideological lens, and both the U.S. and USSR were seen to him as friends."[17]

Another student admits, "I didn't like that we had to study boring political science and Marxism and Russian were obligatory [which spoiled the beauty of that language]. Teachers were seen as gods. There was no freedom of speech [in the classroom], and obedience was expected at all levels. Superiority flourished and every talent of ordinary people was subdued [if their relatives were not members of the Communist Party]."[18] One recalls, "I remember a civics instructor when I was 11 or 12 years old telling us in class that [at an unspecified future period in time] we will be living in pure communism and there will be no money, the goods in stores will be available, and everyone might take as much as they like. As I was listening to this, I recall that I just was not able to imagine this would work."[19]

Student behavior was expected to follow proper political as well as behavioral norms. A Slovak from Bratislava recalls: "Students tended to be very cynical. And we were often forced to read newspapers in order to keep up on current events, which only increased our cynicism towards the 'official' view of things. One day, we presented our teacher with a tee shirt that we had made for him. It was highly patriotic, and displayed the words 'civics and citizenship' prominently. Well, he became very upset with this gift, seeing it as a disguised, critical slight against the communist regime, which it may well have been!"[20]

University Education

Recent scholarship has suggested that both Czechoslovakia and Poland escaped some of the more extreme Stalinist measures to "rid the university of bourgeois elements," by removing faculty and encouraging a larger peasant- and worker-based student population, especially when compared to East Germany. As a case in point, students in Czechoslovakia led much of the protest of 1989, while in East Germany, students remained faithful to the university and state. Nevertheless, the influence of the Soviet Union on higher education ensured that Russian was typically the most offered and hence most studied foreign language.[21]

University education in Czechoslovakia under the communist regime displayed several distinctive characteristics. There was, for example, the degradation of white collar (professorial) work, which was regarded as a sinecure. As a result, manual labor was given a higher pay structure and better chances for advancement than intellectual work, which was seen as bourgeois and superfluous. Second, the university was politically driven, particularly in the liberal arts and sciences. As a result, ideological evaluations, litmus tests and even intradepartmental spying occurred frequently.[22] Finally, students were routinely discouraged from demonstrating critical or creative thinking in the classroom. Conformity and submission to the authority of the professor were considered the norm: "There were two rules in school. First, no one failed. A failing student was seen as a negative reflection of the entire class as well as the teacher. Instead, poorly performing students were often assisted by their peers. Second, no one was to excel or stand out. That too, was seen as untoward; an indication of a show-off."[23]

In post–World War II Eastern Europe, the Soviet Union exerted considerable control over higher education, but that control was uneven and varied widely among Communist Bloc states. East Germany established a higher education system based, to a large degree, on the Soviet model. This was facilitated by the presence of large numbers of Soviet troops in East Germany after the War, and by a student and professional class that had been largely discredited with their support for National Socialism. Communist educational ideas could thus fill a vacuum of societal "moral capital."[24]

Czechoslovakia did not experience the same degree of initial control by the USSR over its higher education system, as "benign Nazi backing in the form of professional passivity," coupled with a traditionally ambiguous stance by the Czech Communist Party, led to a very different system of organization, when compared to the East German model. In Czechoslovakia, communist students often created "action committees" to design and administer university policies, but both Party indifference and rural opposition to higher education, hindered the students' efforts.[25]

University Admission

If one followed the traditional university track, the first step towards higher education was getting admitted to a university. Admission was fraught with obstacles that did not necessarily relate to academic ability. Czech geologist Jiri B. describes his experiences applying to universities in Prague:

> I wanted to be a biochemist after completing gymnasium [secondary school for the university bound]. I applied at Charles University, to the Faculty of Natural Sciences. I waited for the results of my exams to see if I had passed and been admitted. No result ever appeared, only a recommendation that I "go into agriculture." The statement to this effect was unsigned—it had merely been officially signed *for* some anonymous person. My father appealed the recommendation and was told subsequently that our family had been found to be too "bourgeois" for me to be admitted to my chosen field of study. The odd part was that my family was not very well off financially![26] In the end, the field of geology was suggested to me, as Czechoslovakia had only five professional geologists at the time. Russian intervention into the application process facilitated my admission, and soon after, I learned that the number of professional geologists (and those in training) in Czechoslovakia had been raised from 5 to 80.[27]

Denial of higher education to citizens deemed "bourgeois" was standard practice. Future Czech president Václav Havel grew up in a wealthy family and was denied access to higher education, instead being forced into menial labor.

A second account, this from Beáta, of Banská Bystrica, tells a similar story:

> I had trouble applying to university because of an arrest when I was 17. As a high school student, I used to collect jokes and write them down. Many of these jokes were political in nature. Some of them were very simple, such as "What are four enemies of socialism?" Answer: "Spring, summer, fall and winter." Others were wry or ironic

> statements, such as "We live in a society where workers don't work and governors don't govern." A friend took a copy of these jokes, translated in English, to a sports club, where an undercover government agent saw it. Shortly after, two men in black suits came to my house and arrested me—or, more to the point, they drove me around for a while. No charges were yet mentioned. They then asked me who gave them [the jokes] to me and who had translated them into English. I was interrogated. The two men played a game of "good cop, bad cop" with me. This action was, in fact, illegal, as I was only 17, and was entitled by law to a parental chaperone. Much of the questioning focused on my ability to speak English, and how the jokes came to be translated.
>
> My parents were not notified of either my arrest or my detention and interrogation, but they supported me throughout the ordeal once they had been informed. In the end, my mother was watched, and the government tried to have her salary reduced. To his credit, her boss refused to do so. But I was given two choices: to be expelled from school, or to finish the school year and leave the school. Later, this arrest delayed my ability to enter university. After 1990, I came to discover that my state record was empty and that no mention of my arrest existed. My records had either been lost or expunged, and my State "folder" was empty.[28]

Admissions tactics could also be suspect in the neighboring Warsaw Pact countries. In Poland, the entry rate for applicants was about 10 percent, as competition was intense. In addition to State exams, similar to those used in Czechoslovakia, aspiring students were asked to write an essay on "values" as an effort to assess the moral leanings of aspirants. Corruption was an issue as well, although, as Ela K., a graduate of Kraków University, explains, while it "certainly existed, it was also a powerful urban legend that parents (and students) used to explain away rejected applications. One aspect of the application process was the requirement for inclusion of a photograph with ones application. Students submitted the best—or sexiest—photos of themselves that they could find. We used to joke that the female students chosen for university tended to be unusually pretty. My father was an officer in the military, so I probably got some special treatment as a result. I know that I was given a top dorm choice based on my father's military status."[29]

In Czechoslovakia, certain application rules and strictures applied to university admissions, but, in theory, higher education was available to all who qualified. As described by Pavol V., "I received a full scholarship to study at university. This could never have happened in, for example, the United States, because my status was working class. I was not from a privileged class, yet I was given the chance for higher education."[30] University exams were often set up to provide extra advantage to applicants from humble backgrounds. Points were given on an application to "laborers" and Communist Party members, especially if both parents were members.[31]

The University Experience

Tomáš K. commenced university studies in the late 1950s and describes his experiences:

> I was not a great student, but the university tended to focus on rote memorization, so there was little incentive to study. My brothers had "black marks" against them in school, and this followed me around from time to time. I chose to go into engineering. Student housing cost me about 50 crowns per month, and I received a university salary of about 900 crowns/month [each figure was barely more than a few dollars]. My diet included little more than bread and jam. Attendance was not required in class, but the exams at the end of the term were what really mattered. Professors were treated as gods, and deference was the rule. About one—third of my fellow students were female—and this was in the late 1950s. The exams were truly brutal as there were about 40 of us in a class, and maybe four passed the exams, which ran about 14 hours.[32]

Students who failed an exam had one opportunity to retake it. In a few cases, they could petition the rector for a third chance. Those who came from Communist Party families had a certain level of protection, and there was some accompanying corruption as well. Some of these (party) students would stand up to professors and demand preferential treatment. Tomas K. recounts: "In one case, I saw a student throw his index [a student's record] in the face of a professor, demanding special treatment. This could be very intimidating to professors, who feared standing up to Party members. In the end, though, there was a very strong sense of community among students, whether communist or not. In our group were also considerable numbers of foreign students. I remember a particularly large group of students from Mongolia, many of whom were either rich or connected to the Soviet army."[33]

Universities subjected academic departments to varying degrees of oversight. Generally, the more potentially controversial the field, the more oversight was imposed. Strictures on research became increasingly severe in the mid- to late 1950s, and by the 1960s, the breadth of subjects in certain fields had grown quite limited. For example, no political science departments existed as such; rather, one studied "scientific communism." Some political science departments were called Departments for Marxist Leninist Studies. Sociology, too, was a controversial area, and only Marxist–Leninist theories were permitted (the only exception being the occasional inclusion of non–Marxists, who were critical of "bourgeois" theories).[34]

Student Retention

By 1960, the Czechoslovak university system had run into issues that struck at the ideological, as well as the qualitative character of the national universities. The problem was that the issue of "academic mortality" had reached epidemic levels. Too many students were leaving university without having completed their studies. At issue was *why* students were failing to finish their studies. On September 16, 1960, an article, authored by Josef Havlín, a CPCS functionary, tried to explain the high dropout rate at universities throughout the country.[35]

Statistically, the problem of "student incapacity to master subjects" was extant; 30 percent of students throughout the country failed to complete their course of study, while 50 percent of part-time students also failed to finish. Higher rates still existed in the sciences, engineering, foundry, building, and agriculture.[36] Havlín's article attempted to place the blame for student failure at the hands of forces outside of the students themselves—all within the orthodoxy of traditional Marxist–Leninist "principles." Teachers, tutors, and university officials were seen as culprits, while "capable and proven workers who had decided to sacrifice part of their own time to study at university" were portrayed as victims. Failure was said to come from inadequate study facilities, particularly at work places. Overall, Havlín suggested that education was becoming "too individualistic," ignoring the collective interest of the working class and of the Party.[37]

Articles subsequent to Havlín's tended to take a more diversified approach to the issue of university student failure. An article from *Mladá Fronta*, in October 1960, noted that each university student cost the government 17,000 Czech crowns (*koruna*) annually. Dropout rates approaching 30 percent in the sciences could not be sustained. However, in some regions, rates were even higher; Brno reported dropout rates of 48.6 percent in mechanical engineering, at the technical college, in 1960. The medical faculty in Brno incurred a loss of nearly 28 percent of its students, while 62 percent of physics students failed in their first year, and 27 percent failed in descriptive geometry. Slovakia did not fare much better. By 1960, students in the mining program at Košice departed at a rate of nearly 60 percent within their first few years. *Mladá Fronta* stated in its article that problems of retention were caused by multiple factors; one was that many students had been accepted into the technical faculties only after having been refused to the faculty of arts, during an admissions process that was often politicized. Therefore, a student might take up chemistry only because he or she had been refused admission to study law. Curriculum was also attacked in the *Mladá Fronta* piece, particularly with regard to the sciences. New information, it was said, was integrated into the schooling process without having rendered older theories and data obsolete—thus forcing a meaningless burden of information onto students.[38]

Intertwined with the issue of superfluous information was the matter of Marxist–Leninist studies, which were considered part of the core curriculum at the time. Such studies were vociferously defended by Party regulars as "[not merely] a set of theorems, but as an inseparable part of all subjects on the curriculum." Compounding the curriculum issue was the matter of Brigáda work, the required physical labor for university students, to inculcate a sense of working-class solidarity among all classes. Compulsory labor was first introduced to the schools and universities in April 1959. CC Secretary Jiří Hendrych stated that "manual labor helps to educate people towards the socialist cooperation as distinct from bourgeois individualism."[39]

A piece from a 1958 edition of *Rudé Právo* reveals the prevailing attitude within the Communist Party at the dawn of the new decade: "Teachers should not judge their pupils in a narrow way. They should know where they grew up, how their political opinions were formed and what their attitude is towards the Socialist Republic. Only thus can one ensure that people will not go to the universities if they are not guaranteed to serve the working class exclusively and faithfully."[40] This passage illustrates the problem facing the regime. On the one hand, many capable students were kept from university based on their (or their parents') political or ideological records, but, at the same time, the "ideal" student population, being drawn from the working classes and rural areas, were often unwilling or unable to leave their locales for the university. Thus, by the early 1960s, the Communist Party was unwilling to compromise either on the Brigáda work requirement for students or on the inclusion of Marxist–Leninist principles in the curriculum.

Adult Education

In addition to the traditional university, Czechoslovakia had a long tradition of adult education. This system, severely disrupted by the German invasion and World War II, was invigorated after the passage of the Adult Education Act of 1959. The Act formally placed adult education into the hands of the Communist Party, which was then undergoing a critical period of examining Stalin's crimes and the Cult of the Personality. Adult education was progressively localized and liberalized under the control of elected officials, who would devise policies for the "scientific" education of the "New Socialist Man."

By 1964, new initiatives were adopted at a national conference for the Ministry of Education and Culture, stressing both quality of work and the need to follow "needs and wishes" of people "in planning adult education activities." Between 1960 and 1964, adult education was introduced as a faculty in the Charles University in Prague; at Comenius University in Bratislava it became a separate discipline and was granted independent departmental status at Šafárik University, in Prešov.[41] By 1963, one out of seven adults participated in some form of adult education in Czechoslovakia.

Recent research suggests that "vocational" education at the high school level did not necessarily preclude university education during the socialist period: "During the liberalization in the 1960s, the probability of going to a secondary school was higher for non–Party children. This continuing liberalization culminated in 1968, just before the Warsaw Pact troops invaded Czechoslovakia."[42]

Nevertheless, some literature suggests that Party members had favored status in university applications—at least during periods of tumult or Communist Party orthodoxy. "The consequences that parental involvement in the CP held for children's education display remarkable historical variation, which is unambiguously responsive to modern Czechoslovak history. Children of active communists were advantaged in the two periods of the most explicit communist orthodoxy: after the revolution between 1948 and 1953, and then after the Soviet occupation of Czechoslovakia between 1970 and 1974."[43] Unfortunately, the data used here does not further adjudicate the two competing explanations of the effect of CP affiliation.

The system of education in Cold War Czechoslovakia was highly funded, highly monitored, and dedicated to the goals of the state. Early education was tied closely with recruitment for the Communist Party, the Pioneers, and other "social" organizations as well as games and competitions, which helped to socialize students in the interest of their future advancement.

Promotion in education was, of course, also related directly to the family—and to the appearance of cooperation with the State political structures. Exclusion from higher education could be arbitrary, and, also, circumvented. For some, such as Václav Havel, who was denied higher education because of the perceived high social position of his family, higher education was simply blocked. For others, a gray space persisted.

Chapter Three

Culture, Entertainment and Leisure

Overheard in Prague: At what time should a proper lady be in bed? Answer: By 7:30, so that she may be home by 10.

The traditional stereotype of Eastern Bloc life was that of a dreary, grey mass. The reality, in fact, was quite different and considerably more complex. This chapter looks at the various ways Czechoslovaks spent leisure time, enjoying themselves through music, shopping, art, and other forms of social activity.

The Secret Studio

During the academic year of 1998-1999, I began my second year as a guest professor of history and politics at Prešov University, in the eastern portion of the Slovak Republic. Slovakia had been independent for barely five years, and many changes were underway. As a historian, I was quite interested in the Old Regime, and I often asked my students, friends and colleagues about how life manifested itself during those times. One Slovak friend noted my curiosity and offered to show me something that he said "would really blow my mind." I took him up on his offer, and he escorted me to a small town in the far eastern portion of the country. There, I met his father—an English speaker and music enthusiast—who welcomed me to what he called a "nicely kept secret." After exchanging pleasantries, I accompanied him to a block of uniform, staid, decaying flats from the 1960–1980 housing boom era.

He directed me to a ground-level entrance, from a back door. We entered into a long hall, typical of such buildings, normally used as basement storage areas for the apartments. My friend took me down the hall and then paused at a door on the right. This was no ordinary door. It was, first of all, massive and thick, like a bank vault or entrance to a giant refrigerator. Second, it had multiple locks. The father of my friend opened each of the locks, and we entered.

What appeared before us was a kind of secret garden—early 1970s style. In the first section of the entrance was an area for depositing shoes, umbrellas, or other accouterments. Just to the right of this area was a fully stocked bar, complete with four or five seats. It made me think of a kind of "hip" speakeasy. But the bar was only the entry room. Beyond lay the true treasure—a large, paneled, music listening room, complete with couches (circa 1973), shag carpeting, top-quality stereo speakers, turntables and other equipment from the same period. It had dimensions of about 6–9 meters long by 3–4 meters wide, and was lush, in a '70s sort of way. Huge amounts of work and heavy investment had gone into crating such a musical oasis. Here, he told me, was where local music enthusiasts got their (private) "fix" of popular music from the '60s to the '70s and '80s, when many bands (local or international) were either banned or otherwise frowned upon.

This was a club, and a selective one at that. Membership was required, and secrecy was imperative. The sole *raison d'etre* of this secret locale was the sharing of prohibited music. During my visit, my host shared with me a "cache" of old albums (still maintained in 1998)—the Beatles, King Crimson, the Grateful Dead, Bob Dylan, Pink Floyd, and many other bands that were difficult, if not dangerous, to possess in Czechoslovakia. From old American blues standards to controversial Eastern pop acts, this was a venue for opening minds and defying authorities. My friend's father told me that the police were aware of the club, and the members knew that the police were aware. Raids were fairly common, but police were paid off in a routine manner to maintain the peace. The stocked bar also helped to ease opposition from local authorities. Interestingly, the club still exists—a relic from a distant past, still replete with its pristine albums, turntables, refrigerator, plush carpets, and comfy couches.

Childhood Revisited

Representations and recollections of youth are highly useful in that they reflect an innocence of experience, devoid of political or social commentary. Childhood recollections allow for a unique and often revealing view of a culture and its values. Following are several largely verbatim interviews that reflect the communist-era Czech and Slovak lands, the small town, the big city and the countryside. What emerges is an image of an integrated, safe and stable society that allowed for a very healthy relationship to develop between child and nature. The first narrative reflects small-town living in Slovakia:

> I was born in 1965 and raised in a village in the west-central Slovak region, near Trnava. As children, we worried about nothing. Our lives were simple; we lived on a small farm and had pretty much everything that we needed. As young kids, we never worried about parents not being around, because all mothers were given a state income from the birth of their child until his/her entry into primary school. There was no need for daycare. In our village, all types of kids played together—even of different ages. Our play was usually [like most play] without much direction—but it could take place anywhere. Often, we would head to the woods—even the deep woods—and play all day long. There was no danger because there was no crime.
>
> In the old days, we often used large bottles to store vinegar. Children would often take the old bottles to sources of mineral or spring water and bottle it for their families. In the mountains we had many varieties of water, and each child had his own favorite. In a funny sort of way, the empty bottles were our toys. We didn't really have toys, in the modern sense of the word. We didn't really have much in the general sense of material items. What toys we did have were usually homemade. Either our parents would cobble something together or we kids would improvise something ourselves. A stick could be a gun, and old clothes (or those of siblings) became "dress up" outfits for us to pretend that we were kings, queens, or princesses. Once in a while we received some actual items with which to play. For example, I received a set of dishes, which I used to hold tea parties with my friends. These dishes were precious to me. The tea was often served with mud cakes from the garden that we "baked" and served with tea. I did have one toy of which I was very possessive. My father visited the Soviet Union and brought me a "walking" doll. It was about two feet high! If you held its hand, it would "walk" beside you. I was very protective of my Russian doll.
>
> Kids were generally not very fashion conscious—we tended to wear hand-me-downs from older siblings. But it didn't matter because everyone did the same thing. It was a custom to receive a new dress for Easter. We were able to keep tradition in our lives and families. Children did not have bank accounts because they didn't have money. We rarely used cash as kids, and it was unusual to have any with us. We had to do chores around the house, but we didn't receive any money for it. From time to time, our parents would give us a few cents for gum. Village labor was often donated for free by adults and children—if a project required large numbers of bodies, kids would be recruited. The expectation was that one's own family would need the community to help them one day.
>
> In the woods, we would play teacher (my sister was a teacher), or often, we would play war. The sticks from trees comprised our guns. From time to time, we would see a plane flying overhead. I always wanted to fly in a plane as a child. But the planes often scared me, because—although we knew little about the enemies of our country—we had heard rumors that America wanted to attack us from the air, and it scared us sometimes.

As a teenager, I became deeply involved in the "folk" ensembles that were popular at the time. It was the most beautiful time of my life. I was a dancer. The folk programs had considerable government support; we would dance at political meetings and gatherings. We called ourselves "40 brothers and sisters," and we felt an incredible camaraderie. We practiced every day and worked very hard—but we were never forced to join or to continue participating. There was no ideological pressure, either.[1]

Everything was free of charge. There was a certain amount of control from the top, but, with all of the benefits and holidays, the authorities sort of threw us a bone. Most of us joined the Pioneers [youth collective] as teens.[2] There was no consciousness of the fact that we were entering the first stages of grooming for the Communist Party. We felt free. Overall, however, despite the fact that I would not want to return to that old system for many reasons, what a wonderful life we had![3]

The second narrative reflects rural life and describes a pastoral, traditional style of living, where children assumed considerable responsibility in relatively safe environs:

The communist period leaves me with many conflicting feelings. As an adult, I can certainly understand the horrendous oppression that took place during the 1970s and 1980s, while I was growing up. I would never want to live under such a regime again. Still, there was a "sweetness" to my childhood under the old system, and I would not trade those experiences for anything in the world.

Our lives revolved around nature. We were free to explore anywhere we wanted to go—the woods, the village, nearby towns. Nobody controlled us. Furthermore, we didn't need money most of the time. Our joys were not material, but aesthetic. For example, I always loved animals and I enjoyed spending time around them. My family had a herd of cows, which grazed outside of our village in an idyllic field, close to a forest. As a ten year old, I was allowed to manage the cows during the day, ensuring that they stayed in place and were eating and drinking properly. It is funny to think about, because, as a ten-year-old girl, I was responsible for about thirty cows. Nobody gave it a second thought at the time. They were the most pacific and pleasant creatures I have ever seen.

After I watched the cows, my uncle would take me to our small *chata* [summer cottage] where he produced brandy. My uncle used plums, which he fermented. He then created liquor which was both strong and fragrant. I wasn't much of a fan of drinking it, but it was always a thrill when the slivovica was ready each year.

Life today is very materialistic, and people everywhere are interested in making money. Today, I practice yoga and other spiritual rituals, but I would attribute all of them to my experiences as a child, in the field with the cows. We were untouched by our neighbors, by government, by anyone. As a child, I was free.[4]

The third and final narrative describes an urban childhood in Prague, and touches on some of the politically-charged decisions that each family had to make:

My father was a communist, but he never told his family. Under the Old Regime, we felt a sort of "freedom," but looking back, we didn't really know what freedom was.

Unlike most of my friends, I was not a Pioneer. My father had spent time in prison, having overspent his visa allotment. The term was three years in prison, for the charge of having overstayed his visa. Thus, the family had some resentment towards the regime.

Nevertheless, as children, we never felt oppressed or deprived. It is true that we lacked some basic necessities—such as sanitary napkins and toilet paper—but we never really felt a need to complain about it. In the end, it was humor that united us.

My father was a dissident, but he was not "active" in the typical sense. Mom stayed at home—which was very unusual at the time—and he would work on his translation service, mainly German. I remember as a young child feeling that I was being evaluated not so much by who I was but by what others said I was. As a result, we often felt that that we lived "double lives," based on ostensible dissidence, but also on our own community. We assumed that our home was bugged. In 1989, it was confirmed to us—as three bugs were discovered.

We never really felt held down, as kids. Quite the opposite, really, as by the 1970s, we generally thought that "peace had been made" with the communists. This was good news, and we wanted to believe it—as it suggested fewer regulations and inconveniences—negative qualities that we associated with E. Germany. Our secret place where we could be free was the *chata*. For both parents and kids [although for different reasons] the *chata* was often viewed as a secret paradise. There was less work in those days—and child care was provided by the state.

Summers were fun—we would travel to Croatia, Bulgaria, or to [the East German island] Rügen. The drive to Croatia was usually in our [Russian-built] Lada, which was an awful experience. At least we could fly to Bulgaria.

We liked our Slovak neighbors, for the most part, but there were often regional jokes. I suppose that they had them too. For example, we used to ask: "How is a Slovak different from a Czech?" The answer was "If a Czech has 100 [crowns], he will pretend that he has none, while a Slovak with 1 crown will try to make you believe that he has 100."[5]

From these brief descriptions of life in Czechoslovakia, one can immediately perceive the importance of social relations such as family and friends, limited materialism, close contact with nature, and an appreciation for the daily and seasonal rhythms of life. One gets a sense also that young children lived a rather safe existence, free from external dangers, and were tasked with many responsibilities (such as watching the cows or helping to make slivovica). The lack of money, or for that matter, the lack of concern about money, is a theme that reappears in narratives of diverse communist regimes. Deprivation of material wealth might have been a fact, but it was not viewed as an inconvenience. Finally, a "sense" of freedom prevailed, whether real or not, combined with a limited but very real private sphere, such as the *chata*. The narratives suggest the state maintained a careful balance between authority in the political realm, and limited local autonomy in the cultural and private spheres.

Marriage and the Family

Marriage rates in communist Czechoslovakia stayed consistent until the early 1970s, when they began a steep decline that has lasted until the present day. Between 1973 and 2011, the overall numbers of people getting married dropped by approximately 50 percent. During the communist period, much attention was paid to the institution of the family, at least in official pronouncements. The unity of the family was seen as essential to the proper functioning of the socialist state.[6]

Historically, economic considerations loomed large when a young couple decided to marry. A steady and adequate income was essential, as was a dwelling, either as a newly-purchased private flat, or at minimum a shared apartment with extended family. If one or both of the newlyweds were well connected to Party politics, they might expect an apartment provided by the state.

Reproductive concerns also played a role in marriage up to the 1980s. The raising of children was foremost in the minds of many. In addition, birth control was unreliable and not readily available in much of central Eastern Europe until fairly recently, and many brides were pregnant when they married. Only marriages approved by the local municipality were legal. Church weddings were not considered valid. Divorce also required the acknowledgment of state authorities.[7]

The traditional marriage was driven by a desire for children and economic stability. An unplanned pregnancy could be successfully navigated by a wedding. Women were expected to marry by age 20, lest they be called "old maids." Men married slightly later, on average. Over time, the economic motivations for marriage (and as well for single status) lessened, as women became increasingly independent and mobile. Co-habitation became increasingly common by the 1970s and 1980s, and marriage from World War II onward became a more secular event, rather than representing a religious ideal. After the events of 1968, the society turned inward towards the "private sphere," and the family unit took on a new significance, becoming the representation of the *private* realm of consumerism, popular culture and withdrawal from the regular influences of the state. (In fact, this phenomenon was driven by official state *normalization* policy that will be discussed further in Chapters Six and Seven.) Facilitating this transition was a housing construction boom in the 1970s, allowing additional material opportunities for newly-married couples.[8]

From the Second World War through the communist period, divorce became increasingly common. (This trend continues today.) Increased affluence, "declining morals," individualism and perhaps a more casual attitude towards the institution of marriage, were some of the contributing factors. In some cases, however, mutual economic dependence kept some marriages together that would have otherwise failed: "For some people, survival on a single income was difficult or impossible. If a couple shares a flat and an income, it might make more sense for them to remain together, even if they are seeing other people and are not really a couple anymore."[9] Unlike the past, marriage and divorce have, since the 1960s, become increasingly treated as consensual, emotionally-driven commitments, rather than economic, family-oriented or religiously-driven obligations, as they had been previously.

Going Out

To place Czechoslovak entertainment in its proper context, it is useful to explore the spatial dimension of the country during the latter Cold War and to examine the locus of both daily life and popular entertainment. Private space, at least internal, domestic private space, was limited. Many, if not most, urban families lived in hastily constructed post–World War II high-rise apartment complexes. These concrete towers were scattered throughout Eastern Europe; principles of "socialist architecture" were employed even in Paris and London, as a means of relieving an extreme housing shortage after the War.[10]

Initially, these massive housing projects were highly popular, providing free, decent and modern housing in return for quiet acceptance of the prevailing political regimes. Old, historic central neighborhoods were often razed or abandoned, many falling into neglect as vestiges of "bourgeois sentimentalism," in favor of the new suburbs of the high-rises. (Often, the old historic areas were occupied by local Roma [gypsies], who continued to live there for decades, until the private real estate market returned, and property values soared after 1989.) The construction of these huge concrete neighborhoods peaked in the late 1980s. Today, they continue to clutter urban areas in various states of disrepair. Some have been torn down, others rehabilitated.[11]

One rather grim association with "socialist architecture" was its impersonal nature—and its extreme functionality at the expense of aesthetics. Large numbers of strangers were grouped together in social circumstances antithetical to traditional village values, within the concrete jungle, and the results were often negative. For example, the alienation of the high-rise often led to high suicide rates among inhabitants. Petržalka, an enormous public housing complex established in Bratislava, and home to more than 100,000 residents, became the leading region of suicide in the Slovak territory and one of the highest in Czechoslovakia.

Similarly, by the late 1980s, Hungary's suicide rate (4,000 out of a population of just ten million, with another 40,000 attempted suicides) had become the highest in the world. The most common means for suicide was jumping from high places—easily accomplished in the high-rise structures, which had a disproportionate rate of these deaths. Clinical depression has been ascribed to the phenomenon in both countries, and while the Czech and Hungarian governments were traditionally loathe to attempt connecting "socialist architecture" with suicide and mental illness, there is an almost immediate anecdotal association in the minds of the general population.[12]

Thus, one may extrapolate from the above that high rise living in the Eastern Bloc was, at best, a mixed experience. But one may also suppose that the desire to get out, to seek entertainment venues outside of the house, might well be highly desirable—and necessary.

Music

Listening to music in communist Czechoslovakia was not always risky—as certain styles were tolerated. But enforcement was arbitrary. Pop music, the musical style most associated with the West, was often the most controversial form. "The Beatles were fairly safe," says Ľuba S., "at least until they became increasingly politicized. But you could never be sure. We listened to quite a bit of Pink Floyd and Led Zeppelin in high school. Because I lived in Bratislava at the time [just across the border from Austria], we listened to a lot of Austrian and western radio, and taped much of it."[13] A local resident from the central Slovak region of Banská Bystrica, Beáta, concurs: "We listened to and taped a lot of 'forbidden or controversial' music. These tapes were usually hidden under our beds. In addition to music, there were routinely published lists of banned books. We were sometimes able to obtain them, as smugglers brought them in over the mountains from Poland. Some people had contacts with others in the United States, too. Aleksandr Solzhenitsyn was banned, but we could find his works. Bibles, which were legal, could be obtained as well. The problem with bibles was that the state was required to approve a version before it could be sold [or read] openly."[14] Taping was an option in areas of the country that were in radio signal range to the West (particularly Radio Luxembourg, which was a great source for Beatles songs), but for the eastern areas of the country, taping was less of an option. "It was sometimes possible to buy western cassettes in Budapest, and sometimes at flea markets" says Paul V. "Classical music was easy to obtain, as we had access to Deutsche Grammophon but finding western pop in stores was almost impossible."[15]

But enforcement ebbed and flowed. "It wasn't so much a matter of bad lyrics or behavior that could get you into trouble," says Paul V., "but any relationship with a western band or musical culture. Connections could be very damning. The deepest period of censorship was in the early 1980s. That was the period of the 'heaviest' communism.[16] The government used a 'carrot and stick' method to control music. They kept us off balance by never making it clear what was permitted and what wasn't. Sometimes, they loosened their grip, only to tighten it later."[17]

The "normalization" period after 1968 saw some new regulations; bands could no longer use English words for their band names, and lyrics could not be written in English.[18] Some bands and artists were blacklisted; the criteria seemed to be applied to those who were too active in saying things that were not in the interest of the Party. Of course, contacts with the West could also create significant problems for artists.[19]

While in the West the popular music worlds of the 1960s and 1970s were often associated with prevalent use of controlled substances, drugs were largely unknown in Czechoslovakia. During the 1960s, Czechoslovakia was slow to acknowledge the seriousness of drug abuse in its society. Most official pronouncements from the 1960s and 1970s more or less denied the existence of illicit drug use in the culture. In October 1987 officials held a press conference to publicize efforts to combat drug abuse in Czechoslovakia. In spite of these efforts, the regime continued to disallow the publication of comprehensive data regarding drug abuse. In 1988 approximately 6,700 individuals were officially registered as drug addicts in Czechoslovakia. It was estimated that upwards of 60,000 people were "using narcotic substances," although official estimates provide no data on the incidence of or the specific substances consumed. The secret report of an official conference on drug abuse held in Prague in 1983 (smuggled out of the country and publicized by Charter 77) and data published in the State press offer radically differing perspectives on drug abuse: The official report speaks of "tens of thousands" of individuals "addicted" to "hard drugs" (without specifying precisely what drugs). Another government source estimates that upwards of 400,000 individuals abused various amphetamines and barbiturates. "The official report indicates that youths predominate among those who abuse, or are addicted to, drugs. Males aged 15 to 19 constitute approximately one-half of all individuals officially considered addicted. The percentage of marijuana smokers among 12- to 13-year-olds is reported to have increased by three to five times between

1971 and 1980. Finally, children are trying drugs at ever younger ages. Charter 77 claims that throughout the country, 91 drug-related deaths occurred between 1978 and 1981."[20]

Jazz was both the most musically dissident musical style, and, oddly, one of the most accessible forms of music. This may have been because jazz musicians were cheap. Paul V. explains the jazz scene: "We were able to get Chick Corea and Dave Brubeck to perform in the early 1970s. Music was a showcase for the communist regime, a chance for the government to 'show off.' There was much government support for music—especially classical—and musicians were sometimes allowed to travel abroad." Western classical musicians were invited and treated like royalty, all a big show for the authorities. Pop and classical music had historically been on par with one another, but by the late 1960s, pop gained the upper hand. Czechoslovakia had its own hit parade in the early 1970s.[21]

One of the most influential musicians of the late '60s and early '70s was Marián Varga, a conservatorium dropout and free thinker who fused classical, rock, and other styles. Varga owned an early Hammond organ and also possessed a rarity in Czechoslovakia for the period—a Moog synthesizer. He was tolerated by the authorities, as his music was not overtly political or socially controversial. Perhaps the most popular band of this period was Elán; they performed songs with topical relevance, and their four band members had a Beatle-like appeal. Peter Lipa was a well established artist, as was Gabriel Jonáš and many others. Well established pop stars in Czechoslovakia, like Karel Gott, often did covers of Beatles and Rolling Stones songs without fear of reprisal. After all, they had an incentive—there were no worries about paying royalties.[22]

The club scene was pretty lively in 1969–1970, before the post–1968 normalization really took hold. Many artists who had fled the country in the 1950s and early 1960s returned to Czechoslovakia, under an amnesty program. Later, when it became harder, some musicians organized underground concerts. If authorities made inquiries, one could just plead ignorance. The underground concerts had no advertising—only word of mouth—and attendance was free of charge. Some musicians had their own clubs where they performed—Dežo Ursíny, for example, had the "Orolanda" Club on Hlavné námestie, in Bratislava.[23]

The Saga of the "Jazz Section"

By the mid 1980s however, there were signs that the music scene was actually becoming more closely monitored and controlled. At issue was a group of officers of the "Jazz Section," a social youth organization, detained by police, and now threatened with a trial in Prague. The seven were arrested in September 1986 and were subsequently charged with the illegal publication and printing of commercial materials. Prison terms for such activities ranged from two to eight years. While in custody, the Section's office was locked by police.[24]

Youth clubs were encouraged by communist authorities, and the Jazz Section had come into being through legal means. The Communist Party considered such officially sanctioned clubs as instruments by which to exert influence. However, from the 1960s onward—particularly during the "normalization" period following the events of 1968—many such clubs became highly suspect as bastions of lingering "reformist" sentiment. As a result, the post–Dubček regime of Gustáv Husák purged all such clubs, preferring to start anew with a "clean slate."

New clubs were set up in the place of the pre–1968 ones. The Jazz Section made an application in 1971 for a union of jazz musicians, but their request was turned down. Applicants were told instead to join the extant Czech Musicians Union. Due to an administrative glitch, the new members were allowed to set up their own section within the union—much to the chagrin of central authorities. Further complicating matters were rules that stated that, once set up by the national ministry, a group could be disbanded only by the union members themselves.[25]

Czech authorities had also failed to ensure that the chairman of the section be appointed by the ministry. A privilege enjoyed by officially sanctioned social clubs was the right to publish internal leaflets, brochures or newsletters—without having to endure strict censorship rules. (This guideline was driven by the seemingly benign nature of the subject matter, jazz music, and the presumably minuscule readership.)

A publication called *Jazzpetit* emerged from the Section in the mid–1970s, and readership burgeoned by the 1980s to nearly 100,000 readers. Meanwhile, the Section itself had grown to more than 7,000 members, quite in excess of the original cap of 3,000. The Jazz Section had, over time, evolved into an instrument of expression for multifarious artists throughout the country, many of whom were opponents of the regime. In July 1984, the entire Union was disbanded, with the demand that the "Section" be removed from its ranks.[26]

However, previously in 1980, the Section had applied for membership in the International Jazz Federation, an organization accredited by UNESCO. The new international recognition afforded the Section legitimacy later on, even after the group had been officially disbanded, and membership in the federation brought considerable international attention to their situation.

Arrests followed. Four days after the arrests of Section members, the wives of five of the accused protested their concern in a letter to Gustáv Husák. They argued that the arrests: "Raise the question of why the Czechoslovak authorities have found it necessary to come down so heavily on this seemingly innocuous group of musicians. The answer can be traced back to the origins of the 'normalization' rule in Czechoslovakia."[27]

Comedy and the Regime

From the 1960s onward, one of Czechoslovakia's top comic entertainers was Július Satinský. Satinský made a name for himself, particularly, when teamed up with fellow comic Milan Lasica. The two were mainstays of Czechoslovak television for several decades. Satinský, publically portraying the persona of a male chauvinist pig, actually preferred the company of educated, independent women. "Július called himself a monarchist," his wife Vierka recalls. "He claimed to admire the Swiss because of the way in which they delayed granting suffrage to women. He would regularly say (in public) that a woman belongs in the kitchen. The truth, however, was that he really respected strong women."[28]

Satinský went as far as to establish an "Old Women's Club" as a means of facilitating meetings and conversation. Older, independent professional women were his favorites. It was said that feminists hated him for his outspoken, politically incorrect statements about gender relations, and Vierka would often be asked how she could stand living with him. Satinský himself used to muse that, if ever anyone put a bomb under his car, or found some other means of doing away with him, "it would probably be a feminist!"[29]

The politics of comedy was complicated in Czechoslovakia. Lasica and Satinský rarely if ever touched directly upon political topics and never engaged in political satire. Instead, they were more interested in word play, double meanings, and "devising topics and interpretations where the listener or watcher could find the meaning that they chose to find." The authorities regularly accused the two of being covertly political, a charge that his wife refutes—mainly: "The authorities did indeed think that they were political, but really, they simply dealt with broad topics. Július enjoyed creating illusions—through words and scenarios that were not, strictly speaking, political. Perhaps they touched a nerve here and there. But it was only later in his career when he did, in fact become overtly political."[30]

Satinský enjoyed illusion—the illusion of sexism, of monarchism (he was a democrat). Early in his career he ran afoul of the authorities, the result being that he was unable to complete his university education. While Lasica was able to complete university in 1959, Satinský was blocked by his (later dissident) Marxist professor, Milan Šimečka. Because of a single failed exam, Šimečka prevented Satinský from graduating.

From the late 1960s until the early 1970s, Satinský and Lasica were banned from performing in Slovakia. Oddly, they were allowed to continue performing in the Czech lands. "Perhaps the Communist Party of Slovakia understood Slovak language (and humor) better than their Czech counterparts," Vierka muses. However, even in the Czech region, Prague was off limits for the duo; they proceeded to set up shop in the mid-size Czech town of Brno. "Comedy in the 1970s and 1980s in Czechoslovakia was not dangerous—just inconvenient."[31]

Satinský's heroes were numerous; Laurel and Hardy posters still grace his apartment, as do images of Buster Keaton and Don Quixote. He had hoped to complete a comic novel prior to his death in 2002 but became too sick to write. Lasica was not only his professional partner; the two were very close friends and lived together for many years. Like Václav Havel, Satinský received offers from political parties and even an offer to run for the presidency.

Dramatic Art

The early 1960s witnessed a reaction against intolerance and dogmatism in the areas of literature, theater, and film, particularly during the Third Congress of the Union of Czechoslovak writers, organized between May 1962 and May 1963. The Third Congress created a new sense of freedom and liberation for young dramatists. The official Party apparatus looked, however, with some consternation on the reform developments and dealt with them using traditional formulas. For example, an effort to slow the "de–Stalinization" process was led by the Ideological Commission of the Communist Party to purify the cultural front "from below," meaning that the "voice of the people" would be used to challenge liberalization in the arts.[32]

During this period, many young dramatists began to ignore the self-imposed censorship that had been prevalent before the 1960s. Alfréd Radok, founder of the famous *Magic Lantern Theater*, was a model for the young generation. Radok wrote that writers should "be bold and avoid self censorship! To describe the inner life of the individual. To grasp the world within and around us. The theater cannot answer questions; it can only incite us to ask questions."[33]

In the early 1960s, dramatists were sometimes broken into several ideological groupings. The first group comprised a set of young playwrights, many in their 30s, such as Václav Havel, Ivan Klíma, and Milan Uhde, all of whom pushed boundaries and were often accused of being "reactionary" by the regime. Second were the older and more established writers, a less radical force, but a group willing to create controversy. Individuals in this group included Peter Karvaš, Milan Kundera, and Jiří Robert Pick. Finally, there were the "regime" playwrights, who were in retreat by the early 1960s. They included Miroslav Stehlík, Jan Drda and Ludvík Askenazy. Differences among dramatists included but also transcended politics, often owing more to generational differences than to other influences.

Plays by the "revisionist" dramatists focused on issues of politics, society, morality, and responsibility. Peter Karvaš, for example, authored *The Scar,* dealing with unresolved societal issues. The immediate matters included the show trials of the 1950s; by the early 1960s, many of those accused of crimes had been officially "rehabilitated." *The Scar* deals with hidden complicity, and the responsibility borne by those who refused to speak out. The play is not about the trials *per se,* but about those who served the Party by a "conspiracy of silence" over the lies that were spread. In the end, the play intended to illuminate "how it was possible for such a total conflict to arise between the most humane philosophy of all times, which, in practice, was so inhumane."[34]

Milan Kundera's *The Key Holders* typifies a major piece of dramatic work in post–World War II Czechoslovakia. Thematic emphasis includes questions about everyday life and the role of responsibility and civil courage among ordinary people, in a World War II occupation setting. The play also references the political tumult of the 1950s.

J.R. Pick was a dramatist who had formerly worked under the prevailing ideological cult of personality characteristic of the Stalin years but who moved beyond it in his later works. Pick's work *How I Was Murdered* was a thriller, openly criticizing Party bureaucracy and unqualified *apparacheks.* The play was prohibited in much of the country but was allowed to run in Prague. Milan Uhde aimed biting satire at the contemporary political and economic situation in Czechoslovakia, with his *King Vávra,* in 1964. This work is set in Ireland, where a king with long ears keeps his secret from his subjects until they eventually find out. The king lashes out at all who might compromise his authority by exposing his secret. The play is an attempt to point out the lack of qualifications within the ruling class and to reveal the deep—rooted hypocrisy of Czechoslovak society.

Václav Havel, another of the "young" dramatists of the early 1960s, produced a work called *Garden Party* in 1963. Havel had, because of his middle-class background, been prohibited from studying at the Academy of Dramatic Arts but went on to receive excellent practical training, first as a stagehand, and then as an assistant to Alfréd Radok. *Garden Party* ridicules official Party jargon and makes fun of degrading, anti-social mechanisms found in Czech society, as old dogmatisms gave way to new ones, in the name of reform.[35]

Ivan Klíma produced a major work of symbolism in 1964. *The Castle* involves a group of scientists and artists who inhabit an unnamed castle; each has profited from the Stalinist period, and now all reside in a castle, doing nothing. While their level of living comfort is high, they share an undefined anxiety. A young man (a representative of the younger generation) dies in the castle—as the symbolically "old guard" will stoop to murder to protect its status. The residents live in constant fear of everything new and everything different. They trust nothing and seem unable to acknowledge, much less slow, the march of time. *The Castle* has been called "Kafkaesque" in its structure.[36]

Klima's *The Castle* might have been the last straw. In January 1965 the Party ideological biweekly *Život Strany* printed the CPCS resolution from a district committee in Ústí nad Orlicí, which had criticized television programs, theater productions, and writers as "doing damage to the working class." The call for a "voice from below" (the "voice of the people") was again raised to protect the society from outside corruption. A secretary to a regional committee of the CPCS in Hradec Králové issued the following critique of modern Czechoslovak television and theater:

> An attempt to bring various pro–Western tendencies into the present development of our culture is apparent. This is clear from the views expressed by some artists who want to achieve pure art, classlessness, formalism, and abstractionism.
>
> There is a tendency to yield to the pressure of bourgeois ideology and to the Western way of lifting the Working People protest against the attempts to belittle the achievements of our people, and to undermine trust in the strength and faith of the policy of the Party and its Central Committee.[37]

By April 1964 the CPCS Central Committee secretary for the Bohemian region, Jiři Hendrych, overtly attacked "disobedient" artists: "I have in mind those who act as if they wish to shake the very foundation of our society instead of seeking its constant regeneration. Such tendencies cannot remain unanswered; we must take energetic steps and severely censure those who spread incorrect ideas."[38] One year earlier, the Communist Party had made a half-hearted attempt at acknowledging the wrongful actions of the Stalinist Slánský trials a decade earlier. Fourteen individuals had been accused of treason, and 11 were executed. A brief blurb appearing in newspapers announced that those executed after trial had been "rehabilitated." The announcement was a gesture towards de–Stalinization, but it in no way implied a retreat from Party unity and orthodoxy. The Ideological Commission proceeded to ban a play by Jaroslav Dietl, *A Young Lady for His Excellency, Comrades!*, a thinly veiled account of modern life after Stalin, and growing discontent with the status quo into the 1960s.[39] In fact, the origins of the events of 1968 have been traced to a revolt among writers and a growing tension between impatient and rebellious literary figures, nominally reformist within the Party, against the literary establishment.

Such tension reached a crescendo during the 1967 Writers' Congress, in which many reformists criticized the failures of the Czechoslovak Socialist Republic to solve basic societal ills. Many expressed disillusionment with the aspirations that they had felt at the close of World War II. Significantly, however, diatribes against the Old Guard were not demands to end socialism. Instead, there were calls to incorporate elements of reform without "wading to the other bank of the [ideological] river" (a reference to Dietl's play). Party leader Antonín Novotný did not share this nuanced interpretation of the possibilities of reform socialism, instead seeing such criticisms as a threat to the system itself.[40]

Film

The slogan of the state was to "do all for the people in all spheres," such as culture and sport, and to do so in a manner that was affordable. Film clubs were prevalent and showed both new releases (including some Western films) and many classics. The quality of the films tended to be high, with serious artistic merit, and cost about 5–6 crowns a negligible fee to attend. One negative aspect of the film exhibits was the occasional showing of ideologically "correct" films. Before a film would begin, an MC would greet the audience and describe the film, director and plot before the show began.[41]

The varying and often complex world of a film director in Communist Czechoslovakia is depicted below, with four leading directors, Jakubisko, Menzel, Herz and Forman providing perspectives in interviews regarding their experiences in the 1960s film industry.

Miloš Forman

During the 1960s, an avant-garde style of film—commonly known as the "new wave," developed in Czechoslovakia among a young cadre of film-makers. Miloš Forman was one of these. The Czech film industry had dwindled during the 1948 communist takeover to about three films per year. During this time, however, the film school continued to produce new graduates. Thus, by the time that Nikita Khrushchev made his famous speech denouncing Stalin and Stalinism, the stage was set for a revival of the industry. "Khrushchev said that 'we have to give more confidence to young people,' and this traveled very slowly—you know it took a few years before it came to the heads of Czechoslovak Communist Party bosses."[42] Prior to that time, the level of censorship was always touch and go. Forman recalls how censorship "has hiccups, has spasms, you know, so one day one thing is possible, and the next day it is not possible, but they don't tell you really." He describes a moment at the Cannes Film Festival of 1967, on the terrace of the Carleton Hotel, where a Czech secret service man approached him and said, "'Oh guys, you know—talk, talk, talk today is permitted—just keep talking, today it is permitted.' It was so strange that he said that. Of course, it happened later when 'Thanksgiving Day' arrived!"[43]

Forman recollects that there had always existed a "schizophrenia" within communist culture; a posture commensurately both dogmatically pro–Western and anti–Western. On the one hand, "they just publically and internally scorn the decadent, evil Western culture which is in the garbage bin of history; on the other hand, they were fascinated by any success with the Western intelligentsia. The French film critics probably saved us because they were ready to choke us, because we took work away from the old Party members, who deserved to be working."[44]

Forman acknowledged that his own experience with censorship was relatively benign as his films were, ostensibly, "comedies." However, his final film in Czechoslovakia, funded by Carol Ponti, was banned for 20 years for being "against the common man." Ironically, Forman's sponsor also disliked the movie, withdrawing his funds from production. In this case, Forman argued, "the west helped to do what the east did," by canceling the production. His explanation for the artistic environment for film makers at the time was this:

> It had become unpopular [after the Khrushchev speech] to administer a bureaucratic ban on films. Suddenly it was not popular to do that. Thinking that they were clever, they [the authorities] arranged a meeting in a small town, for the working class people of the film, and they sent a few of their people there, who said, "Dear comrades, we just saw this film and have to talk a bit as we want to know your feeling."

They knew how to slightly shift what they wanted to hear. Afterwards, if a working class "objection" was raised by such leading questions, the film was banned.[45]

Later, Forman produced the film *Fireman's Ball,* interpreted by many as a political statement. In fact, he says:

I just wanted to have fun knowing that you were bugging these idiots, like Biľak and Jakeš and Novotný, these totally corrupt people. In this case, authorities tried to show the picture locally showing it "in town," but things went wrong. Although a few firemen [workers] in the audience expressed the belief that perhaps the idiotic presentation in the film of firemen degraded them, more expressed the belief that, in fact, many firemen were routinely drunk and disorderly, and that the film was on the mark. "The Communists forgot one thing; *that in the moment, these firemen were not any longer firemen, they were actors, and they were defending their film*."[46]

Interestingly, in 1996, Forman became embroiled in a controversy over his film *The People vs. Larry Flynt.* Forman sought to portray Flynt as "libertarian" in orientation; others saw a more pernicious side to Flynt's character. In the end, the film was, for Forman, a depiction of the evils of censorship.[47]

Jiří Menzel

A leading figure of the Czech "New Wave," Menzel received an Oscar in 1966 for his first film, *Closely Observed Trains*: "At that time, he says, it was like Europe in 1848—the whole world went mad. Everyone had different reasons. In the US, people were against the Vietnam War, the French were against I'm not sure what, and they were both unlike our own well-mannered revolution. We never demonstrated. Until the Soviet tanks arrived, it was very quiet."

Menzel remained in Czechoslovakia after Miloš Forman departed for the U.S. His film *Larks on a String,* shot during the Prague Spring, was banned until 1990.[48] His take on Czechoslovak history is pointed: "We got our liberty a little too cheaply after WWI. We didn't earn it, and we lost our independence very easily in 1938–39. Then, when the Russians arrived, we adjusted again." Menzel's themes combine a skeptical look at Czech and human history, along with a combination of dark themes and slapstick comedy. Menzel claims to have been influenced by Buster Keaton and Charlie Chaplin. "People need comedies," he says.[49]

Juraj Jakubisko

Fellini said of Juraj Jakubisko that "the irrational, the miraculous and the fairytale appear just as naturally as life itself." Jakubisko's best known works include the trilogy *The Deserter and the Nomads, Birds Orphans and Fools, and See You in Hell, Fellows!* The three works move between tragedy and farce, focusing on the weaknesses and foibles of the human condition in the context of the 20th century world. Jakubisko was a Slovak, and grew up in a small mountain village. His period of greatest success coincided with the Prague Spring of 1968, resulting in a ban on his early movies until the 1990s. During the "normalization" period, he was banned from producing films until 1979. In 1983, with German backing, he made *The Millennial Bee*, which depicted life in a Slovak village from the turn of the century until the conclusion of the Second World War. His work was backed by German support for several subsequent projects.[50] This backing, he says, allowed him to make quality films rather than the expected "socialist-realist" style.

Jakubisko attended the FAMU film school in Prague during the communist period but says that "our professors made sure that we saw the films brought in for the authorities to look at. For example, we were able to see what Fellini was doing." After the Prague Spring, censorship was eliminated for a time—but, following the Soviet invasion, "our freedom was replaced by a kind of self-censorship. We became responsible—and afraid. Directors would take their wives, kids and friends to the projection halls to ensure that there was nothing in the films that could be used against them. Over time I found that it was better for a director to be close to his subject—that distance changes things and that is not good."[51]

When asked if he believed in the existence of a "Slovak" school of film, Jakubisko responds that, in some ways, the notion was valid.

> Slovak cinema is full of feeling, whereas the Czech approach is more rational and ironic. I wanted to use the symbolism of the village as a means of returning to our roots. Religious images and rituals, such as weddings, inspired me, along with their use of color and choir singing. You see, that in the early 1960s, official folk culture was like an operetta with little connection to real life. I was from a village where there were no cars, because there were no roads. Once, when a policeman brought the first bicycle to town, women cried and claimed that the "devil's wheel" had appeared. I prefer to draw from my own life experiences in my films.[52]

The years following 1968 affected his work greatly. He was transferred to an agency for the production of short films for 10 years; it appeared that he would not be allowed to make further full-length films. However, in 1979, he was allowed to make *Build a House, Plant a Tree*. "The main character was a thief, but I made him into a hero. Almost everyone stole things under socialism—there was even a saying: 'He who is not stealing from the state is stealing from his family.' I changed the story to illustrate this principle."

Juraj Hertz

One of the most memorable films of the 1960s was 1968's *The Cremator.* As a quintessential representative of the Czech New Wave film movement, Juraj Hertz portrays a black humor sensibility, featuring a lead character actor Rudolf Hrušínský, who plays the part of crematorium attendant Karl Kopfrkingl, a bizarre and dedicated man. (This film stands in contrast to the war-weary cynics popularized in Jir Menzel's films. Menzel himself plays a small part in the film.) In essence, the lead character, Kopfrkingl, believes that the burning of corpses is a means by which those spirits might attain a higher state of being, "a higher plane." The movie is set in 1938 Czechoslovakia, the year of the Munich Accords with Moscow, and Kopfrkingl is converted into an ecstatic Nazi sympathizer.[53]

Public Challenges to Artistic Standards

Czech and Slovak directors, writers, and poets walked a fine line with regime standards, which ebbed and flowed as circumstances in the regime dictated. The flaunting of convention by a visiting outsider—an American, an artistic radical, and a Jew no less—was cause for a more complex confrontation that was played out in Prague in the mid 1960s. At the center of the controversy were American beat poet Allen Ginsberg and folksinger and political activist Joan Baez.

On one occasion, in the 1980s, singer Joan Baez was on stage performing at the "Bratislavská Lýra," the International music festival in Bratislava. At one point, she began to talk to the audience, perhaps about politics. Shortly thereafter, her microphone was turned off. "It was whispered throughout the audience that 'they' had dared to turn off the microphone of somebody as well known as Joan Baez."[54]

In early spring 1965, Ginsberg was effectively thrown out of Cuba for protest activity. Ginsberg, a supporter of the Cuban revolution, had spoken out against one Party rule, censorship, and mistreatment of homosexuals in the theater. Cuban authorities also noted that Ginsberg had too much contact with local Cubans, which was not permitted under the law.[55] As a result, he was put on a plane to Prague and expelled.

While in Prague, Ginsberg set up shop in a poetry cafe called Vinárna Viola, which was popular among poets, jazz musicians and students. The café was renowned for its weekly poetry readings. Many of Ginsberg's works had already been translated into Czech, and he found that he was already quite the celebrity there. Throughout his initial stay in Prague, he found "nice persons" (that is, undercover police) appearing in various places, such as the Vinárna Viola or his hotel room, watching him and questioning those with him. At the time, Ginsberg was interested in challenging orthodox Marxist dogmatism, which dictated all art should emanate from the Communist Party as the representative of the "people." To this end, he employed, at a major poetry reading at Charles University, a "vocalized" reading of some of his major and minor works, both in Czech and in English. This technique was drawn from literary trends in the United States at the time; it was well received by the throngs who attended.[56]

Ginsberg left Prague for Russia and Poland, where he spent an extended period of time. On his late April trip back from Moscow, Warsaw and Kraków, he stopped in Prague once again, for what was to be a short stopover of a few days, before heading to New York by way of London. However, he was not able to book a plane until May 7. During this unexpected sojourn, he met with Czech writers, such as Škvorecký (sometimes called the "Jack Kerouac of Czechoslovakia"). On or about April 29, Škvorecký asked Ginsberg if he would like to be the candidate for the King of May, at the Polytechnic University. Apparently, his name had been floated among many students. His first concern was whether the May Day Parade was a political event—to which he was told that, in fact, it was an alternative parade to the standard May Day celebrations. This celebration would be more of a traditional Middle European fertility festival.[57]

Czechoslovakia had a history of such May celebrations long before the communist period, as did Russia and other Eastern states. By 1965, however, most of these fests had been banned. Notably, they were still tolerated in the Czech lands by President Novotný. Ginsberg accepted the nomination (each university or technical school put up a candidate) with the understanding that the winners (there was a Queen as well) could sleep with any person they chose in Prague. It was, after all, a fertility festival.[58]

In the end, over one hundred thousand people showed up in the park for the festival, and Ginsberg was, in fact, elected. With the crowd at a level much higher than had been anticipated by authorities, the political overtones to the event were palpable. Shortly after his election, Ginsberg was approached by some burly apparatchiks, and, still sitting on his king's throne, was carried off stage, having been told "you are no longer the King of May." After spending some brief time with the new wave film director Juraj Jakubisko, Ginsberg was arrested on Cuban charges of having written items "counter to the state." He was promptly booted out of Czechoslovakia.

Ginsberg went on to London, where he met with Bob Dylan, Donovan and the Beatles to discuss his recent experiences in Prague.[59]

Writers, whether musical, stage or literary, found expression through the regime, navigating often arbitrary, changing standards dictated from above. Certainly, the events of 1968 led to a formal tightening; during other periods, however, the whims of local authorities might expand and contract, as if to control a theoretical leash on artistic freedom. Still, many provocative works saw the light of day, often travelling under the radar in the form of metaphor, farce or dark comedy. Areas of limited private space (such as Petržalka) forced people out into public areas. By the same token, avant-garde art and poetry often attracted the same people back into the privacy and intimacy of a thriving club scene. The West factored into the film and musical scene in ways seen both as positive and negative, as curiosity drove a desire to seek out what was available abroad. At the same time, Czechoslovak music, drama and film developed—and often thrived—in a context that was national and contemporary with the realities of life in central Eastern Europe. Internecine tensions within communism and the Party, between reformers and true believers, further complicated the themes that emanated through the visual arts both before and after the events of 1968.

CHAPTER FOUR

Consumerism

"The Czechoslovak Communist Party just held its annual raffle. First prize is a week's vacation in the USSR. Second prize is a two week vacation in the USSR."

In this chapter the focus will be upon on the important and often arduous experiences of shopping and travel in Communist Czechoslovakia. Availability of goods, quirks of "market relations," and the always unpredictable experience of travel abroad reveal in Czechoslovak culture the frequent tension between consumer demands and Party policy.

Shopping and Consumer Culture

Obtaining Goods

The regime always spoke of material equality, but in fact there functioned a two-tiered system of privileged access to consumer goods. Material goods would pass through many layers of control before appearing in stores. Retailers, warehouses and producers could all claim a share long before anything actually appeared on the shelves of a store. Often, these goods were sold, bartered or traded to friends and relatives. Service employees had privileged access to scarce goods such as bicycles, exotic fruits and electronics. This access was typically bartered for other goods. One analysis has broken the exchange framework into three sections. The first of these is the circle of colleagues and connections in a work environment. This was particularly useful if one worked in the retail sector, where trade shows or new product displays could provide valuable insider information.

The second means of establishing insider status was through school relationships. Groups of individuals would establish consumer relations within cities: "A year after graduation, basically what did we become? No matter what store I went in, there was someone I knew there. My classmates, you see. So there was an advantage ... when a person was trying to find something. The girls would say 'yes we've got that,' and they would set it aside for us."[1]

A third level of contact was one's community relationships: local contacts, such as one's neighbors, local business owners and friends. These connections would keep an eye on developments with store merchandise. Selected persons would receive preferential treatment. Bribes also helped to grease the wheels of the underground economy, and were based on the value of the service being rendered. A surgeon might expect ten thousand crowns to bump a patient up in line for major surgery. In most cases, however, small "bribes," often called "tips," were given to expedite services such as home or car repairs. The alternative was simply to wait or to go without. "If you didn't know anybody in the shop, you wouldn't get what you needed. Really. Let me tell you about the refrigerator. It was a Hungarian refrigerator. For three days, we took shifts standing in line, morning, afternoon and night. For three days we waited in line! Well, finally, I got one. And it was the same thing with the washing machine, one of those 'Romovkas,' a little one with a spin cycle. There were always queues unless you knew someone."[2]

One might receive a bribe and use the same money to bribe another the same day. It must be added that the use of bribes was not endemic to the communist regime. Rather, the practice of consumer favoritism, use and misuse of connections and even tolerance for theft can been explained historically, having been culturally inculcated much earlier by the injustices of the Austro-Hungarian Empire and Nazi brutality, long before the forced expropriations by the communists in 1948.

Earning Money

Despite official policy, there existed always a "shadow" economy, a means of finding goods and making money. Many of the rich tycoons from the post-communist 1990s got their start earlier in the shadow economy. Certain elements of this shadow economy were legal and legitimate. Most jobs and professions provided salaries sufficient for subsistence living, while social and economic benefits from the State filled the gaps. But the shadow economy allowed revenue for the creation of profit and even wealth. One needed a *družstvo*, a word that indicates a cooperative, also translated loosely into "friend." These "friends" often appeared in the form of collective communes. Within these structures, it was possible—and even encouraged—to produce excess quantities of products. This excess of items—furniture or agriculture, for example—was allowed to be sold at a profit, using market forces to supply prices. The system allowed such arrangements because they tended to be very efficient and corrected weaknesses in planning schemes.[3]

Tuzex

Western items may have been difficult to procure in Communist Czechoslovakia, but they could be found. One of the leading sources of Western goods was *Tuzex*, a specialty store set up by the government specifically to sell Western items—in hard currency. The goal was to attract hard currency into the country; foreigners were invited to shop at Tuzex for jeans, chocolate, Western liquor and cigarettes, in exchange for their Deutschmarks, dollars—and even Yugoslav dinars, which were considered hard currency in Czechoslovakia.[4]

Tuzex used its own currency, the *bon*. A *bon* (or *bony*, in the plural) was worth about 5 Czechoslovak crowns. *Bony* could be obtained only from official government outlets in exchange for hard currency. Buying private or black market *bony* was illegal but commonly done. Some had access to hard currency, and these people became conduits for Western goods. For example, truck drivers carried an allocation of hard currency for travel meals; foreign students often carried hard currency; expatriate families sometimes mailed cash, though this was fraught with risks. One of the most reliable sources for private *bony* was elderly pensioners (often women) who had inheritance or foreign pensions paid in hard currency. Money that they received from abroad would be converted into *bony*; these women would then sell their *bony* back for hard currency outside of the Tuzex shops.

The biggest advantage that Tuzex offered was availability. Products were on the shelves for purchase (even houses/apartments). The name of the game was hard currency—Tuzex, while frequented by many Czechs, was never intended to function for the benefit of residents. Instead, it was a means of generating hard currency through three distinct groups: *tourists* bent on returning home with authentic Czech products; *pensioners* who drew their sums from the West in hard currency; and *émigrés* who "gifted" family members in the home country. Even a person of modest means in Western Europe could appear wealthy and benevolent by gifting through Tuzex. Large items (such as apartments) tended to be even cheaper than on the local economy. Eastern Slovakia possessed a disproportionate number of Tuzex stores, owing to the high number of earlier émigrés to America and elsewhere.[5]

The *bony* culture was time sensitive as the special currency was valid for only six months. Only those who possessed the *bony* vouchers could enter a Tuzex shop, and, as privileged consumerism could be perceived at odds with official socialist ideology, shops were often found in remote areas or little trafficked side streets. The Czech word *klid* (*kľud, pokoj* in Slovak) was used to represent a state of mind in the parallel economy. It referred to a means of "going with the flow." All participants in the bony economy, from pensioners to consumers to (often corrupted) police, understood this sentiment. Sellers of *bony* (often Roma) were called "*vekslák*," and they served a variety of purposes. For example, in addition to providing *"bon"* for hard currency, they also sold hard currency to Czech residents who wished to travel abroad and needed amounts of hard cash not necessarily available for good rates at local banks.[6] "Tuzex was a way to keep foreigners happy, and to inject hard currency into the state treasury," says Zora V. "I remember that my most desired items were Puma Shoes, Twinings Tea, Tic Tacs and western toothpaste. The tea was the greatest luxury. Our two domestic teas were known as either '*Pigi*,' which looked like dust—and tasted worse—or '*Club*,' a foul tasting tea that came in a yellow package with red letters."[7]

> Jeans were a big thing. We didn't have a great sense of material success. But we knew that others did. There was a tremendous sense of accomplishment when we acquired a CD or an LP of a major artist. The major gain was a car—that was a feat—other items came about twice per year. We managed to purchase a boom box in 1987.[8]

Of course, Tuzex was exceptional. Most actual retail took place through more or less normal channels. In this system, connections were extremely important; regular market relations did not often apply, especially to high-priced and hard-to-find items. Pavol explains:

> We did not ever feel as children that we were poor—certainly not in any abject way. We had what we needed—the essentials were covered. But there was always a feeling that "something was missing." Some of us had bikes and cars, and some did not. But to obtain these items, one did not "shop" as one would normally. A high-demand item was almost never for sale. By this, I mean that the "grey economy" took over in such cases. One didn't *buy* things; one *got* them.[9]

Through connections with a proprietor or perhaps a store cashier, one could ascertain the delivery date of new cars or bicycles. By making a contact, paying a bribe, settling an advance contract, or bartering some other goods, one could insure that they would receive an item when it came in. In Komárno, where I lived, there was only one dealership for Škoda cars and one for bicycles. Nobody ever *bought* anything; the stores were always empty—all of the items were "gotten" prior to delivery.

Pavol V. describes the key role that store workers and cashiers played in the consumer information chain:

This was also true with food items, like certain cuts of meat. A store cashier had an enormous amount of power in sharing shipment details with preferred customers. Even with a contact, the waiting time for a car or bicycle could be three to six months. Some towns were favored, and the population was treated to "getting" items that were hard to find elsewhere in the country. One city, Komárno, was a center for heavy industry, as we had shipyards on the Danube. Tank wheels were manufactured here. Hence, one's city was known as a "Center of Interest" of the state; workers were paid higher wages than elsewhere, and rare foods like bananas were easy to find. Such a designated town was looked after.[10]

Zora V. adds: "Throughout the country, shopkeepers had enormous power. When shipments came in, they would call their friends, who would buy and trade for the incoming goods."[11] Peter D. recounts the peculiar nature of the "extant" economy, where nothing was quite what it seemed: "The underground economy even had a term, *podpultový tovar*, which referred to goods which could not be 'seen' in a shop. Perhaps they are quite valuable, or in high demand—or perhaps the shopkeeper has only a few of them. In this case, it was useful to know a shop assistant, and if you gave the clerk 'some extra money,' you could have it. This means of purchase was obvious for [large scale] items like a washing machine, furniture or an ice box, and you sometimes made a deal on the spot—in your first visit to the shop, in some cases."[12]

Bartering

Consumerism in Czechoslovakia was driven by a desire for shops to "reserve" products for favored customers. (In fact, many will tell you that this practice is still widely condoned within the culture.) Another operative slogan of the times was *Čo Dávajú*, which translated into "What (in exchange) do you give?"[13] In the end, "shopping" for products, especially high-end items, often devolved into a sophisticated, *de facto* bartering system.

Food shopping involved different strategies. While food was generally plentiful, variety was poor, with many fruits and vegetables available only occasionally during the year. In this context, the most important person to know was one with knowledge of a delivery vehicle. Rumors could become rampant, and throngs of people would surround arriving trucks, based on insider information (often erroneous) about their cargoes. Individuals were limited typically to a purchase of one kilo; as a result, entire families would stand in line, one by one, to maximize the individual allocation limits.[14] Some items, like bananas, mandarin oranges or figs "were only available in pre–Christmas time. We would hurry to the store—all of us—to maximize our purchasing power. But we were happy when we got it—and could prepare sweets and fruit bags for the children."[15]

Consumerism was taken seriously by the authorities. In fact, consumer advocates occasionally challenged Party policy. In 1965, a Slovak "publicist" published an article in which he tried to demand reforms benefiting consumers. Eugen Loebl had been an insurance executive as well as a communist before World War II and was part of the communist group in exile in London during the war. Loebl had been caught up in the Slansky purges of the early 1950s and was sentenced to life in prison. By the mid–1950s he was out of prison and was considered "fully rehabilitated" by 1963.[16]

Loebl's argument began with a question: He asked, "Why should we not say that the advantage of socialism is that it is able to satisfy the needs of the consumer better than capitalism?" From this premise, he laid out arguments that stressed the satisfaction of consumer demand as the guiding principle of all economic activity. Consumers know their needs best, he argued, and should be free to consume what they wish—and their demands should be met by state policy. "The consumer should be sovereign," he stated. In doing so, he undermined a prevalent view in more orthodox communist quarters that the "view from the center" should be held in higher regard than that of individual consumer preference.[17]

With regard to competition in the consumer realms, Loebl argued that monopolies must be limited—in both their productive and distributive aspects. Consumer sovereignty, he argued, would be better served by economic competition. Further, he noted that price controls should be abandoned by the central government; "Price fixing from the center introduces alien elements into the consumer world. The center should not determine prices or demand, as this is the function of industry."[18] The issue of markets and prices was revisited several years later by the CZ deputy prime minister, Antonín Cervinka, who stated in an interview that "with centrally planned economic management, it is necessary to solve the following problem: the planned tasks have to be assigned to the companies via market relations between them, that is, in the form of demand by consumer companies." He added quickly, however, that market forces must be in a form that manifests the relationship to the plan, the relationships to central management. In the national economy, market relationships should not be allowed to have their own "autonomy," their own closed mechanism. Several months after Loebl's provocative article, the Czech regime admitted that, throughout the country, there existed the problem of "excess purchasing power," or that consumers had "unsatisfied" purchasing power, which, it was feared, could set off a round of panic-buying.[19]

President Novotný announced in 1965 that prices of raw materials would be connected to wage norms and profit; subsidies would be reduced or eliminated wherever possible, and market flexibility would be encouraged in consumer items (up to this point, only Yugoslavia had encouraged the market flexibility of raw material prices). Overall, prices would now tend to be set at a lower level rather than at the central governmental level. Novotný was cognizant of the controversy of his reforms—and certain reforms on enterprise freedoms were eventually repealed—but policy on prices and centralized decision making had certainly taken a turn. Comparisons with Yugoslavia were apt, as Tito visited Czechoslovakia, along with the GDR and the USSR, in 1965. The trip served to increase trade between Yugoslavia and the other Comecon countries. By 1966, Western trade with Yugoslavia had, for the first time, taken second place to trade with Eastern countries.[20] In fact, "operative decision making" was to be systemically decentralized as "enterprises and sector [branch] management [are] to take responsibility for the solution of the concrete problem of production and economy." In the end, a Commission for Finances, Prices and Wages was set up to negotiate issues associated with income, standard of living and general economic issues.[21]

Foreign Shopping

Sometimes, Czechs and Slovaks would opt to shop outside of the country. The logical destination for many in the central and eastern sections of the country was Budapest, Hungary, as it offered a better selection of boutiques and clothes. As noted previously, the chances of finding diverse styles of recorded music improved in Budapest. In order to enter Hungary, a passport was required, and a declaration of goods had to be made upon return. Customs duties were assessed on some items like alcohol and cameras. As Zora notes, "the most difficult items to afford at the time were coats and boots, as they were very expensive. As a result, people tended to be less interested in fashion than in durability."[22]

The culture of the Czech system was also peculiar in the manner it valued materialism and consumer items generally. In the first place, the societal norms tended to emphasize the equality of all non-elites. This had the effect of "freeing" people from the stress and tension of work, as competitive individualism was discouraged. Salaries tended to be higher for manual laborers, but the differential between professions was not excessive. As a result, the prevailing mentality lead to creativity, as people managed to make do with less.[23] As noted by one individual, "the materialism and its accompanying stress were simply not worth it," and comparisons with American "competitive" culture and stress were often emphasized. For most, the security and relatively consistent standards of living minimized the competitive aspects of material culture.[24]

Post–1968 "Normalization" and Consumerism

By the early 1970s, a concerted effort was made by the state to pacify reformist ideas and to ease citizens into a sense of comfort and security. For example, in the 14th Congress of the Czechoslovak Communist Party in 1971, it was declared that the "political crisis" was over and that "socialism" was reborn. At this time, the government set out to devise state policy to "ensure the fuller satisfaction of the needs of the population." In practical, consumer terms, this meant that prices on basic consumer goods were to be reduced. In fact, on May 3 of that year, across-the-board price cuts took place. The plan was intended to "raise the living standards" of the general population.[25] The realization that political order might be maintained by improved material standards came to be known by the early 1970s as "real existing socialism." Of course, this was an official term propagated by the post–1968 regime in the interest of recreating an orderly society.[26]

In the years between 1968 and 1969, nearly 107,000 Czechs emigrated to other countries. The borders were officially sealed by the fall of 1969, but during the previous 12 months, it had been possible to get out. After autumn 1969, anyone "missing" from Czechoslovakia was tried in absentia as a "deserter" of the Republic.[27] Several amnesties were offered, most notably in 1969 and in 1973, but few returned home. At Ruzyně Airport, in Prague, official contingents met the returnees, few as they might be, and comments were carefully recorded. One follows:

K. Vaník: [I should] find out back home if I too could return. I didn't kill anyone; I only went a little crazy in 1968.

A. Nosková: I ask you to please send me a letter about the conditions back home, I'd like to see my grandchildren before I die.

J. Švenlák: I left a girl behind in Prague, I didn't even say goodbye to her. If only I knew if she's still single.[28]

Moreover, by the 1970s, a powerful movement roughly translated as "If You Abandon Me," took hold as a measure for explaining high emigration from the reform period and to control the "normalization" regime. Émigrés were at once considered patriots who could return within the strictures of the Husák regime. But, more typically, émigrés were considered traitors who left their homeland under the pretense of a better life under a foreign regime. In fact, such culturally embedded ideas of traitors (both redeemed and condemned) became central in the concept of Czechoslovak nationalism.[29]

Few accepted the offer to return to Czechoslovakia. But for those several hundred who did, full honors were conferred at Ruzyně Airport. Returnees were seen as true patriots; stories abound of those who had tasted the savory treats of the West, only to find that the culture was, in fact, shallow and materialistic. The stories that they presented were often fantastical—that western countries offered no help whatsoever to unemployed workers, for example. Regular criticisms were made of the "western" system as inhuman and inefficient: "For the Janoček family, it was the conditions of life in America, rather than the tightly sealed borders of post–1968 Czechoslovakia, that functioned as a prison from which one longed to escape. In contrast, the social benefits available in Czechoslovakia pointed to security, and therefore, to freedom."[30]

The 1970s also heralded a "retirement" to the private sphere by many citizens, possibly as a reaction against the tumult of 1968. The State encouraged the retreat to the private sphere by promoting consumerism and deemphasizing political involvement and ideology, both of which had dominated the reform period of the late 1960s. Some reformers, notably Václav Havel, found the new consumerism distasteful and penned a public letter to President Husák arguing that materialism was creating both an "escape from the public sphere" and a loss of social responsibility.[31]

Travel

The ability to travel outside of Czechoslovakia could be a complicated ordeal, particularly if the trip was outside of the Eastern Bloc of communist countries. If one wished to travel to the West, they needed to obtain several documents that were difficult to acquire. The first of these was the travel permit. A permit could only be obtained after having received official approval from local Communist Party officials. Any record of political activism or other behavior regarded as suspect could result in a request being rejected. Indeed, lack of political convictions, or Party membership could doom an application. Approval from one's employer was required as well. Furthermore, applicants had to apply for a travel voucher that would permit them to exchange Czech crowns for German Deutschmarks or other western currencies. Strict limits applied to the amount of money that could be converted. At any stage of the application process, a request to travel could be turned down, up to the moment that the trip began. Many individuals found it easier to book a trip with a state agency as a means for easing the endless paperwork involved in getting a trip approved. Families travelling were often required to leave one family member behind, as a guarantee against defection.

Traveling Within the Eastern Bloc

Vacation travel in Czechoslovakia tended to follow certain patterns. Yugoslavia was a top destination, as it afforded landlocked Czechs and Slovaks a chance to visit the sea. Particularly popular destinations included the coastal cities of Zadar and Split. Lake Balaton in Hungary was also a popular stop, as were Bulgaria and the Black Sea beaches: Balaton "was our 'sea.' Actually, it's a large lake, but it was nice and something totally different from home. We lived in cabins, and I already liked it when I was a child. Then I was there again with my kids, and they liked it too. The only difference was, now I had to look after them. When I was there as a child with my mom, she looked after me."[32]

Foreign currency was usually controlled, with maximum limits of about 500DM. Czechs in the north found Rügen Island in eastern Germany a desirable destination. Travel restrictions were tight until 1965, when both eastern and western travel restrictions were relaxed. In 1965, Czechoslovak citizens were legally allowed to apply for a passport for travel outside of the Soviet Bloc for purposes other than specifically approved work assignments or conferences. While some travel restrictions continued, and hard currency for travel remained difficult to come by, the chance to travel was suddenly available and Czechs and Slovaks grasped the opportunity at unprecedented rates—in 1964 alone, 2,078,645 people traveled abroad on holiday.[33]

Citizens, in turn, were able to use comparisons with the West to formulate their own attacks on the government. In 1967, one angry reader of the newspaper *Lidová demokracie*, who signed himself as F. Novák, countered an economist's bogus explanations of the national economy by writing: "Today every fox terrier can see that our standard of living is decreasing rapidly." The economist responded by saying that Novák (an avowed construction worker) appeared to be a member of the intelligentsia trying to provoke the government, as his letter had contained no grammatical errors.[34]

A trip to the USSR was considerably more difficult to arrange. It was a given among Czechs and Slovaks that the standard of living there was considerably lower than that of Czechoslovakia, and the permissions granted to visit Russia were rare and conditional. For example, Dorina and her friend received permission to travel to Russia in 1972. However, they were instructed to take a specific driving route from Bratislava to Moscow and to record the exact mileage that the car had traversed on the trip. After a deviation during the voyage of "about 10 kilometers," a helicopter began to follow them and eventually stopped them for questioning.[35] Even travel to the (former Czechoslovakia before the Stalinist annexation) border area of Transcarpathia was fraught with difficulties. Juraj K. recalls "traveling to a city such as Užhorod was hard, because the Russians didn't want foreigners to see the lower standard of living."[36]

Stories of travel in the USSR suggest that, in addition to material hardship, information about the outside world was very limited there. Jeans and warm-up suits were the highest-demand clothing items. Another story involves a Slovak woman who went to a Russian dentist. When the dentist saw that she had white implants (added in Czechoslovakia), he called in all of his colleagues to see them, having never even heard of their existence. Still other stories refer to Soviet hospitals, where patients were not provided food and had to sneak out just to eat. Zora recalls a conversation with some very nationalistic Russian workers who had bragged to her about the superiority of Russian "astronaut machinery," recalling the voyage of Yuri Gagarin. In what was supposed to be a bit of levity, she mentioned (falsely) that she had been to "Honolulu" and made up stories about life there. Entranced, the workers insisted that she continue, and they hung on her every word, evidently completely ignorant about a place they knew nothing of and which, in any event, she had never visited. "Compared to us, they were so unaware of the world," she adds.[37]

Travel in Yugoslavia

Yugoslavia elicited a different sort of response from Czechs and Slovaks. Yugoslavia was nominally communist, but with aspects of market economics, beautiful beaches (Czechoslovakia was landlocked) and a high standard of living that shocked many who visited. A limited sum of money was allowed for the family to take out of country and at a good exchange rate (an artificially high exchange rate was maintained for the Czech koruna as a means to demonstrate a strong economy to the outside world). Whole families were rarely allowed to travel together. Generally, one member had to stay behind as "insurance" for the family's return, as described by Juraj K.: "My family applied for our vacation to Yugoslavia during the summer of 1988 in the standard manner. We appealed to the central government through the local, 'district' unit. We decided that my mother would not join us. We waited for a few weeks for our applications to be processed. We knew that the customs officials would be very tough as we crossed borders, and indeed they were. There was no room for niceties. In anticipation of this, I bought—ahead of time—a shirt with the Soviet Union name written in Cyrillic on the front—'ČSSR'—as a means to show my 'loyalty' to the Czechoslovak state."[38]

During the trip to Yugoslavia, Juraj K. purchased a short wave radio and cassette player: "I could listen to Radio Free Europe, which would broadcast in Czech and Slovak. What was interesting about the programs is that they would discuss events of the day but would provide two or more perspectives. Our local media would not discuss many events, at least not providing differing viewpoints. The activities of Vaclav Havel were one such example. I must admit that the fact that listening to Radio Free Europe was forbidden made it all that much more attractive."[39]

Those who could not afford (or were not granted permission) to visit Yugoslavia could travel within Czechoslovakia. The high Tatras provided great opportunities for hiking in the summer and skiing in the winter. The large artificial Šírava lake in the east provided an opportunity for swimming, picnicking, and camping.

Nearby were Poland and Hungary, each possessing attractive tourist and shopping opportunities at and beyond the border areas. Patrícia L. recalls travelling to these destinations, within easy reach of her eastern hometown of Košice: "Outside of Czechoslovakia, many of us knew little more than the Polish flea markets in the border areas and the Hungarian spas in places like Miškolc. And even short trips to these places involved thorough checks by customs officers. For example, they would count how many blankets we were carrying, how much luggage we had, and how much pocket money we had brought. The experience often left us feeling disrespected."[40]

Traveling in the West: One Family's Story

In 1984, a request from Malta was received by the Czechoslovak government. Malta was seriously short of doctors and other health care professionals. As a result, they asked Czechoslovakia for assistance in "loaning out" health care professionals. (Czech and Slovak doctors were also "loaned" during this period to "socialist" countries, such as Libya, as well as to the socialist and non-socialist Third World.)[41]

A family from Banská Bystrica, in the central Slovak region of the country, was invited to participate in the program, a true honor for any qualified professional. After all, they would represent (in a professional and technological sense) the triumph of the socialist regime back home. Five of Mirka's family members prepared for the voyage; stipulated in the contract was an understanding that one family member would be required to stay behind. Fear of defection from the Czechoslovak state drove this policy. In the end, Mirka's father remained behind. The rationale for choosing him to remain in Czechoslovakia was that he possessed limited English language skills.[42]

The move to Malta proved a torturous one. In the first place, the trip was to be done by train—a trip that would lead the family from Czechoslovakia through Austria, Hungary, and then the full length of the Italian peninsula before traversing Sicily, finally arriving at Malta by boat.

Travel to the West involved a four-stage process. To begin, a traveler had to secure a letter of invitation from a person or an organization abroad. Without this letter, no permission could be granted. Second, each traveler, if working, had to obtain permission from his or her "employer" to commence the voyage. If an employer refused consent, the entire travel process came to a screeching halt. In many cases, not only was the immediate supervisor's approval required but also that of the chief manager, foreman or "boss," who, in some cases, had no relationship or even knowledge of the affected employee. Without a doubt, many travel requests were turned down at this level, simply as a matter of expediency.[43]

Next, a traveler had to obtain hard currency, which was virtually impossible to possess in Czechoslovakia. An application could be filed with a local or national bank to procure needed funds in German Deutschmarks, French francs, Italian lira, or whatever Western currency was required. Once permission was granted, the traveler could begin the next phase—the visa process. Much hard currency was obtained (or augmented) through the black market. A baseline figure for value was the 1968 British pound, which fetched 100 Czechoslovak crowns in that year. (This figure was a common popular reference point for some time after.)[44]

Mirka's family managed to clear these hurdles and make it to Malta. The trip was long; many hours were spent on hot, packed Italian trains. Perhaps the most interesting episode of the voyage occurred early on, towards Vienna, Austria. A Czech man with a walking stick entered their cabin aboard the train. He placed the walking stick above, in the carry-on luggage rack, and sat down. After a short period, he got up suddenly and exited the car—without his walking stick. After the train had cleared Austrian customs and was entering the station at Vienna, he re-entered the car and reclaimed his walking stick. Mirka and her family watched the entire event unfold, surmising that the walking stick (in a Czech tradition that dated back to the Second World War, when valuables were stowed away in the legs of furniture) probably contained money or other valuables—or possibly a gun.[45]

In Rome, the family took a break and visited the Vatican. There, one of the family members had the good fortune to see the pope as he passed by, "so close that she could have reached out and touched him."

The trip to the Vatican and the story of the pope were never broached upon the family's return to Czechoslovakia:

> We never spoke of seeing the pope, much less being so close that we could have spoken to him. The reasons were multiple. In the first place was the obvious; one traveling outside of Czechoslovakia did not want to be associated with religious practice, particularly foreign and western.
>
> Secondly, our family was Jewish, and the tacit understanding of all Jews (particularly those who had survived WWII) was to avoid calling attention to yourself and your identity as a Jew.[46]

Returning Home

The return from a trip abroad could be an ordeal. Items purchased abroad were carefully examined. Even food was opened up to check for smuggled goods. Oranges were a rarity in Czechoslovakia, so travelers often brought some oranges back with them. However, customs guards routinely split them open as they did tubes of toothpaste. Entire car racks were dismantled so that authorities could check the screw holes into which the rack was fastened to the car. Of course, possession of illegally obtained foreign currency, or "black money," was a major offense. Alica recalls a trip that her brother took to Sweden. He had obtained a significant sum of "black money," and had sown it into the skin of a chicken that he took to Sweden with him. The "surgery" was performed by a local friend (an eye surgeon), and the cash was placed just under the skin, next to the bone and was subsequently transported successfully to Sweden.[47]

Defection

Some travelers chose not to return to Czechoslovakia. The means by which they achieved defection was typically a secret maintained within a given family and not shared with even the closest of friends—for their protection. For children, a defection often manifested itself as a "disappeared" friend. In the spring, one would befriend a classmate who, for reasons left unexplained, would fail to return in the fall. Jana T. recalls sudden disappearances from her school:

> It happened several times at school; a moment where someone "disappears" after summer vacation. Kids travel with their parents during the summer months, and some went abroad, to the seaside—though only to "socialist" countries—Bulgaria, Yugoslavia, Romania. So I was about 11 or 12 years old when we returned to school September 1, and one student did not come.
>
> Later, there was talk that the entire family had left, their apartment was taken and given to someone else. Months later, one of my classmates said that she had received a letter from the boy—he had written from Australia that he was ok. I know now that one of the ways to leave was to go to Yugoslavia—and from there cross into Austria. As a child, I was dimly aware from time to time that something was not quite right—when people suddenly leave and nothing is talked about.[48]

Popular Media

How well were Czechs and Slovaks informed of the world? What was the nature of the media from the 1960s until the collapse of the regime? With regard to the West in general, and to the United States in particular, a long history of fascination with what might be called the Myth of the Wild West dates back to the founding of the Czechoslovak Republic. Founding Father Thomas Garrigue Masaryk used the American governmental system as a model for the new Czechoslovakia, which emerged in 1918, following the First World War. American silent Western films were shown at that time, with actor Tom Mix a favorite among viewers. Further, the Czechoslovak *Tramper* movement of the same period was inspired by the American Boy Scouts and Girl Scouts, and songs and poems reflected widely the traditions depicted by names like Hiawatha, Wigwam, Dakota, and Gold River.[49]

Westerns disappeared from Czech theaters after the German invasion in 1940, but resurfaced in the early 1960s, with such films as *High Noon*, *The Magnificent Seven*, and *The Big Country*. In 1964, the first Czechoslovak Western appeared, titled "Lemonade Joe: A Cowboy Story Such as it

Should Be." Jiří Brdečka had created the character some 20 years earlier, where he could be found in pulp journals. The film itself could be seen as both a tribute to and parody of the American Western genre, with references to "Stetson City," the "Trigger Whiskey Saloon," and characters with suggestive names as "Dag Badman," and a *femme fatale* named "Tornado Lou, the Lark of Arizona."[50]

Lemonade Joe, as a symbolic savior, is dressed in white, drinking from a bottle of Kolaloka Lemonade, which gives him superhuman force as well as the ability to accurately shoot a fly—or the pants off of a villain. Joe provides a Puritan driven humanity that serves to remove social and class barriers from the now-liberated Stetson City. Some look back at the film as a parody of the East; some as a parody of the West. Either way, it was reflective of a period of increased media tolerance that came crashing down with the events of 1968.

One of the major films that attempted to portray the events of 1968 was *Hippopotamus* by director Karel Steklý. The film portrayed a man being swallowed whole by a hippopotamus at a zoo, who then continued to live in the hippo's belly. Prague Spring political leaders were spoofed in the film as both opportunists and as undermining the societal order.[51]

The Role of Television

Television became a major instrument of influence throughout the 1960s. By 1970, most households owned television sets. The events of 1968 were stoked by television messages of reform, and the normalization that followed 1968 foisted its own vocabulary and narrative after Dubček's ouster. "1968 was a wakeup call," said many normalization leaders, realizing perhaps for the first time the power of TV as mass media.[52]

In fact, the (post–1968) Husák regime used the medium to promote a normalized perspective of socialism that had slipped from the establishment's grasp during the events of 1968. It sought to portray a new "private citizen" experiencing the "quiet life" through consumerism and private, passive entertainment, a major component of what was to be television. Throughout the 1970s and 1980s, subtle messages of reform and cultural/political criticism vied with orthodoxy and official doublespeak on the home television screens of millions of Czechs and Slovaks. It contributed to the development of a critically minded public as well as to the process of "remembering and forgetting," a phrase used by Milan Kundera to describe the post-communist period.[53]

Czechs and Slovaks living within the reach of signals from West Germany and Austria could enjoy Western broadcasting. In fact, until 1971, when they suddenly disappeared from store shelves, a firm in Pilsen manufactured antennae. Later, an "anti-aerial" campaign was instituted, whereby owners of antennas were asked to voluntarily remove them. (Later, in the 1980s, the arrival of satellite television and video cassette recorders threatened once again to flood the East with Western media.)[54]

By 1975, a new television series, *Major Zeman*, made its debut through a cooperative effort between the Czechoslovak Ministry of Interior and Defense and Czechoslovak Television. The show spanned 30 episodes, each conforming to a year since the communists seized control of the government. Historic events were given an official spin—for example, events of 1968 involved the hero, Major Zeman, a tough, honest, square-jawed law enforcement agent, being demoted by "reformists." The episode demonstrates his resolve to set the record straight and to restore order to the chaotic country in his new role as patriot dissident. Throughout the series, the Communist Party, or CPCz, is a reliable ally to his unquestionably patriotic efforts. *Major Zeman* was propaganda with a military and nationalistic edge—and it was enormously popular. To be sure, the general director of Czech TV, Jan Zelenka, had been instructed that *Major Zeman* needed to "advance socialist society."[55] The *Zeman* series was distinctive in its attempts to be apolitical; Major Zeman was merely fighting for the right—he was not a politician—and for the country, in an effort to bring it back from the brink of irrationalism and mayhem.[56]

In addition, the decade of the 1970s saw a rise of pop culture and increased celebrity within the major media. By the early 70s, nearly three quarters of all citizens owned a television set, and many (particularly in the southwestern Czech regions and western Slovak regions) could pick up either West German or Austrian television. Although the government tried to regulate the use of antennae, they did not meet with much success. In the early '70s, it was estimated that a majority of those who could reach Western programming watched mostly Western television.[57]

The television work from writer Jaroslav Dietl expresses, artistically, many of the trends of the "private life" period during normalization. Dietl's work was enormously popular throughout Eastern Europe, as it refrained from overt political themes and controversy. Dietl's characters tended to be average, responsible people the viewing audience could relate to. Show themes included many day-to-day problems played out in a somewhat idealized socialist world.

Shows like *A Hospital on the Edge of Town* and *A Man at the Town Hall*, from 1977 and 1976, respectively, dealt with highly charged emotional issues that were resolved between close communities with tight bonds. The Communist Party and politics are generally prominent in the shows, although it is clear that the quality of life displayed (somewhat fictitiously) is a result of Party work and ideology. By focusing on family life and private values, Dietl's work could be said to take controversy out of public life and to encourage private reflection and discussion in the private sphere, as noted by the comments below[58]:

> I have often recognized myself, my colleagues; all of us who had experienced and overcome certain problems daily. Maybe even those who had stood on the other bank of the river [i.e., anti-communists]—either with their way of thinking or else in their actions—also recognized themselves. And there were more than just a few of them. But it made me happy that the series was able to portray them openly and even courageously. It was also wonderful that the Party was able to admit its own political mistakes.[59]

> Not without reason do we call them a family series, and that's just because more and more are becoming just some chronicle of one single family, and a family, moreover, that seems to be removed from the surrounding world, a family that exists "in and of itself," that seems to be unconcerned about almost anything else that takes place around it ... with its home-baked joys and tragedies.[60]

Like television, radio programming often allowed for people to listen to foreign shows, particularly in the western portion of the country. But one had to exercise a certain degree of care. "We had a radio that picked up western European shows," says Beáta, "and my parents listened to it all of the time. However, we could only listen to the radio in one room of the house—the bedroom. My parents told us to be quiet and to keep the volume turned down for fear that neighbors might hear."[61]

A significant portion of the Czech population listened to foreign broadcasting stations, entities often termed "seditious" by the state controlled media. The stations included the BBC, Voice of America and Radio Free Europe, among others. Thus there existed a means by which individuals could compare news of the world as reported both locally and internationally.

In the end, entertainment in Czechoslovakia, though always under the watchful eye of the Party apparatchiks, was an erratically policed phenomenon as well as one that evolved over time. External politics, political stability and consumerism ultimately drove State policy towards social standards, with very mixed results.

Chapter Five

The Communist Party

Question: "Is it possible to foretell the future?"
Answer: "Yes, that is no problem: we know exactly what the future will be like. Our problem is with the past: that keeps changing."—Soviet anecdote

Despite this study's attention to popular culture, one cannot escape from the fact that the Communist Party, along with an orthodox ideology and its commensurate political extensions, held enormous influence over society that cannot be divorced from the popular culture. The fact remains that the Communist Party exerted significant social and political force in Czechoslovak society.

Membership in the Communist Party was a privilege, not a right or responsibility. Only a minority of citizens became members. Reasons for joining the Party were complex and multifarious and suggest many explanations and justifications. Most decisions were not taken casually. For example, as Ela K. recounts, a family might desire university education—or a particular university education for a child (entrance "assistance" was also a consideration—and Party membership could facilitate each of these processes). Professional considerations also factored in. Professional advancement in many fields was facilitated by Party membership—the field of criminal justice representing a salient example.[1] In some cases, Party membership was seen as providing "credibility" for an individual or family and, as a potential form of "insurance" against potential police surveillance. Of course, individuals who wished to pursue a career in politics had little choice but to join the Party. Often, married couples would make a strategic decision about which family member should join. In many cases, the wife was the consenting partner.

The early steps towards Party membership began early in the lives of students. Typically, by the first grade, up to the fourth grade, young students signed up to be *Iskra*, or "sparks." These were the "small pioneers," the rough equivalent to the American Cub Scouts. Membership was not voluntary. The name *Iskra* derives from a speech given by Lenin and quoting Russian poet Odoevsky that "out of a spark will emerge a flame that will flare up, the flame of the revolution." At age 12, the Iskra could become "full" pioneers. By high school, they became *Svazák* (Czech) (*Zväzák* in Slovak), continuing through university study. Most students joined the Pioneers; membership was free, and activities were numerous and wholesome. In fact, it would be considered suspect if a young child did not join. Peter D. recalls "membership in Pioneers was one of the conditions if you wanted to go on to school to a gymnasium (university bound high school) or a university." Peter referred to membership in the youth organization as "forced," though this is disputed by others. In fact, social pressures (and perhaps implicit threats) towards joining may have exerted a sense of being "forced" or, at least, coerced.[2] Membership was an honor. "You wanted to be in—you wanted to belong."[3]

Nevertheless, some chose not to participate. Jana T. recounts:

> I remember one of my fellow pupils sitting alone. When we were given a break for a few minutes, I went to sit down next to her, and I asked her why she wasn't practicing with us. She said, I will not be joining the Pioneer Organization. I was very surprised, and I think I asked her why not. I don't think she gave me an answer. However, I remember later that she just disappeared. We as a class were told that her family moved out of the city. I didn't think about it as a child—but later I was wondering if the regime moved them somewhere. And I was also wondering—what was the thinking of her parents? It seemed to me that they were creating a confrontation with the political system through their daughter at a time when she herself would not have been able to make a decision for herself and didn't really have a say in it.[4]

All Pioneers got to wear sharp uniforms. Zora V. explains that young adults considered themselves members of the "Socialist Union of Youth" or *Socialistický zväz mládeže*. They had slogans, much like their American Boy Scout counterparts. For example, the unifying Pioneer slogan went: *Budovat' a brániť socialistickú vlasť buď pripavený*, which meant "Be ready to build and protect [the] socialist homeland." When this statement was issued by a Pioneer leader in a public setting, the youth would then respond in unison *Vždy pripavený*, meaning "Always ready."[5] (The similarities between the traditional American Boy Scout slogan, "Be Prepared," is noteworthy.) This slogan was not just said—it was *shouted*. The militarism exhibited by the speak-and-respond ritual was intended to serve as a reminder that the homeland was sacred, and was under constant threat both from "enemies within" and from the West. The slogan originated in the USSR and was appropriated by Czech authorities as a (somewhat paradoxical) means of conveying national pride and sovereignty.[6]

Activities within the Pioneers were fun for kids and allowed them a healthy (and economical) outlet for many athletic, social, and even charitable activities. Sometimes, for example, each pioneer would be asked to contribute one crown to assist a charitable cause. Typically, these causes were designed to benefit other socialist countries.

Contests were common events in the pre-communist membership societies. Pavol recalls that some of the more prestigious contests featured topics such as "What Do You Know about the USSR?" and "Pushkin's Memory," a poetry contest. Such competitions were taken very seriously; participants were required to attend special classes, often at 7 a.m. before their normal classes commenced. Prizes for the competition were typically books, or other academic, non-ideological items. In order to build suspense, schools often did not reveal the winners of the contests until the end of the current school year. Winners had their achievements noted within their report cards; having such a mark in the class record could be a very useful feather in one's cap when applying for secondary school admission.[7]

At the center of the Pioneer movement was the moral authority of the Soviet Union. "The Russians seemed great," Pavol adds. "They seemed to possess a moral authority about them."[8] When a Soviet delegation would visit Czechoslovakia, Pioneers would typically line the roads to greet them, waving to the delegates as they drove by. The Pioneers were often anything but ideological, and official gathering and ceremonies were often dull events to be tolerated as best as possible. As Zora V., an ex–Pioneer, notes, "our [Pioneer] meetings were parties, and we enjoyed great times. We would often poke fun at officialdom—such as the parades—and then, just after the bigwigs had passed by, we would return to our partying. The 'waving' was all done in good humor. Despite our irreverence, however, the possession of a *zväzák* shirt was highly prized among young people."[9]

Pioneers also attended numerous meetings—some of them related to the national defense issue of preparing for nuclear war. Former Pioneer Soňa C., explains "we were taught how to run, how to throw a hand grenade (boys and girls), how to fasten and utilize a gas mask, and how to properly lie down if a nuclear attack were to take place."[10] Implicit in all of these preparations was the threat of the West, particularly of the United States. America was routinely demonized in official circles. The Czechoslovak propaganda apparatus devoted considerable energy towards criticizing various American actions. For example, the catastrophic events of the 1986 Challenger space shuttle launching was repeatedly referred to by the local media as a "careless" error, typified as a reckless attempt of the U.S. to speed up the space race with the USSR. The Strategic Arms Limitations Treaty (SALT) talks of the 1970s and 1980s were also portrayed typically in pro–Russian terms.[11]

Party Elections

It may surprise some to learn that Communist Czechoslovakia had regular, monitored elections. And it might be even more surprising to hear that opposition parties were permitted—and even encouraged—to participate in elections. Voting was obligatory; all adults 18 or older were expected to vote. The façade of elections was that they represented the "democratic" will of the people. Patricia L. notes that *how* one voted was significant, however; voters choosing to vote for an entity other than the Communist Party risked being punished—through a "downgrade" at work or school, limitations on future travel, or prohibitions on their children's opportunities for higher education.[12]

Ideology

Basic indoctrination to the tenets of Marxism–Leninism took place in the State education system. History was taught from age 10 to 14 in elementary school, and then for an additional three years in secondary school. History lessons corresponded to the Marxist theory of social, political and economic evolution through various periods of development. Assurances were granted that the communist ideal would be reached in the indeterminate future, as explained by Beáta: "I remember a civics class teacher telling us when I was 11 or 12 years old that we will be living in pure communism [at an unspecified future point] and there will be no money, the goods in the stores will all be available, and everyone will take as much as they need for free. As I was listening to this, I recall that I was not able to understand how this world would work."[13]

Equality

At the heart of Marxist–Leninist doctrine was the belief in equality in the social, political, and particularly economic spheres. Literacy programs and redistributive policies (including expropriation of property) were exercised as a means for leveling the economic playing field. Manual workers, on average, tended to make better salaries than "bourgeois" professionals and were entitled to other societal advantages as well. In fact, literacy rates climbed under Communist Party rule as did access to health care. To some, these apparent successes came at a high cost. A former manual laborer, Beáta notes that "literacy and equality were terms that were used to manipulate the population. They encouraged obedience and identity. Real equality didn't really exist."[14]

This was particularly evident in the ways women were treated. Salaries for women, to cite one example, were always much lower than those for men. In other ways, however, women did in fact benefit. All women had access to child care and were even able to demand time off to take care of their children. This all disappeared after 1989. "My mom was from the old school of thinking and didn't realize this," says Beáta. "After 1989, she continued to insist that women had the right to child care—a right that they no longer possessed. She didn't realize that the system had changed."[15]

"All were, in essence, equal under the old regime," Juraj K. argues. "Everyone was stuck in a similarly low economic position. Economic equality was a fact of life, more or less. Cultural equality was a different matter, however. Some professionals were held in high esteem—especially doctors. These professionals realized, however, that they could not carry themselves in an elitist manner; they needed to respect workers and provide services." Regarding services, Juraj recites an old joke:

> A man walks in to a car shop to buy a [Russian] Lada. He is told to pick a color for the car that he is ordering, which he does.
>
> He is then told that there is a ten-year wait for the car and that it will be delivered on June 21, ten years hence. The man agrees and requests the car be delivered in the afternoon as he has a plumber scheduled to arrive the same morning.[16]

Official propaganda used models of Western and American inequality to further the State's legitimacy. In the 1980s, the West was portrayed as particularly aggressive, unequal, racist, and unjust. U.S. president Ronald Reagan was depicted widely as a warmonger. May Day celebrations often portrayed the West in less than flattering terms, at parades and other public gatherings. Parody was common. For example, one such May Day parade in Slovakia featured a display of American "rockets," accompanied by a group of "prostitutes" keeping them company. Some of these prostitutes were men—including Juraj's father, as he recounts. All "Americans" in the parade display were both cigar smoking and morbidly obese. The creators of such spectacles were often local artists; many were considered useful for promoting the ideology of the regime, through murals, paintings, statues, or, in this case, parade floats. Cash prizes and competitions were often part of the effort to streamline a political message—and it worked for some segments of the Czech population. "Fear often achieves success in that way. In the end," Juraj K. concludes, "if we had not been such friends with the Soviets, we would have been much better off."[17]

The Czechoslovak Communist Party Defines Itself to the West

One means of assessing external, "outside-the-system" conceptions of communism is to look at the ideological export of the regime itself. How does a system wish others to see it?

It has been theorized that although the West distorted the meaning of *socialism* by defining it through a monolithic, moralistic perspective, so too did the Eastern Bloc. By equating Stalinist Communism with Marxism, the State thus provided its own rationalizations and distortions. The Czechoslovak Communist Party had, of course, considerable means of propaganda at its disposal, and this apparatus was used to support the system and, after "normalization" in the Post-Prague Spring period, to re-educate the populace to the true meaning of Marxist–Leninist Socialism.

Perhaps the best place to start looking for official views of the Czechoslovak Communist system is in the official history of the Party, published *in English*, for a Western audience, in 1985. Earlier versions existed as well, and were periodically updated. (The USSR had its own English language history available from the time of the Revolution.) Here, one may peruse the origins of socialist working class movements through nascent socialist ideas, subsequent "revisionism," and the emergence into "true" socialism. In the first place, the history of the KSČ (Communist Party of Czechoslovakia) is presented as a historical struggle to overthrow capitalism and to develop a socialist alternative. A second tenet of this historical mission is that the working class may complete its historical mission only if led by a Marxist–Leninist revolutionary party. The founding of the Party in 1921 is noted as a turning point in the ability of the working classes to oppose and bring down the bourgeoisie.[18]

In essence, the key to the success of the Communist Party represents the confluence of two factors: first, the scientific nature of Marxist–Leninist theory, which posits the inevitable end to capitalism, and second, the revolutionary character of the working class, which organizes itself on the principles necessary to see through the fundamental changes that must take place, given the specific needs and history of the Czechoslovak circumstances.[19] References to Lenin and to the need for the implicit links to the Soviet Union are repeated themes: "The Communist Party of Czechoslovakia fulfills its historic role as a revolutionary working-class party of a new type. Logically, it had to undergo a process of Bolshevization in which, in the fight against opportunism, revisionism and dogmatic sectarianism, it acquired the features of a revolutionary Leninist party and has consistently improved itself."[20] The Communist Party is able to maintain order and stability through its loyalty towards and support from the workers and the general population. Farmers and workers are said to share harmony of interest, an essential precondition for the development of what is called its "leading role for the most progressive class of modern times."[21]

The role of the Party has both a national and an international function; the fight for workers' rights is portrayed as an international function, whereas the fight for national rights is seen as inextricably connected to the international context. For example, the origin of the KS is "linked to the victory of the proletarian revolution in Russia and to the Communist International." Throughout its development, the KSč has drawn on the rich experience of the CPSU (Communist Party of the Soviet Union; KSSZ in Czech). The existence of the Soviet Union and the rise of the world socialist community created favorable external conditions for the victorious advance of the socialist revolution in Czechoslovakia.[22]

The official history is not without reference to "undesirable" or "revisionist" developments that have hampered Party development. The term "Prague Spring," is, understandably, never used in the official Party history, but considerable space is devoted to the "Non–Marxist Crisis of Political Disunity" that arose in 1967–68. During this period, "revisionism" and "anti-socialist" ideas predominated, such as the allowance of political pluralism, the reduction of the Party's authority, and the tolerance of the "autonomy of [bourgeois] culture." During this period, the relationship with other Eastern socialist countries was said to be severely strained, class relations became increasingly ambiguous, and "right—wing opportunism" became rampant, creating false impressions in the minds of the people by manipulating the mass media.[23] The removal of Alexander Dubček in 1969 was described as a means by which the whole of society could emerge from the cycle of one crisis followed by another. Warsaw Pact troops on Czech soil were justified as the means by which "the forces faithful to Marxist-Leninism inside the Party, who were determined to defend the benefits of Socialism in Czechoslovakia, to reform their ranks and to struggle to surmount the counter-revolutionary threats by political means."[24]

In the end, the "historic road" of the Communist Party of Czechoslovakia is described, by the Party itself, as an enormous success, the culmination of glorious "national and revolutionary traditions" of the Czech and Slovak working classes. The official history ends with an admonition that the second half of the socialist century will shine brighter than even the first—as working people build an "advanced socialist society."[25]

"Official" Folk Tales and Popular Myths

Propaganda was employed at all levels of Party indoctrination, and, as such, it took on many forms. In some cases, folk tales, often with political themes, were employed. Perhaps the most famous of these was the infamous "Potato Bug" tale, known by all Czech and Slovaks. In this tale, the potato bug was introduced as an insect originally unknown to Czechoslovakia. When it appeared in the crops, it was said to have been dropped by American spy planes over Czechoslovakia as a means of destroying their agriculture.

The potato bug saga dated from 1950 when, in an effort to score propaganda points against U.S. involvement in the Korean War, a campaign was introduced accusing "American gangsters in airplanes" of intentionally dropping the potato bug pest on Czechoslovak crops. An official proclamation was issued by Prague on June 28, 1950, to this effect. Edited sections are reproduced here: The statement read:

> Every day our working class farmers—and, along with them, the entire nation—oversee the ripening of the grain and the harvesting of the crops with the joy and conscientiousness of tillers of the soil. They work in unison with the heartfelt and industrious participation of our entire nation towards the second harvest of the five-year plan. And precisely at the moment when joyful preparations are underway to begin harvesting the fruit of the yearlong constructive work of our small and medium scale farmers, news is arriving from the western and southwestern parts of our republic concerning a serious threat to this year's potato crop by the potato bug. This year over the course of a few days, the potato bug has suddenly and on a massive scale laid low all of the western and southwestern regions of the republic bordering the occupied zones of western Germany. From there, the potato bug is spreading throughout the nation. In several districts, the potato bug has been found primarily near roads and highways. Boxes and bottles have also been found filled with this beetle. All of this is irrefutable evidence that the present potato bug peril did not arise, and could not have arisen, through natural and normal routes. The dangerous parasite was transported to us artificially, intentionally, and on a massive scale with the assistance of the clouds and winds of Western imperialism and their agents and saboteurs sent to dwell among us.[26]

It was not only the Czechs who were alarmed; on July 2, 1950, the USSR made a formal protest against American potato bug infestation of the German Democratic Republic (GDR). The timing of the protest is significant as the hostilities of the Korean War had commenced only two days previous.

Over time, the potato bug became a symbol of the imperialist and aggressive West. The "voracity" of the bug was compared with the "imperial appetite" of American global expansion impulses, and the eradication of the crop pest became commensurate with the vanquishing of the American enemy. A popular ballad went as follows:

> A crisis is looming over Capitol Hill
> Where Mr. Dollar mediates on war
> He would shatter his sword against the iron shield,
> The wickedest of weapons is not foreign to him:
> The pestilence itself seeks to exterminate us with pestilence.
> The insect himself sends to us his fellow insects.
> And wonders whom to send into the field:
> Find him—it's difficult to go oneself, he's afraid.
> He would shatter his sword against the iron shield
> The wickedest of weapons is not foreign to him
> The pestilence itself seeks to exterminate us with
> pestilence the insect himself sends to us his fellow
> insects[27]

More broadly, the potato bug came, over time, to represent the "world of evil" as conceptualized by the Czech authorities, and this sometimes led to condemnations and demonizing that went far beyond the Unites States. Critics of Joseph Stalin ranged from reform-minded Communists like Joseph Tito in Yugoslavia (who broke with Stalin in 1948), to Rudolf Slánský and Milada Horáková (two Czech politicians accused of betraying socialism in the show trials of the early 1950s—both of whom were executed).[28]

Overall, however, the "American Beetle," that "six-legged Ambassador of Wall Street," was an American symbol typifying the supposed excesses of American capitalism, imperialist expansion, and even fascism. This sentiment was expressed in verse:

> Potato bugs and roaches, this is it,
> Invade our fields and try to cross our fences.
> No matter what, you'll end up in the shit.
> I really meant to say, that is, our trenches.[29]

Pioneer groups were encouraged throughout the Cold War to do their part to eradicate the potato bug. In some cases, pioneers would pick the bugs by hand from the fields in organized, "civic" actions. These group activities, carried out in areas of greatest exposure, were praised highly for their patriotic value.[30] Claims by authorities that scientists were developing a "potato bug-resistant crop" were common, as were frequent flyovers by Russian jets as a demonstration of agricultural "protection" from the West.[31]

The UFO Scare

There are certainly elements of the past that stand out—the outrageous, the unbelievable and the sensational. The potato bug saga instilled a sense of insecurity and sabotage amidst the general population. In the popular mind, *paranoia* is well remembered, particularly as it related to the West. Images of the West were as distorted as images of the East were for Westerners. In the early 1950s, the sense of "otherness" was magnified to include aliens from other planets. In the Cold War West, the James Bond genre served to concretize the "Other," using traditional Cold War themes. But perhaps nothing served so well the prevailing ideals of the Soviet enemy as both "sub-human" and "super-human" as the science fiction and horror movies of the 1950s. A recurrent topical theme during this period was *mimicry*, the ability of an alien invader to assume the behavior of normal American citizens, as well as to control their minds. Infiltration of American institutions, values and culture was a constant in the sci-fi genre, and it reflected cultural fears of vulnerability at that time. Indeed, the metaphor of a superior invader from outer space reinforced the paranoia and feeling of helplessness prevalent during this period.[32]

Of course, a populace conditioned to fear an enemy will eventually learn to see that enemy around every corner. Thus, the UFO phenomenon was a logical outgrowth of the Soviet narrative that had been cultivated since World War II. In the U.S., UFO sightings surged in June and July of 1947. In addition to the many individual sightings around the country, a United Airlines crew went on record as having seen unexplained bright lights in the sky one evening. American businessman Kenneth Arnold also reported witnessing UFO activity. In a celebrated account, the American FBI began an investigation in 1947, its targets the "best" U.S. sightings in recent memory. Up until this time, the American media had typically referred to unexplained aerial sightings as "flying saucers." The term *UFO* was introduced in 1952 as a means to better explain aerial phenomena seen as too diverse to be categorized merely as "flying saucers."

Interestingly, the fear of UFOs in America was paralleled by both the fear and the incidence of UFO activity in the USSR during the same period.

In 1959, two dramatic UFO sightings occurred; one in the Soviet Union and one in Poland. In the Polish case, a UFO was said to have crashed into Gdynia harbor on January 21, 1959. A "small humanoid" was said to have been seen walking around "in a confused state." The Soviet sighting originated in Sverdlovsk, which was the headquarters of a tactical missile command. Ground personnel at the site reported seeing UFO activity hovering over the base to such an extent that the base commander eventually ordered the "intruders" to be chased away. Soviet authorities tended to view UFO stories as "bourgeois propaganda," or as "capitalist" phenomena. On the other hand, there is considerable evidence that the higher echelons of Soviet society remained quite interested in UFO reports.[33]

The Communist Life and Death Myth

In 1953, both Joseph Stalin and Czech president Klement Gottwald died within days of each other. (In fact, Gottwald became ill while attending Stalin's funeral.) These events sent shock waves through the socialist world as the deaths seemed to symbolically to betray the millennial goals of orthodox socialism. "Socialism was, in its symptomatically and eschatological conception, seen as the final achievement of an ideal realm of happiness and earthly bliss, and the natural fact of death came into sharp contrast with this notion."[34] Both leaders were embalmed, to "preserve" their immortality, in much the same way as Lenin had been after his death in 1924. From the 1950s onward, various attempts were made to abolish, symbolically, the deaths of socialist leaders. Abolition of death assisted the goals of permanent revolution, authority, and stability.[35]

The National Monument, on Vítkov Hill in Prague, became the final resting place for the prominent "living dead." The deceased statesmen placed there were kept as much "alive" as was technologically possible; hence, their "memory" could be interlaced with the more important principle that, in fact, they were immortal—they still lived. The ritual preservation of the corpses of Lenin, Stalin, Gottwald and others had other, non–European origins. But the political function was clear; the living dead carried a message of life in death; they united a people in a life struggle through bodily death. Much care was taken by major media at Gottwald's funeral to note that the leader "looked as good in death as he had in life," and friendship with the Soviet Union was a constantly recurring theme: "this is not only an act of mourning ... it is a grand manifestation of a hundred million hearts of the loyal and eternal unity of our nations with the Soviet Union."[36] Hundreds of thousands of Czechs and Slovaks filed by the

"Worker's President," whose coffin was then placed on Vítkov Hill at the National Monument in Prague, a location with strong ancient religious significance dating back to Jan Hus. The music accompanying the ceremony was Bedřich Smetana's "Tabor," employing a Hussite hymn, "Ye who are the soldiers of god."[37]

The denial of death as a means for the Socialist state to maintain a form of internal consistency and control of its population was later reflected in jokes that abounded in the 1960s, 1970s, and 1980s. These jokes typically interchanged subjects, some featuring Lenin, Stalin, Gottwald, or others. The punch lines may seem almost incoherent to an outsider, but their cultural and historical origins are within the cult of death defiance. Three examples are provided by Pavol. The first involves a teacher, who is showing pictures of animals to her students. In one case, she shows a picture of a zebra and asks her students to comment on it. No one seems to know what it is, so she begins to spell out the name of the animal: Z ... E ... B.... One child stands up and exclaims, "Maybe Lenin?" ("*žeby*" in Czech means "maybe").[38]

The second example is a commonly told joke about a Slovak, a Czech, Hitler, Lenin and a Roma (gypsy) who find themselves surrounding a great hole in the ground. The Slovak pushes the Czech into the hole, Hitler then pushes the Roma in—but who pushes Hitler? The answer is "Lenin, because he is *always alive*."[39] The final example is a bit cruder, with Mikhail Gorbachev and George H.W. Bush in a conversation over the relative merits of U.S. versus Soviet technology. In the first case, a visiting Gorbachev sits in America with President Bush before three buttons. Bush asks Gorbachev to push the first button. When he does so, a pile of feces falls into the room. The second button presents a second pile of feces. The third button brings a robot to clean up the entire mess. Soon after, Bush visits Gorbachev in Moscow. Three buttons appear again. Bush pushes the first, but nothing happens. After pushing the second, again there is nothing. Even a third button produces no reaction. Bush, at this point quite bored with seemingly poor Soviet technology, announces that he is going home, to which Gorbachev says, "But where are you going home to?"[40]

By the mid–1980s, a comic syllogism, penned by Vladimír Kusín, began to spread through the country. It was titled "The Seven Wonders of Communism":

1. Everybody holds a job.
2. Even though everybody holds a job, no one actually works.
3. Even though no one actually works, the plans are being fulfilled.

4. Even though the plans are being fulfilled, there are shortages.

5. Even though there are shortages, one can somehow obtain everything.

6. Even though one can somehow obtain everything, everybody keeps stealing things from the state.

7. Even though everybody keeps stealing things from the state, no one misses anything.[41]

The Communist Party was no joke, however. Many Czech and Slovaks had family members who, by the 1960s, had already served lengthy prison terms from the Stalinist period of the 1950s. Jan recounts how his mother's father had been imprisoned ten years (though her grandfather had been sentenced to 20 years). His grandfather had been a Catholic literary critic. In the orthodox atmosphere of the 1950s, this was considered a high crime for both religious and political reasons. As a result, a "show trial" was held in 1951 and his grandfather convicted. Jan recalls that "from an early age, I realized what fate had befallen my grandfather, and I was instilled with a strong sense of danger about the culture in which I lived. My father later continued my grandfather's work in the 1960s, publishing the works of Catholic poets, writers, and thinkers. But I was told, strictly, to avoid discussing his work with any of my friends or school mates."[42]

Joining the Party

It was widely understood that being a Party member—or knowing local Party loyalists—could be a significant advantage, even if one was not in the Party, as friends could always be taken into confidence for benefits accrued to Party members. For example, Party adherents might inform their non–Party friends about economic and social plans of the Party ahead of official announcement. A Party member friend could, in effect, offer a "heads up" to friends about policies that were about to be implemented.

For most people who joined the Party, ideology was rarely a consideration. Rather, concern for career development and opportunities for family members weighed heavily in the decision to join. For families that had a tradition of Party membership, there was significant pressure to continue tradition. Jan H. recalls: "I was born into a fairly hard line community. I don't have bad memories of that time. We didn't give it much thought as children."[43]

Others joined to avoid being continually hounded for membership.

Many were motivated simply by the desire to be left alone. Of course, careerism and the opportunity for advancement drove many to join the Party. A job, a letter of recommendation, an application to a university, or even a new apartment could all be favorably expedited by Party membership: "That's how it was. And that was part of the reason why there were so many people in the party. They simply thought that it might buy them some benefit in the future."[44]

One had to be mindful always of the occasional demands of the State to administer loyalty oaths of one kind or another. After the signing of the anti-communist Charter 77, many professionals came under pressure to prove their loyalty to the state through the signing of the Anti-charter. Educators, in particular, were pressed to sign the Anti-charter. One teacher recalls:

> There was a special meeting called of teachers at our school. We were all asked to sign the Anti-charter. The director did not give us an ideological lecture on that—he just said "here is something that we need to sign." I had a child and thought that I needed to simply sign it. I didn't even know what was in the Charter that was supposedly contradicted by the Anti-charter, and I felt sick when I signed it. I felt at the time that each of us has a little light somewhere inside, like a pair of compasses. And each of us knows when we are doing something when we are self-violating, going against that light within.[45]

The Diplomacy of Avoiding Party Membership

Without question, Communist Party membership conferred privileges and advantages on adherents. Pressure to join the Party was subtle but persistent. Many joined the Party in order to create opportunities for family members—or to avoid undue conflict with authorities. But others, particularly university grads and others on a professional track, found that Party membership, for various reasons, was something to be avoided if possible. An outright refusal to accept Party membership could result in a lifetime of sanctions against both the individual and the family. Thus, many chose to take a third path; neither join nor refuse—simply stall, passively if possible, and by other means if necessary.

Pressure towards Party membership often increased at university. Soňa, a philosophy student in the late 1980s, found that the pressure to join was unrelenting. "I felt almost forced to join," she admits. However, as Party membership was considered both a privilege and a force of elevated status, an escape route existed for some. For Soňa, the answer was to argue that she was not yet ready for Party membership: "I argued that I was not yet ready—not yet prepared (an acceptable response at the time)—because it acknowledged [at least tacitly] the prestige and responsibility associated with membership of the Party. From a Communist Party perspective, then, a 'declination' on such grounds might only enhance the prestige—and thus the desirability—of eventual Party status."[46]

Indeed, there were even slogans to indicate ones' personal preparatory status towards Communist Party membership. A common response was "I am not ripe enough yet" ("*nie som na to ešte dost zrelý*").[47] In fact, this justification was a cover phrase for those who wished to avoid Party membership altogether. Ivan discusses her mother's experience in 1963:

> My mother was invited to join the Party in her final year of high school. She used exactly that line—"I am not ripe enough"—as a means to avoid having to make a decision about joining. She was an excellent student and was respected by her teachers and those who knew her. After one year of "candidacy" she was supposed to be admitted to the Party in her first year as a university student (studying history and Russian language to become a teacher). Her refusal in her first year of university study caused a scandal at the university, as the local Communist Party organization.... Up to this day my mother says that it was completely unpleasant and horrifying, to be standing there alone in front of the Committee, many of whom were in utter disbelief how dare she refuse the *honor* of having been invited to join.
>
> The intervention of a professor at the university, who intervened and spoke on her behalf was the only reason that the refusal was not entered into her *kádrové materiály*, or permanent record of "aptitude" and "political reliability." It was almost criminal to refuse to join the Party after a one year candidacy.[48]

There were other, more elaborate methods for avoiding Party membership—short of defecting from Czechoslovakia. Jan C. describes a difficult situation at Charles University, Prague, in the late 1980s. Jan had been a faculty member for some time but had never joined the Party. Now he found himself cornered. In order to remain in his faculty position, he was told that he would have to become a Party member. (Technically he was considered "three interviews away from taking a vow to the Party"—a final stage.) As usual among resistant Party joiners, the principal issue was how to stall, how to buy time. Jan enlisted his childhood friend George to assist him. Jan and George had shared a devotion to Catholic doctrine as children, and they remained close from that time. "George had considerable job security," Jan recounts, "so he was in a position to offer help."[49]

The two devised an interesting scheme; they would use an old typewriter to draft a letter to the Communist Party chief. This "anonymous" letter would purportedly have been sent by a disgruntled colleague of Jan's, with an axe to grind. The letter described Jan as a "product of his grandfather" (who had been imprisoned by the Party for religious activity), and suggested that he could not be trusted. The goal was to create the conditions by which he would be fired from the department for incompetence—but not for failing to join the Party.[50]

The letter was received later by Jan's department, but the director of the department, a chronic alcoholic, did not recognize that the letter was a fake (Jan recounts that the quality of typing, writing, and professional reproduction were abysmal). In the end, the department chief made the decision to "retain" Jan, but "to remove him from the promotion process." No punitive actions were taken.[51]

Membership in the Communist Party involved a myriad of considerations—family, career, education and, most importantly, one's future. Although non-compulsory, membership conferred educational and social privileges that were difficult to turn a blind eye to. The avoidance of harassment was a negative incentive, as well; "legitimacy" for oneself and one's family could be achieved with Party membership. Still, for many, religious, generational and ideological considerations made taking the step towards inclusion in the Party unacceptable. The tools that were employed to stave off "inevitable" membership were both shrewd and calculated; in some cases, the candidates used the criteria for membership as dodges.

In the end, each candidate had to balance that which might be gained against that which could be lost, for one's family, one's friends and, ultimately, one's reputation and sense of self. Each potential candidate had to ask themselves the most difficult question of all; who am I and who do I wish to be within the present regime?

Chapter Six

1968

How do the Russians visit their friends?
In tanks.

Black humor, circa 1968: "One night, Dežo and Milo headed home by foot. Martial law had been declared, and a strict 10 p.m. curfew was in order. They walked quickly though a Prague neighborhood at 9:45, when a soldier raised his gun and shot Milo. Dežo cried out, "Why did you shoot my friend, as it is only 9:45!" The soldier replied, "It's ok—I know Milo and his family—and I know where they live. There is no way he could have made it home by the 10 p.m. curfew deadline!"

The story of the Prague Spring has been told many times. Reformers, led by First Secretary Alexander Dubček, attempted to create a new socialism by promoting increased press liberalization and political reform. The events of 1968 and the "normalization" process that followed resound with poignancy as experienced by Czechs and Slovaks who lived through it.

In late 1967, reformers, notably Dubček and Ota Ŝik, challenged First Secretary Antonin Novotný in what became a significant power struggle. Novotný was a devoted Party member who had attained fame in the early 1950s as a prosecutor during the Slánský Trials, in which numerous top Czechoslovak Communist Party officials, under intense pressure from Stalin, were accused of treason. Many were executed or given long jail terms. (The accused were given formal pardons in 1963.)[1] Novotný invited Soviet Premier Leonid Brezhnev to Czechoslovakia to shore up Novotný's political base. Upon his arrival on a trip to Czechoslovakia, Brezhnev quickly realized that Novotný had little popular support, and issued his famous phrase that "this matter is your [Czech] business." Abandoned by Brezhnev, Novotný was replaced by Dubček in January 1968 as First Secretary of the Communist Party. Dubček, a Slovak, was seen as an ideal compromise candidate, given a weak economy, complaints from many in Slovakia for more autonomy, and his acceptability within different wings of the Communist Party.[2]

Pressure built for both the repeal of a 1966 censorship law and for the removal of President Novotný (who had retained the presidency even after removal as First Secretary). Further economic reforms were promoted by the Communist Party, and Ludvík Svoboda, a military man and war hero, was elected as the new President. On April 5, the so-called Action Program of the Communist Party was published as part of an effort to provide "socialism with a human face." It called for the "democratization" of the political and economic system and described a "unique experiment in democratic communism," in which the Communist Party would now have to compete with other parties in elections.[3] Such changes led to popular demand for additional reforms, such as censorship (which would be abolished in June); Dubček had to steer a difficult course to contain the momentum at home and relations with the Soviets abroad. At the end of May, the Soviets hosted the Czechoslovak leadership in Moscow, expressing displeasure with many of the recent changes as well as issuing a veiled threat of possible Warsaw Pact exercises on Czech soil.

Within a month, the "Two Thousand Words Manifesto" had been issued, signed by reformers (including some Central Committee members) and published widely, calling for "democratization," the re-establishment of the Social Democratic Party, and the setting up of citizens' committees. The manifesto, a more radical alternative to the Communist Party's *April Action Program*, was rejected by Dubček and other top leaders.[4]

National polls from the period suggest a high support for the Dubček government and a sense that material prosperity was on the upswing. A poll from July 1968, just prior to the invasion, shows relatively high support for socialism and the current government:

1. Would you prefer Czechoslovakia to abandon further development of socialism and to enter the road of capitalist development?

For capitalist development 5%
For further socialist development 89%
No opinion; don't know 6%

2. Are you satisfied with the work of our government, or partly satisfied, or unsatisfied?

Satisfied 33%
Partly 54%

Unsatisfied 7%
No opinion 6%

3. *Considering present developments in the country, how much confidence do you have in the Czechoslovak Communist Party?*

Absolute confidence 11%
Confidence 40%
Not for, not against 33%
No confidence 12%

4. *Do you believe that the Communist Party is a political power able to ensure development of socialism and democracy in our country?*

Yes 52%
Don't know 27%
No 21%

Trends in Czechoslovak public opinion in the extraordinary (post-censorship) period from January 1968 to March 1969 have been documented by the Czechoslovak Institute of Public Opinion. The Institute, headed by Dr. Jaromíra Zapletalová, had a staff of approximately fifteen persons. Its work was professional and careful. As in most East European countries, the interviewing was done by volunteers who were motivated by the prospect of clarifying the desires of the populace. Quota sampling was used. As an institute of the Academy of Sciences, it received a fixed annual budget, which was used at its discretion, asking questions that seemed most important. The results were released to CTK, the Czechoslovakian press agency, and published in newspapers as well as in scientific reports.[5]

In a poll taken in January 1969 during the post-invasion period, but still under the leadership of Dubček, 22 percent of respondents said that their "Christmas table" was more plentiful with food and gifts than previous years, while 67 percent reported that their level of prosperity was "about the same," with 12 percent reporting a deteriorated condition. On the question of personal income, 33 percent indicated higher income, 54 percent about the same, and 12 percent lower. Standard of living was reported as improving in 22 percent of cases, lower in 24 percent, and about the same in 53 percent. When asked about their "greatest wish" for the New Year, fully 45 percent of all respondents indicated either "sovereignty and freedom" (24 percent), or the "removal of Soviet troops" (21 percent). Overwhelming numbers supported the suppression of censorship, as well as the rehabilitation of those caught up in the political show trials of the 1950s.[6]

The very fact that public opinion polls existed at all during the period of the Prague Spring was a testament to the reformist impulses that allowed for the "pluralism" of "bourgeois thought" that would have previously been unthinkable. Fully two thirds of the 34 major polls taken between 1967 and 1971 came from the 1968 reformist period prior to the Soviet invasion. The decline of such polls during the normalization period was equally dramatic, as conservative forces sought to re-establish order.

One particularly interesting study from 1967 sought to measure the attitudes of younger people, between the ages of 15 and 40. Not only would this group have no memory of pre–Communist Czechoslovakia, but they would also comprise the age group most likely to engage in the events of 1968:

> Not surprisingly, the surveyed citizens of socialist states experienced a lower level of personal efficacy (political influence) than their Western counterparts. Even so, both Czechs and Slovaks were socially engaged (as measured by high rates of participation in social organizations), and exhibited optimistic expectations about the role of the younger generation in shaping a better future.
>
> The combination of a frustrating sense of political powerlessness, social engagement, and heightened expectations leads [the author] to the conclusion that there was "latent popular support for reform" in the period immediately preceding the Prague Spring.[7]

What kind of reform was envisaged and acceptable to most citizens? Researcher Pat Lyons distinguishes between what she calls internal (intra-party) and external (intelligentsia and society-based) proposals for reform. In doing so, she is able to discern that a majority of Czech and Slovak citizens supported reform, although through the perspective of pragmatism and "realism." The reform program of Dubček fit this "realistic" conception of change, including the enhanced political role given to organizations like the National Front. Most citizens were in favor of a more competitive pluralistic system although they expressed a preference for preserving socialism, rather than surrendering to economic market forces.[8]

> One of the most interesting parts of [Lyons] book is the diachronic comparison of the attitudes of Czech and Slovak citizens in both 1968 and 2008.... There is a supplementation of mass public opinion with an analysis of elite attitudes and a network analysis designed to gauge the level of elite cohesion during the Prague Spring. Contrary to the widespread perception of orthodox communists confronting liberal reformers, Lyons uncovers a much higher degree of consensus among the Prague Spring elite, notably around questions of its own social reproduction, gradualist reform, corporatist governance, and the value of political stability.
>
> To be sure, there is no way to verify such counterfactual propositions, but Lyons' survey evidence demonstrating the strong preference of the majority for full freedom of expression and political pluralism renders plausible the view that a political showdown would have occurred sooner or later. If that was indeed the case, the Soviet

rulers may not have been unjustified in thinking that the Czechoslovak example could become the germ of political ideological contagion throughout the Soviet Bloc.[9]

The Invasion Begins

In late July, representatives of the Communist parties of the Soviet Union, Hungary, Poland, East Germany and Bulgaria met in Poland. From the meeting came a warning that events in Czechoslovakia were threatening to undermine other socialist governments. Immediately afterwards, Brezhnev summoned Dubček and other members of the Presidium to the far eastern, Ukrainian-bordering Slovak village of Čierna nad Tisou. There, a meeting was held in an old train carriage. Dubček argued that reforms did not endanger the role of the Party but actually built public support. The Soviets reacted coolly to his arguments and remained critical of Czechoslovak moves, again threatening the possibility of invasion. Shortly thereafter, the neighboring countries of East Germany, Poland, Hungary and the Soviet Union announced that they would hold military exercises near the Czechoslovak border.[10]

On August 20, five of Warsaw Pact Nations and over half a million troops invaded Czechoslovakia, occupying Prague and arresting Alexander Dubček and other leading reformers. Shortly thereafter, the arrested Party members were flown to Moscow, where they were pressured to sign a protocol stating that they renounced reform and agreed to the occupation of Czechoslovakia by the Soviet Union. Czech leaders were under enormous pressure in Russia. Fear of summary execution was always present, as was the memory of Imre Nagy, the Hungarian leader who had been executed by the Soviets after the 1956 invasion. Only one delegation member, František Kriegel, refused to sign the accord. Czechs often recount that when Dubček made a radio address to the nation from Moscow, though calm in manner and his message, his voice was shaking noticeably.[11]

During the first days of the invasion, the only public communication that escaped control of the Russians was Czechoslovak Radio. When this organ was forcefully taken over, communication devolved to leaflets and "special issue" newspapers. A network of underground "verses, songs, graffiti, slogan anecdotes and satirical compositions" arose quickly, "rejecting the occupation as well as Stalinist-Brezhnev's conceptions of politics."[12] Rules applied, however, and sloganeers and graffiti artists were admonished to avoid certain excesses, and to emphasize certain themes:

> Be clear and understandable; do not paint things that foreign soldiers could interpret differently than you intended (no swastikas or similar symbols).
>
> Currently, one tour of invading military personnel is being replaced with another—try to write in a foreign language. Very few Russians, for example, read Latin alphabet.
>
> Explain exactly what is at stake and what we are fighting for—that is, for the occupants to leave our country, for the freedom, sovereignty, for the freedom of our government. We do not regard slogans, such as "death to occupants," as noble or worthy. Please speak as intelligent people—we need to communicate to the soldiers that the invasion is not just, that they were lied to by their own government.[13]

The official propaganda—as indicated in leaflets and public announcement—was that the Soviets had been "invited" to Czechoslovakia for the protection of socialism and the working classes. People were told not to resist the occupation forces, and the Czech Army was told to stand down and remain in their barracks. Shortly after the invasion, crowds and Soviet troops confronted one another on Old Town Square and Wenceslas Square. Tanks appeared at the Museum and began to fire at nearby buildings and the National museum.[14]

A short time later, censorship was reintroduced, and the 14th Communist Party (reformist) Congress was deemed "invalid." Protests continued, and, in one celebrated case, a student, Jan Palach, publically self immolated in a central Prague square. In April 1969, Dubček was removed as First Secretary.[15] Czechoslovakia would be occupied by Soviet troops for the next 22 years.

Experiences from 1968

The Soviet invasion created enormous cultural confusion, resentment, and feelings of betrayal for millions. A pro—reform professor noted that "with few exceptions, the Soviet comrades do not understand the situation in our country. They are not familiar with Czechoslovak history, the composition of Czechoslovak society, the mentality of our people, or our democratic traditions." His sentiments were borne out of the belief that few of his countrymen were bent on eliminating socialism and that the invasion would, in fact, do irrevocable harm to socialism.[16]

Recollections of the image call up very graphic and painful memories. Vladimír, formerly an economist at a Czechoslovak university, recalled that "1968 is very hard to understand from a rational perspective." "It was," he said, "a very emotional time. One lived many lives in one life" as a result of the period. He continues: "There was, first of all, significant support for the Communist Party in Czechoslovakia from 1960–68, as there was more freedom than before." Novotny, the First Secretary, was said to be "fearful of intelligence and intelligent people around him," whereas Dubček (a Slovak) brought in a number of highly competent Czech politicians who did some positive things, such as releasing political prisoners, providing for freedom of the press, and ensuring freedom of religion. "The leadership of the 1960s," he said, "was more human than previously. They visited factories, spoke with workers, and seemed to most as sincere."[17]

The invasion was a shock for 18-year-old Vladimír; his mother woke him up with the words "there is war here." At first, he simply could not believe what was happening, preferring instead to believe that it was a product of American propaganda; he assumed that what was actually transpiring was a "capitalist" invasion. Indeed, one widespread rumor was that U.S. President Lyndon Johnson had made a secret deal with Khrushchev before the invasion. Czechs felt that the U.S. played a "dirty" role and had actively assisted in betraying Czechoslovakia. This view had a historical antecedent; many Czechs saw this as a *second* betrayal by the West, the 1938 Munich Accords with Hitler setting the precedent. Perceptions of the West prior to the 1968 invasion were generally positive; this view soon changed, however, Vladimír notes. When informed that it was, in fact a Russian invasion, he could not make any sense of it. Perceptions of the USSR were "not negative" among most Czechs. In fact, the Soviets were often seen as a "big brother" or "tutor" to the Czechs. "In retrospect," says Vladimír, "the Czech authorities could not [or would not] see that there was a power shift underway. When the Warsaw Pact countries [minus Romania] surrounded Czechoslovakia, ready to fight, Czech officers were not even consulted."[18]

These sentiments are echoed by others. Jan G. describes his feelings at the time that the Russians "would never—and could never—invade Czechoslovakia. It was unthinkable. After all, Dubček had lived in Russia before the Second World War; he spoke fluent Russian." There was, however, a generational split within the Czechoslovak Communist Party, and this may have contributed to the conditions that led to the invasion.[19]

The sense of disbelief in the invasion often escalated into fear of all out war. Said Daniela F.: "of course today we know that there were casualties, but that it was not a war. But nobody knew that the first day ... people were really worked up because they assumed that it was the beginning of a war ... and there (in the hospital where she was recovering) in the TV room, everyone was crying and the expectation was that the tanks would be there in no time. And where could we escape on crutches and in wheelchairs? Nowhere."[20] The invasion itself had moments of chaos and even humor. Vladimír lived near Branisko, in the east, a formidable Slovak mountain pass that had to be traversed by the Russian tanks as they made their way west to Prague. In one case, a tank drove off of the steep, narrow road and plunged down a cliff, to the cheers of locals. As Soviet troops passed through the villages, locals spoke Russian with them, sometimes providing incorrect directions. In other cases, street signs were taken down or changed to confuse the invaders. Other signs appeared, such as "Invaders Go Home," which was printed on a plaque in front of a Branisko pub. Vladimír recalls that many of the young troops manning the Russian tanks *did not know that they were in Czechoslovakia*, as their officers had not informed them of the purpose of their mission.[21]

What has become known as the "politics of renaming" was nowhere more evident than in Prague, where the issues of city space and institutional power became intertwined. From the first few days of the Soviet invasion, multitudes of Prague residents participated in a semi-organized campaign to confuse and disorient invading troops. One contemporary wrote:

> Who came up with this splendid idea? Hundreds of thousands of anonymous, unknown people tore down the signs with the names of streets and squares. Plaques with house numbers also disappeared. On some buildings, there are no longer even the names of tenants. Prague, for example, no longer has a Vodičková Street or a Karlovo náměstí [Charles Square]. The Prague of names and numbers has become extinct. Someone who wasn't born here, who hasn't lived here, will find an anonymous city of a million people, in which the occupiers may perhaps find only a wide variety of appeals written in Czech ... the postman will find it, but the bastards won't.[22]

Further east, in Banská Bystrica, the birthplace of the Slovak National Uprising during World War II, the Soviet invasion was greeted with considerable fear by residents. Beáta, six years old at the time, recalls that she, along with many other children, were taken into the woods and kept there, where they would be safe. The local radio station was closed, and the tanks and soldiers rolled through: "I remember the Russian soldiers would pass out candies to the children. The soldiers seemed very young. At the time, I had a doll that I had named Ivan—and during the invasion, my friends would not speak to me, because 'Ivan' was a Russian name! We were very angry—why did they do this to us? We all felt a sense of betrayal. Why didn't the Czech government do anything to help us? Why didn't they stand up to the Russians?"[23]

Soňa, a child in the eastern city of Prešov, recalls talking with the invading Russian soldiers: "They were very young, and they asked me my name. I was very pleased at the attention that they gave me. My parents were far more reticent. They hated the invasion, but pitied the soldiers who were being forced to carry it out. The truth is that many of those young Russian troops had no idea where they were."[24]

Juri was a young boy in the Hungarian border town of Rimavská Sobota at the time of the Soviet invasion. His father was an officer in the Czechoslovak military, stationed in the western Czech city of Olomouc:

> We were told to stay at home, and there was a complete news blackout. We didn't really know what was going on. We did know that many Russian aircraft had landed in Olomouc, as there was a good airport there. But my father had a very difficult time communicating from Olomouc with us back home. We learned later that the Russians generally stationed troops only in larger urban areas, as the villages were considered too dangerous. The strangest development was when the Hungarian [Warsaw Pact] invasion troops from Hungary entered into Czechoslovak territory. Many of the [ethnic Hungarian] Slovaks in our border city initially welcomed them as *liberators*, as the Russians were considered to be the bigger enemy. We did not realize at first that they were fighting on the same side with the Russians—against us.[25]

A woman from the Slovak region recalls being in the hospital with cancer at the time of the invasion. At that time, the head doctor of the oncology unit paid visits to all patients, even those diagnosed as terminally ill. He was convinced of the possibility of civil war and thus advised his patients to leave the hospital so that they could be with their families.[26]

A Kraków resident, Ela, recalls the 1968 invasion from the Polish perspective:

> My father was a Polish officer and was very ambitious. We had always harbored the belief that the Russians would never invade Poland, in part because of the power of the Catholic Church, and also because of the widely held conviction that the Polish Army would never turn on its own people. However, my father was part of the Warsaw Pact 1968 invasion of Czechoslovakia; he was sent into the Czech territories. Upon his return, many officers were offered considerable promotions for their service. Oddly, my father was not one of them, for reasons that were never entirely clear. During the operation, many Polish mothers congregated and created a support network. There was considerable sympathy towards Czechoslovakia.[27]

Zuzana, a Bratislava resident, was on vacation in the eastern towns of Prešov and Košice when the tanks rolled in: "There was panic in the streets, and many soldiers—and some fighters—sparred. Everyone tried to buy as much as they could, and there was general panic. By November, we had KGB agents knocking on our door in Bratislava, asking questions of family members. The borders were closed in October, after which any emigration was simply not possible. Information during the invasion was always hard to obtain."[28]

Tomas, from the eastern town of Šarišské Michaľany, recounted:

> The streets of [the eastern city] Košice were completely torn up by the tanks. One of the first things that the Russians tried to do was to close down all television and radio

> transmission. In Zlatá Baňa/Dubník, they captured a television station—and then shot it up. When we dared, we would try to listen to Voice of America, or to Radio Free Europe. The Russians tried to scramble the signals, but the cost of doing that 24 hours a day was prohibitively expensive, so they weren't too successful. In addition, VOA and RFE often changed their frequencies during the invasion, making it even harder for the Russians to block them.[29] My own concerns were of a more personal nature, as I was marksman, and in my house, I had 9 guns and 20 kilos of ammunition. My biggest concern was ensuring that the Russians didn't find this cache, or I might have been in serious trouble.[30]

Ľudmila M. recalls the attitude towards Czech and Slovaks abroad at the time of the invasion: "People felt really sorry for us because we were under Russian occupation and so Czechs and Slovaks were really welcomed with open arms…."[31]

Livia, a Hungarian from Budapest, recalls the experience of 1968 from her home country:

> Many Hungarians remembered the events of 1956. What could one do? As Russia loomed, Hungary had hoped for help from abroad, but none came. It even looked like the US would assist us, but in the end it just died.
>
> As for 1968, we didn't have a choice. The decision to invade was not a Hungarian idea. It was an order that we had to follow. I first learned of it in grade school, when it was taught in our history class. My father was a history buff, and used to say that the 1968 invasion was a shameful thing. The sad part is that we wanted the same things that the Czechs and Slovaks wanted—but the Big Red Monster intervened.
>
> These days we don't talk about it. We never did. It was done to us under pressure, yet we still feel intense guilt about it. We are a proud nation and admitting that we are wrong is very hard.[32]

Some, such as writer Milan Kundera, praised what he saw as the resiliency of the Czech and Slovak people to rise above the difficulties of the moment and to continue with the process of political and social reform. Václav Havel disagreed, concerned that normalization would lead to capitulation on the part of the general population. For some, a sense of despair accompanied the invasion, as evidenced by the self immolation of university student Jan Palach. His suicide note described the need for people to "wake up" and "eliminate newly imposed forms of censorship."[33]

One recurring theme from Czech and Slovak commentators was the refutation of the commonly held notion that the Russian invasion was somehow limited to Prague. In fact, it was a country wide occupation. In eastern Prešov, according to one account, a Russian commander called for "all weapons to be surrendered to Russian authorities." What followed was a ludicrous peace offering of lines of children, offering up their sticks, butter knives and stones, in an action of community civil disobedience.[34]

In Prague, the locale that became synonymous with the Soviet occupation, the primary news daily, *Rudé Právo*, described the invasion in an article that drew attention to the Czech past as well as to the previous repulsion of invaders from the Czech lands. In the report, the historic Wenceslas Square was highlighted as a locus of Czech identity and culture: "We anxiously waited for a moment. For a long time before it, Wenceslas Square had been surrounded by the tanks of the occupying forces. They formed a perfect wall at the Museum. They aimed their tanks and machine guns at the pavement. The soldiers looked grim and tough. People came to Wenceslas Square in trucks decorated with flags, the crowds grew, and tension mounted ... would it lead to a massacre?"[35]

Considerable cultural self identification within the "Czecho-slovak" state emanated from Wenceslas, a square that dated from the mid–14th century. Czechs in particular felt this identification. There was no question that Russians did as well. Protest signs from the times are illustrative in their textured and often nuanced messages. In one case, two individuals were photographed with signs pinned to their backs, asking (in Russian Cyrillic), "Why are you shooting at us?" Such messages were dissonant with official Russian "pleasant dialogues," which attempted to portray Soviet actions in Czechoslovakia in a benign light. For example, the Soviet Central New Agency, TASS, on August 21, 1968, announced officially that the sovereign state of Czechoslovakia had "turned to" the USSR and other states as a means of providing "fraternal assistance" to a country besieged from without by the "enemies of socialism."[36] The constitution of Czechoslovakia, and the protection of the country from "counter-revolutionary" forces, would be facilitated by the "request" by Czech authorities for Soviet assistance.[37]

The Invasion Plays Out to the West: Here Come the Russians

Western hostility to communism had a long tradition. The response in the Western intellectual community to the events of the early post-war period was significant, setting the tone for subsequent developments. German intellectual Hannah Arendt, in her seminal 1951 work, *The Origins of Totalitarianism,* argued that modern dictatorship was potentially more highly lethal than authoritarian regimes of the past, chiefly because of the availability of nuclear weapons. Both Nazism and communism could be classified as totalitarian, according to Arendt, as both "strived not towards despotic rule over men, but towards a system where men are superfluous."

Modern tyrannies were removed from the people that they oppressed, and essentially killed off aspiration among the general population. Totalitarianism indicated the end of human freedom, of human resistance, and of any possibility of other choices, of other possibilities. Arendt was writing about now defunct Nazi Germany, but with an eye to the extant Soviet system. In her work *Eichmann in Jerusalem*, Arendt defined and discussed the concept of the *banality of evil*, the means by which the most heinous of events could be "normalized" through systematic and bureaucratic legitimization. Evil acts could be accepted as simply "the way things are done," by faceless and unaccountable modern bureaucracies. In the end, totalitarianism killed off the human essence. Arendt referred to the destruction of the moral, individual, and juridical essence of the citizenry, until nothing remained "but ghastly marionettes with human faces, which all behave like the dog in Pavlov's experiments ... and which do nothing but react." In the same year of 1951, Edward Hunter produced his first book, examining the issue of communism and *brainwashing*. Hunter argued, in *Brainwashing in Red China*, that a key goal of world communism was not so much the eradication of opposition, but rather its cooptation and control through psychological trickery. Hunter's thesis became a major narrative of the Cold War, that international communism was waging a psychological war against humanity in the ultimate interest of world domination. In 1953, the *New York Times* military editor, Hanson W. Baldwin, documented treatment of Korean War American POWs in North Korea as evidence of what communism was trying to do on an international scale: "The Communists are trying to recreate man after their own image. Domination of his mind and spirit is an essential, and usually a preliminary, to physical subjugation. Conformist man—robot man—man cowed by fear or blindness—this is the objective of a world—wide conspiracy implacable in its ruthlessness."[38] The images of robot behavior, of the systematic creation of zombies, puppets, and mindless automatons subservient to the alien Communist Other would become recurrent themes throughout the 1950s.

Scholars' efforts to understand Soviet behavior came from all corners of political and intellectual life, at times to the point of absurdity. In one prominent study, anthropologist Margaret Mead tried to explain why the Soviet Union tended to vote "no" at the United Nations, in the early 1950s. The answer that Mead offered was the concept of "diaperology." Russians, she said, raise their infants in swaddling clothes (tightly wrapped bandages to restrain and quiet infants). As a result, she surmised, Russians developed a negative perception to authority, and thus became functionally oppositional in general decision making.

A Growing Disillusionment

The occupation created significant hardship for many. Serious trouble almost befell Jiří, a Czech geologist who had done his doctoral work at Charles University in Prague.

> We had a saying in 1968—that Czech tanks always point towards Moscow! I worked in the area of sand sedimentology; the regime had brought me to Slovakia—though I was Czech, as there were nearly no Slovak geologists. I recall hosting an international Geology Conference in 1968; some time earlier, in 1967, I was formally denounced by my wife (this was a frequent political pressure tactic), and had to endure a nearly eight-hour interrogation. It was absolutely one of the most brutal experiences of my life. I was nearly arrested.[39] In 1968, I was permitted to travel *by foot* to West Germany for four days, and it was at that time that I made my escape. Before leaving, I remember that Russian troops brought in huge containers for the storage of their vodka; these looked more like giant water containers that you would find at an outdoor festival. It was sad to see what happened. Dubček was a good man, and both Czechs and Slovaks respected him.[40]

Dávid R., a university professor from Bratislava, recalled the events of 1968: "Prior to 1968, we believed in much of the Russian propaganda. We had evidence that they really cared about us. After all, they fought the fascists and died for our liberation. After 1968, Russia lost all legitimacy. All bets were off. Tanks rolled into Bratislava, and people would go up to the soldiers and ask them why they were here. More often than not, they were told that the soldiers were here to protect the Czech and Slovak people, to which they would be asked 'from what?'"[41]

Apologists, many of whom were "true believers" in the system—and the relationship with the Soviets—offered justifications of the 1968 invasion, such as elementary teacher Jana T., who told her students that "the [Dubček] regime was counterrevolutionary, and the fraternal and brotherly assistance of the Warsaw Pact nations" saved Czechoslovakia from certain destruction.[42]

Recording the Events of 1968

Photographer Josef Koudelka is credited with having taken some of the most candid—and courageous—photos of Prague during the Soviet invasion. His vision, tenacity, and sheer will are considered legendary. He says, "In August, 1968, when the big Soviet army invaded my country, everyone was against them, and *everyone forgot who he was.* If he was communist, if he was young or old, if he was anti–communist. *Everyone was a*

Czechoslovak. Miracles happened. People behaved as they never had before; everyone was kind and respectful of each other."[43]

Koudelka was interviewed about the events of 1968, particularly the social dynamic of resistance to the Russian invasion. Here, he offers some glimpses of Prague during the early occupation:

> [In 1968] to be political in Czechoslovakia meant being in the Communist Party, which I was not. But in the period '68, everyone in society became involved in politics. Czechoslovakia had been a country where nothing was possible, and suddenly, everything was possible, and everything was changing very quickly. What was happening was not about revolution. It was about regaining freedom.
>
> With the abolition of censorship, everything started to change. Seven days after the Soviet invasion of Prague, we heard that one of the key conditions in the Soviets' agreement to remove their tanks from the streets of Prague was the re-establishment of censorship.[44]
>
> Milan Kundera's speech in 1967 supporting freedom of expression at the Fourth Congress of the Czechoslovak Writer's Union in June was very powerful.
>
> *Interviewer:* I read a great quote by Ian Berry, who I gather was the only Western photographer in Prague (during the first week of the occupation). He said: "the only other photographer I saw was an absolute maniac who had a couple of old-fashioned cameras on a string around his neck, and a cardboard box over his shoulders, who was actually going up to the Russians, clambering over their tanks and photographing them openly. I felt that this guy was the bravest man around or he is the biggest lunatic around. Apparently, this brave lunatic, Joseph, was you."[45]

Koudelka goes on to describe his experiences taking photos of the Russians.

> I wanted to take a picture of the Soviet tanks and soldiers all alone in Wencelas Square. The Czech people had decided not to demonstrate—so as not to give the Soviet occupiers a pretext for a massacre—the Czech people realized that they were being set up. [Later] I climbed up on one the buildings, and the Soviets saw me. They thought I was a sniper and started to chase me. I lost much of my film during that encounter.[46]
>
> [These] photographs are proof of what happened. Sometimes now, when I go to Russia, soldiers there say: "we came to liberate you." I say: "Listen: I think that it was quite different. I saw people getting killed." [When they see my photos] they have to believe me. Today, more than half of the young generation don't know anything about the events of 1968, and most of the population that did know chose to forget. The first week of the resistance to the Soviet invasion was fantastic, but it didn't last. What happened during the next 20 years was less heroic.[47]

Chapter Seven

Normalization After the Events of 1968

A man is devoured by Leonid Brezhnev and as he goes through his stomach he meets Gustáv Husák. "Comrade President," he calls out "has Brezhnev eaten you too?" "No," answers Husák, "I came from the other end."

The period after the Soviet invasion of Czechoslovakia is commonly referred to as the *normalization* phase, a period during which major reforms were scrapped in favor of stabilizing the political situation in a manner suitable to the invading Warsaw Pact countries. In fact, "normalization" dates precisely from August 27, 1968, at the return of the Czechoslovak politicians who had been abducted and taken to Moscow. The process of facilitating a return to the status quo had a precedent; the Russians had also imposed a period of normalization on Hungary after the 1956 invasion of that country. In Hungary, the reformist Premier, Imre Nagy, along with his associates, were purged (Nagy was later executed), and the Hungarian politburo was almost completely reconstituted with new members by 1957.[1]

In Czechoslovakia, the political situation was considerably more complicated. Russian troops had been stationed on Hungarian soil since the Second World War, but they had never before been deployed in Czechoslovakia. Also, unlike Hungary, there existed no clear Czech leadership structure for the Soviet Union to embrace after the 1968 invasion.[2] No alternative political center existed for the Russians to use, and though, officially, the USSR had claimed written "permission" granted to them by friendly Czech politicians for the invasion, the reality on the ground was an ambivalent one for Russian troops, who were surrounded by a hostile Czech population.

Tellingly, the joint command of the occupying armies issued an order shortly after the invasion which (1) prohibited the disarming of Czechoslovak Army units; (2) called on troops to withdraw from rural areas and from all locations where Czechoslovak troops were stationed; (3) refrained from blocking important government or Party buildings; (4) allowed banks to function normally; and (5) requisitioned supplies only from within the resources of the joint invasion armies.[3]

The Russian strategy was based on propaganda that explained that instability in Czechoslovakia was being "remedied" by the invasion, that the invaders were, in fact, "liberators" or "helpers" against the threat of anarchy. However, the reaction of the Czech population to the invasion made such a position untenable as the society was manifestly *not* out of control; order was maintained, and people went about their normal business. Solidarity was expressed for the reformist politicians, and notice was served that collaborators would be exposed and punished. The call for the departure of foreign troops was made clear as was a demand for the restoration of full state sovereignty. The orderly manner by which the local population reacted to the invasion "dramatically weakened the principal claims of the occupying powers made in justification of their actions, namely that Czechoslovakia was threatened by 'counter-revolution' and that Czechoslovak institutions were incapable of preserving order and socialism themselves, without the assistance of allied military forces."[4]

Public opinion polls from the post-invasion period are difficult if not impossible to locate, as the sampling from the Prague Spring period was discontinued post-invasion. However, early themes appeared regarding Czech resistance to the invasion. The first of these was the monitoring of potential collaborators and identifying their actions with treason. This concern was tied to a second one, that citizens potentially endangered by the occupation forces required protection. Lack of information about Soviet intentions, coupled with a deep distrust, led to both paranoia and the occasional unfounded rumor during normalization. For example, it was believed widely that the Soviets had created master lists of citizens who were to be arrested. In response, Czech radio broadcasted the license plate numbers of cars believed to belong to citizens targeted for arrest, as a means of alerting them to their status. Subscribers to certain controversial periodicals and literary journals were also rumored to be at risk, as claims abounded that subscription lists were being scrutinized. Mailmen were asked not to reveal subscribers, and news-dealers to destroy such subscription lists. Other rumors suggested that the Slovaks might not stand with the Czechs in opposition to Russia—or that the creation of an autonomous Slovak Republic was being considered.[5]

The Soviet position, therefore, was a fragile one in Czechoslovakia. One of the results was the belief that, for political and social order to be maintained, some reformist politicians from the Prague Spring needed to be retained to maintain the legitimacy of the regime. Thus, for seven months after the invasion, the reformist leadership remained in power, largely intact. Dubček remained in power until April 1969.[6] The country's borders were sealed in the autumn of 1969.[7] Significantly, before the closing of the borders, between 30,000 and 171,000 people left the country (less than 1 percent of the population). Many of the top intellectuals and politicians did *not* depart, preferring to remain and continue to organize resistance to the occupying regime.[8]

One of the most chilling and candid depictions of the early normalization period comes from Jan G., who describes the Russian mood both during and after the invasion: "Dubček had deep ties to both America and to the Russians. His father had spent time in the U.S., and he himself had lived in Russia. At the time of the tensions and invasion, the Russians wanted to *hang* Dubček. And he knew it. In a perverse sort of way, Gustáv Husák [a reformer later considered a collaborator], may have saved Dubček's life. Further, Husák may have prevented Czechoslovakia from bloodshed, or even civil war. Husák and Svoboda both benefitted from the1968 invasion; it rehabilitated both of their careers."[9] Reflecting in 1989 on the normalization period, Gustáv Husák commented that "the concept of normalization was not my invention. We all voted for it as the only possible outcome. If some country experiences an earthquake—what then? It tries to normalize life. And what can it do when a 100,000 plus–strong army descends upon it?[10]

Culture Under Normalization

The second half of 1969 witnessed the powerful resurgence of the more ideologically dogmatic elements of the Communist Party; the return of these forces had profound effects on Czech and Slovak culture, art, and communication. The Czech Minister of Culture, Miroslav Brůžek, a member of the dogmatists, insisted that his purpose was to "break down all of the walls of passive resistance" among artists and their associations.

Subversion was also utilized as a tactic, as the ministries of Culture and Interior were increasingly cooperative in their monitoring activities.[11]

University students were singled out for evaluation to determine if they held sympathies with the protestors. One student noted: "They were screening us, checking our political views, but I didn't see them up close ... the only thing I know is that many people lost their jobs and it was a terrible predicament. But in those days, I was happy just watching the boys, drinking my coffee at Café Slávia and telling myself that the world was a lot more interesting than the life outside of Prague that I had known before, because from time to time you could meet someone who was remarkable in some way."[12]

Another student, previously involved in the demonstrations, recounts the lingering effect of Normalization on her schooling and job opportunities: "In 1970, I was expelled from university, but actually didn't feel much like going there anymore. I was wondering what was the point of finishing my studies when I wouldn't be allowed to teach anyway ... my husband was also expelled from school. He wasn't allowed to take the exams ... then I worked as a cleaning lady. I didn't have a choice. My husband worked in property management."[13]

The "Ten Points" manifesto by writers and scientists (including Václav Havel and scientist Jan Tesař), condemning the invasion of 1968, as well as questioning the legitimacy and authority of the Communist Party, was met with bans, threats, and imprisonment. (The Czechoslovak daily press was "advised from above" not to publish it—advice that they heeded.) The first signer of the Manifesto, Rudolf Batěk, along with Jan Tesař, was imprisoned. Batěk's immunity was lifted in order to make way for prosecution. Shortly thereafter, Batěk was charged with "writing and circulating a statement in which he attacked in the grossest possible manner the policies of the socialist states, slandering its leading representatives, and called for an organized resistance to the legal representatives of the state."[14] We know now that the order to arrest Batěk came directly from the Soviet Union.

After January 1970, six prominent representatives in the arts, sciences, and journalism were jailed, including chess champion Ota Filip; many cultural, religious, literary, and political journals were banned, including *Červený Květ* and *Televízní Noviny*. In religious matters, hard-liner Karel Hrůza took over for reformer Erica Kadlecová in "re-establishing the patriotic clergy" loyal to party and government.[15]

New Communist Party chief Gustáv Husák took measures to divide and conquer artists' associations, in the hopes that some members would sign on with the new regime. In one effort, Husák attacked the "Coordination Committee," the supreme body to which all artistic associations were joined. The Committee had been the voice of artists and intellectuals during the National Front. Husák stated that "we do not recognize coordination committees and we regard them as illegal opposition centers."[16]

The Slovak territories suffered comparatively less overt repression during the "cultural normalization" period, as their Minister of Culture, Dr. Miroslav Válek, was an internationally recognized poet and only secondarily a political functionary. Válek proclaimed that, though the state would retain the right to "distribute" cultural values, the creative work would remain within the "domain of the creators themselves." He added that the Union of Slovak Writers had never found itself in the Czech position of opposition to the regime; they had always managed, he said, to "[erect] some sort of barrier to some of the right wing [i.e., reformer] tendencies in the culture."[17]

In May 1971 Communist Party chief Gustáv Husák told national assembly members that the "process of normalization" had been, more or less, completed, and that the country could now embark towards a "higher" form of socialism. In effect, the only remaining feature of the pre–'68 invasion reform was the federalization of the Czech and Slovak Republics. The Federation endured, exemplified by a nominally independent Slovak Communist Party.

However, the normalization process resulted in massive purges of the Party membership; an estimated 1 million people were either purged or questioned during the normalization period. Many of those suffered permanent job discrimination in the aftermath; in other cases, higher education was denied to their children. The arts, media, and bureaucracy were denied the talents of numerous individuals, all banned on political and ideological grounds.[18]

The Party, though reduced in numerical membership, pledged during the normalization period that it represented the "leading role" in society. By 1983, the CPCS membership was at 1.6 million, drawing it close to the numbers of the early 1960s. Membership carried privileges; education, employment and career advancement had, by the 1970s, become the main incentives for Party membership. It may be no wonder that, by the early 1980s, one third of all Party members were young college and post–college aged recruits.[19]

The role of police in the normalization period was striking. Oppression and repression became the defining feature of the political culture during and after 1968. The police force was expanded significantly after

1968; equipment, manpower and funding were all greatly enhanced. A nationwide system of informers was implemented. New criminal codes, such as the 1973 law, allowed for systematic prosecution for ideological and political reasons. Privacy rights were reduced. Religious persecution reached levels considered "second only to Albania" in Eastern Europe as worshippers were interrogated, harassed, and even imprisoned. *Policing* was elevated to a science; candidates at the Interrogation Faculty of the National Police Academy could now achieve doctoral degrees in their specialty. One report surmises that policy decisions in the early 1970s and early 1980s in Czechoslovakia differed in only one major respect. In the early normalization period, the regime worked under the watchful eye of the USSR, to fulfill its dictates. But over time, the same policies were pursued (doubtless also with tacit Soviet approval) mainly as a means to keep the existing Czechoslovak government in power.[20]

The Normalization Bargain

The normalization period ushered in an unofficial political trade-off between citizens and their government. In exchange for the abandonment of reform and liberalization measures demanded by the Prague Spring, the national government would guarantee a material prosperity unequalled in the communist world. In this way, the Normalization period signified a retreat of large portions of the population from the public to the private sphere. A distinct and lasting separation was created between the people and their government. In effect a new social contract was established which promised material prosperity in return for political loyalty. In some circles, this phenomenon was termed "privatized citizenship." As expressed by Milan Šimečka, a dismissed Party member and leading dissident, it was certainly feasible to live comfortably and quietly in the post–1968 Czechoslovakia: "In order to 'integrate into the new society,'" as he put it: "All the citizen needed to do was to come to terms with a few very basic notions: that there is only one party of government; that there is only one truth; that everything belongs to the State which is also the sole employer; that the individual's fate rests on the favor of the State; that the world is divided into friends and foes; that assent is rewarded, dissent penalized … that the State does not require the entire person, just that part that projects above the surface of public life; and that if this part accepts the sole truth then the individual may do what he or she likes in the private sphere."[21]

The "private bargain" could be appealing, leading to what Václav Havel would come to call "living within a lie": "Prague's wine bars, taverns, theaters and concert halls are similarly full of people. At night there is far more street life here than in Warsaw or Budapest. The winding lanes of Golden Prague, the city's Baroque core, invite wandering, even in the cold. Czechoslovaks, generally well dressed, fill the stylishly renovated old cellars, conspicuously eating large portions of duck and dumplings, crepes in chocolate sauce, and drinking copiously available and very good beer."[22] All of this serves as evidence of one side of the bargain that the Czechoslovak government struck with the Czechoslovak people as part of the "normalization" that came after Warsaw Pact troops, under Soviet command, ended the freedoms blooming in the Prague Spring of 1968. The government has delivered on its part of the deal—to maintain a living standard among the highest in Eastern Europe. No challenges, no adventurism.

What was demanded in return was that there would be no room for political innovation, no liberal gestures or challenges to orthodox communist rule, no revisionism, adventurism, Trotskyism or sins of bourgeois democracy. With the exception of a few largely isolated dissidents, this part of the bargain was kept. As the ambassador said, "There is now much more open and interesting debate and discussion going on in the Soviet Union than in Czechoslovakia."[23]

Material standards did, in fact, improve to a considerable degree. By the mid–1980s, there were, for every 100 households, 145 washing machines, 115 refrigerators, 125 television sets and 49 cars. (Many urban Czechoslovaks had tiny country cottages, *chatas*, which accounts for there being more appliances than households.) Energy costs, however, remained high after 1968, and the country's industrial infrastructure was allowed to wallow in neglect. "What we need," said František Kouřil, the government's principal spokesman, "is a goat that gives milk like a cow and eats like a rabbit."[24]

For many, the Normalization "bargain" of material prosperity in exchange for political passivity created an incentive for avoidance of controversy or visibility. One would "stay off the radar" to avoid potential difficulties with the state. One could, for example, join the Communist Party and decline to participate as an active member. Similarly, one could simply not join the Party. While this decision might close some opportunities, one might still live a decent life, one that some called "unheroic survival." "My husband was never promoted to an executive position because he refused to join the party. But then it was not so terrible that you couldn't survive. So we just lived. Being inconspicuous was a big advantage. You could easily survive."[25] In later years, such "unheroic survivors" were referred to disparagingly as "Little Czechs," for their passivity and failure to oppose the status quo.

At the same time, however, the privatization of individual and family life could have an insidious effect on politics and the state. Increasingly, education became bifurcated, with official, Marxist—Leninist principles conflicting with privately discussed ideas within the home. The point of state policy might have been the encouragement of political passivity in its population, but the outcome was different; a citizenry moving between private and public realms. This development was often referred to as *dual education*.[26]

Normalization and the Arts: Music

Culturally, the normalization period led to political and social stagnation. Hopes of reforming the socialist system gave way to a growing despair, an introspective turn culturally, increased materialism and a sense that one had to negotiate survival within the current state of affairs. Music had provided a useful measure of cultural shift since the 1950s. In the early days of the Czech Communist regime, a variety of musical forms were prohibited or severely restricted. For example, religious and atonal music was outright banned until the 1960s. A professor, Alois Haba, instructing quarter-tone music classes in the early 1950s at the Academy of Music Arts, had his course cancelled. Similarly, composer Vladimír Sommer had great difficulty presenting his *Vocal Symphony*, which he had written between 1957 and 1959. Only the intervention of prominent members of the Union of Composers got the ban lifted on the work, which was finally performed publically in 1963. The justification for the ban was that Sommer was said to have employed "pessimistic lyrics" from writers such as Franz Kafka and F.M. Dostojevski.[27]

However, over time, the Union of Composers was given extended discretion as to which performers and works were deemed acceptable. In this way, they exercised a bit of limited autonomy from the Communist Party. However, the Union could also be a highly politically charged body as Party and non–Party members vied for status, career advancement, and, occasionally, vendettas. By 1968, a Rehabilitation Committee had been set up to rectify poor treatment of musicians and composers from the earlier period. Although it was difficult to get many accused and discredited artists to step forward, the Committee did manage to "rehabilitate"

12 artists, in its report, which was issued in 1969. Unfortunately, the Soviet invasion occurred just prior to the issuance of the report, bringing the rehabilitative efforts to an end.[28]

Composers who opposed the occupation were removed from their positions and given menial jobs. For example, composer Jan Kapr, winner of the Stalin Prize, returned the award to the Soviet Embassy and was stripped of all publishing rights. Over time, the Composers Union was gradually purged and controversial artists were removed.[29]

In music and in communications generally, the normalization period led to the development of an indirect method of communication that was designed to circumvent or confuse the monitoring authorities. Some opposition composers began to use ambiguous or symbolic titles to their work, such as *Peace With Snakes* by Karol Odstrčil and *Inclined Plane* by Ivan Kurtz. In some cases, historical, ambiguous, biblical, philosophical or moral beliefs were employed.[30]

Coping with Normalization

Indirect language and ambiguous communication as a feature of normalization form the subject of comments by Vladimír, who lived through the period as an economics professor in the East:

> In a perverse sort of way, the Russian invasion was a kind of huge joke to us. And, given that tough times are often dealt with by the employment of humor, we did find that jokes proliferated during that period. For example, Gustáv Husák [the first Party secretary who was installed to replace Dubček, and who gradually became a puppet of the Soviets] was referred to by many people as "Mustav Rusák!" [one of the Russians, or "Ruskies"].
>
> There was also a popular story of a letter allegedly sent by a Vietnamese student, in support of the Czechoslovak Communist Party against the American invaders. The letter (a play on words) shows the "student" trying to write in proper Czech, saying, "We thank the Party" ("*Děkujeme straně*"), but slightly misspelling "Party" (strana) to *sráni*, meaning instead, "we thank the shit."[31]

"Those who were Party members," Vladimír continues, "had to agree that they supported the invasion, and that it was necessary. If they did not make an outward show of solidarity, they risked losing their job, and the possibility of their children being denied a higher education."

He continues at length:

> The Normalization Committee was charged with keeping an eye on the attitudes and behavior of Party members. Keep in mind, though, that a third of the Communist Party was purged during this period. Over 430,000 individuals were either expelled

or had their Party membership terminated. Many survived by faking their way through interrogations with indirect language; we got very good at saying many words with little substance behind them.

What I am going to say now may seem very strange, but I truly believe it. The invasion may have actually been *good* for the people in one respect; the population became smarter. By that, I mean that we learned the difference between appearances and reality, between political statements and the realities of power and domination. As a result, we learned not to be literal and to understand that reality had many levels. Language was a tool that could be used at a variety of these levels for multiple purposes; we learned [culturally] to use language in a very complex/double manner, and this helped to provoke thinking among the people. It made us smarter."[32]

This contention is refuted by Beáta, interviewed in Banská Bystrica, who countered:

Second level thinking is not a good thing, as it perpetuates distrust of persons, projects, and ultimately government. This fear created passivity amidst a concern for one's own personal security. In the end, it results in a loss of confidence and a passive posture that waits for "someone else" to make decisions and take responsibility.

The invasion was a "crippling" event from which no good came. We did indeed need to learn to express ourselves more indirectly, as a result of fear from what might happen if our true thoughts were revealed. But the damage that was done to the people, the loss of morale, the descent into passivity, and the simmering hatred towards the invaders was the reality.

Yes, we did tell many jokes during the normalization period—privately, of course. Some of them were better than others. For example, one went "What are the four enemies of socialism? Answer: Spring, summer, fall and winter." We used to say also that we lived in a society where workers don't work and governors don't govern.[33]

She adds, "During the period after the people were required to sign a statement that we supported the invasion and the government, which was humiliating. But you had to think not just of yourself but of your family's future."[34]

Cracks in the Edifice: The Radio with Wire

In the period just preceding the 1968 invasion, ordinary citizens commonly possessed what was called at the time the "radio with wire." The radio with wire was simply a connection to the local radio stations through one's home telephone connection. Having such a connection was, for average persons, a great advantage, making the cost for both a telephone and a radio connection very inexpensive. The "radio with wire" was an arrangement that allowed most people to afford its services.[35]

Jan, a Bratislava technocrat, recalls what happened the night of the Soviet invasion:

I went to bed early—as I was a bit drunk—but as I lived in Petržalka [a densely populated section of Bratislava across the Danube from the Old Town], the sound of the Soviet tanks was unmistakable. They came from Hungary. Their trajectory was to enter Czechoslovakia through the neighborhood of Petržalka. I was out late the night before. That morning, I awoke, as if in a dream. All I remember is that I had a hangover and that, watching out from my windows I saw foreign soldiers in our streets. It was not clear to me from which country they came, at first.[36] By 11 p.m., the Soviet invasion was considered legitimate, and most of the major media were forced to stop broadcasting. The overlooked issue was that the "radio on wire" had not been banned.[37]

The Czechoslovak Politbureau voted 7–4 to officially oppose the USSR invasion (though some dispute this, arguing that the body approved an "invitation" to the Soviets). So, as the better part of Czechoslovak media was suppressed, the "radio on wire" was overlooked and continued to operate, in defiance of the Soviet invasion. As explained by Jan, "they forgot to shut down the radio on wire." This raises several very interesting questions: First, whether the Soviets *knew* about the radio on wire; second, whether Czechoslovak authorities turned a blind eye to the continued broadcast from this medium. It is entirely feasible that, while official Czechoslovak policy was to placate the Soviets and to endorse the invasion, a more subtle message was being sent to the general population, suggesting that authorities were willing to allow certain media to continue.[38]

The invasion created internal confusion as "the better part of the population supported Dubček; he was very popular in both the Czech and Slovak regions of the country."[39] Dubček was described by many as "very down to earth" and as "a man of the people" in many respects. For example, it was said that he walked the streets with other average citizens, without drawing attention as to who he was. It also said that he treated those whom he met on the streets as fellow citizens, with a distinctive lack of pomp or condescension.[40]

One of the major points of contention became a generational dispute. Many 1960s communists did not agree with "the reform communism" of the 1970s. In the 1970s, no Czech politician established the legitimacy to displace the legacy of Dubček. During this phase, Svoboda replaced Novotný as President of the republic. "Opposition radio" continued to be itinerant, moving from location to location, and this continued into 1968 as stations tried to avoid being identified and closed.[41]

The Mixed Aftermath

In 1970, a group of prominent Party members and commentators began to examine the question of whether the Soviet "invasion" had, instead, followed from an *invitation* by elements of the Czechoslovak political establishment. This thesis was aided by comments by Radio Prague commentator Jaroslav Kučera, who claimed that the entry of Soviet troops (along with those from four other Warsaw Pact countries) had intervened through "fraternal assistance" from abroad. The entry of the Warsaw Pact troops, he said, was an "act of international help" and a response to "pleas expressed in resolutions by thousands of individuals and collectives." His view was that the invitation of Warsaw Pact armies was "not a fabrication" but a sincere attempt by authorities in Czechoslovakia to save socialism there. Mainstream media speculated that such "research" and "revelations" could simply be a means for laying the groundwork towards legitimizing the Soviet invasion, rendering it more "respectable."[42]

The night of the invasion, August 20, 1968, the Czech Communist Party Presidium was still in session when, at 11:40 p.m., Premier Otto Černík informed the Assembly that five Warsaw Pact armies had crossed the border onto Czech soil. The Presidium immediately adopted a proclamation (which was passed 7–4, according to some sources) condemning the invasion. Voting against the report were Vasil Biľak, Drahomír Kolder, Emil Rigo, and Oldich Ŝvestka. The proclamation was, however, binding on the Party. Within a short period, efforts were made (by whom it is not immediately known) to prevent the dissemination of the proclamation to the general public, which was already firmly behind its sentiments.[43]

Party leader Gustáv Husák was a key player in the events of November 1968 and was, at least initially, opposed to the invasion. Husák was sent to Moscow to work on the first set of post-invasion "negotiations," and he reported back to the Slovak CP Congress:

> Armies of five socialist states have entered our territory. It is necessary to say that the leading organs of our party and state did not ask for this entry ... a tragic misunderstanding, a tragic incomprehension, have occurred. In this context, the question of who invited the armies arises. The CPCS CC Presidium ... [has] issued a declaration that neither the President, nor the government, nor the Party leadership extended such an invitation. The question of who invited the armies is not yet resolved. All members of the CPCS and the Slovak CP leaderships, without exception, gave their words of honor that they had not undertaken such a step and had not known about it.[44]

Other leading Party members, such as Premier Lubomir Štrougal (after Otto Černík's abduction to the USSR), also managed to provide clear evidence of opposition to the invasion, in a radio interview on 26 August 1968, when he denounced the "illegal occupation" of Czechoslovakia. Štrougal also made direct (and risky) appeals for the immediate departure of Soviet troops.[45]

A number of conservative members of the Presidium and Secretariat were long held in suspicion for having issued an invitation to the Russians for invasion. Brezhnev had claimed that top Czech officials, such as Alois Indra, the economy secretary in the Central Committee, had requested help against the "counter-revolution" in Czechoslovakia. Vasil Biľak, first secretary of the KSS, Oldich Švestka, the editor of *Rudé Právo*, Central Committee member Drahomír Kolder, and Antonín Kapek, a candidate member of the KS Presidium, have all been implicated over time.[46]

Biľak, Kolder, Jan Piller, Miloš Jakeš and others declared on August 28, 1968, "on their honor," that they had never performed any action to dishonor either Czech citizens, or the Czechoslovak Communist Party. These officials, along with four other conservatives, were officially "rehabilitated," and accusations against them were laid to rest as unfounded. Interestingly, by 1970 all eight of the suspected collaborator politicians had retained their positions in government; four were promoted, two retained their status, and two others received moderate demotions.[47]

Suspicion remained during normalization that the Soviets were attempting to rewrite history, encouraging the dissemination of propaganda by the Czech government to encourage the view that authorities had invited the Soviets in 1968. The rehabilitation of leading politicians had removed any hope for finding a "smoking gun." What is significant is that the government chose to broach the thesis again, two years after the invasion. Were the Soviets trying to "settle the 1968 question" to their own advantage? One journalist wrote that "the victims of 1968 are now in the process of being transformed into eager and willing hosts."[48]

The Dubček Legend

On July 16, 1970, the major media in both the Czech and Slovak regions (*Rudé Právo* and *Pravda*) published identical versions of a lengthy, 6,000-word article intended to "destroy the legend about Alexander Dubček by historical truth." The article was unique for its length, and for the fact that even the television media announced it the day *before* its appearance—a nearly unprecedented action in Czechoslovakia[49] but certainly one designed to appeal to as large an audience as possible.

Driving the article's creation was the widely held notion in normalization circles that a "legend" surrounding the deposed reform leader had been created, and needed to be corrected. The article noted that "the legend about Alexander Dubček has deeply embedded itself in the minds, of a part of the population, even among Communists," according to *Rudé Právo.* The cure for this misunderstanding, according to the article, was to provide a series of "erudite" arguments, illustrating the "truth." Interestingly, in spite of the invective spilled towards Dubček and his legacy, the article made no mention of any effort to bring legal actions or criminal proceedings against Dubček—although note is made of his having "disrupted relations with other socialist states."[50]

The article begins with a reaffirmation of the officially sanctioned normalization explanation; Novotný, Dubček's predecessor, had instituted policies that had ended in abject failure, creating a period of instability. In the period that followed, "reformers" argued that Dubček was a compromise candidate who might preserve the unity of the Party. In fact, the article alleges, there was no unity at the time among Party members, and Dubček's earlier criticisms of Novotný, along with his support from Slovak CC members (Dubček was himself a Slovak) ensured his quick installation as Party secretary, circumventing what should have been a period of lengthy debate, discussion, and voting. Dubček was merely a "man without a program," placed at the helm of the Communist Party as an "emergency solution."[51]

The second "fact" presented against Dubček was the allegation that he lacked the "disposition" for high office, that he was "ideologically unprepared," and that he lacked the will to carry out his responsibilities effectively. Such an argument must have appeared spurious, indeed, as Dubček had spent his youth in the USSR, having attended Russian schools as well the Moscow Party College, from 1955 to 1958.

More Charges

As part of the charge of dispositional "weakness," Dubček was accused of having played into the hands of the West; the notion of "socialism with a human face" was a mere concoction of the United States in a grand strategy against the Socialist world, with the end result to "confuse" true Communists, while providing opportunities for "rightist, antisocialist" forces. The argument was augmented to suggest that Dubček had created a new *aparát, or* guiding principle to the Party, thus enabling right-wing forces to gain ascendancy.[52]

Next in the litany brought forth by the article was the charge that Dubček had tolerated societal protest to a degree that national security and order had been endangered. To illustrate this charge, the Peoples Militia

Affair was raised. In June 1968, the Militia had organized a massive protest in Prague, throwing their support to Dubček in an effort to increase democratization. The second incident was in regard to the 2,000 Words Manifesto, issued and signed by 70 intellectuals on June 27, 1968. Dubček was said to be at fault for not mentioning the Party condemnation of the Manifesto in his television address on June 29. (In fact, the Presidium had *already* criticized the Manifesto on national television on June 29, *the day before Dubček's speech.*) The final criticisms involved Dubček's knowledge of and attitude towards the Warsaw Pact maneuvers, which were performed on Czechoslovak soil just before the invasion. In the first place, he was accused of "agreeing" to such maneuvers. He was accused of having special knowledge of the Soviet invasion in advance and doing nothing to prevent it. He merely needed to "lift the phone to our Soviet comrades," even as late as August 20, 1968, "to reach an agreement."[53]

The Lesson and the Letter

Over two years from the date of the invasion, the Czechoslovak Presidium released its analysis of the events of the Prague Spring. The report, known as "The Lesson," claimed that Czechoslovakia had created a series of political mistakes that would not be repeated. The "international assistance" of the Warsaw Pact invasion was rationalized as necessary and constructive to the social order. Thoroughly pro–Soviet in its conclusions, the report opened up new wounds, reigniting a controversy over whether the USSR had been "invited" by a formal letter from the old-guard Communists to invade as a means of legalizing the action. The idea had originally been proffered by the USSR, but withdrawn when the Czech population proved hostile to the invaders.[54]

Reflecting on 1968

Many of the leaders of the Prague Spring reform movement departed into exile after the Russian invasion and normalization period. In 1988, interviews were held with a number of them, as a means of looking back and assessing the events of 1968, particularly in light of a system that was on the verge of collapse. The location was Cortona, Italy, and the April 29–30 conference was called "The Prague Spring and Its Repercussions in Europe." A left-wing Milan-based group organized the conference featuring over 100 participants. During the procedures, the prospects for the post–Stalinist Communist world were discussed, as well as both the successes and failures of the Dubček era. Participants included Jiří Pelikán, Director of Czechoslovak television in 1968; Ota Šik, Deputy Prime Minister in 1968 Czechoslovakia (and a leading proponent of economic reform); Zděnek Mlynář, Secretary of the CPCS in 1968; Eduard Goldstücker, President of the Czechoslovak Union of Writers in 1968 and a noted cultural reformer; and Vilém Prečan of the Czechoslovak Academy of Sciences, author of the *Black Book* on the Russian invasion.[55]

In 1988, a regional Italian newspaper conducted an interview with the 1968 Foreign Minister, Jiří Hájek, who was not present at the conference (still living in Prague). In Hájek's view, there was one overriding error in the reform strategies of 1968:

> We were not completely convinced of the conservative, if not reactionary character of the Brezhnev regime. We thought that we could discuss things, not being aware of how little freedom of maneuver we were allowed. Furthermore, the group around Dubček was not homogenous. We spent too much time in discussion, when it was really important to hold a Party conference in February to give reformers effective control of the movement. Thus, the enemies of reform had time to prepare for the military invasion, and we did not have time. Our real mistake was that we thought that the people in Moscow would understand that *our reforms were also essential to them*.[56]

The conference revealed a widespread belief that the reforms attempted 20 years earlier had gradually taken hold throughout the East, and that the USSR itself had become increasingly tolerant and accepting of such reforms. The participatory political concepts of *perestroika* and *glasnost* represented, essentially, the rehabilitated policies of 1968: "Indeed, the Soviet—led invasion was a crime if for no other reason than that it deprived us of the fruit of an unprecedented experience; the opportunity to see how a freer and more open version of Marxism would have handled the complex problems of modern society in a highly educated industrial country."[57]

Such sentiments offer a significantly different assessment of the phenomenon of 1968 than conclusions typically drawn in the West. Czechoslovakia was not embarking on a Western-style parliamentary reform, but rather a democratic re-structuring of Post-Stalinist Marxist–Leninist Socialism. In this sense, the invasion of 1968 ran counter to long traditions within Czech political culture itself. Since the Second World War, it was widely believed that the country could create its own balance of state power, market relations and social justice, based on rationally applied principles and pragmatism. The Prague Spring was an expression of this ethos: that

Czechoslovakia could find a "middle way" of socialism, by fostering internal changes and evolutionary change.[58]

Interview with Dubček: 1989

A late as May 1989, the significance of the events of 1968 were still hotly contested in Czechoslovakia and elsewhere. On April 17, 1989, Alexander Dubček gave an interview on Hungarian television. In it, he compared events in Hungary and the Soviet Union of 1989 with those in Czechoslovakia, in 1968. The response from the lingering communist regime was swift: "Alexander Dubček's views provided the citizens of Hungary with distorted information about the events of 20 years ago and also about the current situation in Czechoslovakia.... This certainly does not contribute to the sense of international community between socialist countries."[59]

The Czech government went so far as to print negative comments from the interview from Hungarians living in Czechoslovakia. Further, the East German regime stepped in, with the SED (Communist Party of East Germany) criticizing the interview on April 25.[60] Within five months, however, the Velvet Revolution would be under way.

Chapter Eight

Religion

Heard: "The Party owned you from Monday to Saturday, and the priest owned you on Sunday—if the Party didn't catch you in church!"

Historical Background: Communism as a Moral/Religious System

Communist ideals long had a following in the West. At the time of the Russian Revolution of 1917, experts on communism were few in the Western world, and the weight of analysis was placed on a few individuals. One of these was a British professor at the University of London by the name of Harold Laski. Laski had spent considerable time in the U.S. as a political theorist, writing in liberal journals, and was a friend of American writer, Walter Lippman. Laski published a work in 1927, *Communism,* which became highly regarded in both communist and anti-communist circles. In the book he argued that communism and religion were fundamentally incompatible, as organized religion tended to stress supernatural forces while the Marxist conception of history concentrated on materialism as the agent of change. In Laski's view, religion tended to render its followers as passive, obedient followers of dogma, whereas Marxism activated and stimulated its followers to challenge authority and to change their worldly lives. The author himself became a communist in 1931.[1]

Reinhold Niebuhr was perhaps the most influential Western theologian at the onset of the Cold War, having examined communism since the 1920s. In 1931, Niebuhr assessed communism from a religious vantage point. Viewed casually, he said, communism gave the appearance of a mere vulgar and material philosophy, posing as science. But examined more carefully, he said, communism could, indeed, be considered as a full fledged modern religious movement. Niebuhr looked to the 18th century Enlightenment, and to the dogmas espoused at that time—which were far from traditional Christian ideas. In this period, he too saw religious faith and devotion.[2]

Niebuhr's comparisons of the Enlightenment to communism were only superficial. In some ways one could discern the predestination doctrine of orthodox Calvinist theology.[3] The Enlightenment, with its devotion to reason, empiricism, and science, had confidence in the establishment of a harmonious and progressive world. Communism, on the other hand, taught that the world was doomed to collapse because of the forces that Niebuhr considered to be central to communist theology, of *historical materialism*—the idea that history is driven not by spiritual but material forces. Redemption was offered through communism but only after the cataclysm of class warfare had subsided. In fact, Niebuhr's greatest concerns were that communist ideas would stand their best chance of germinating not in the West, but in the developing world, where "primitive religious energies" would be released by the certainties promised by communism.[4] To Niebuhr, Marx had written a communist bible, and Lenin's ancillary writings could only serve to promulgate communism much as Thomas Aquinas had influenced the spread of medieval Christianity. Other theologians weighed in during the 1930s. Russian philosopher Nicholas Berdyaev argued that communism was "a reminder and a denouncement of an unfulfilled duty, of the fact that the Christian ideal has not been achieved."[5] Others argued that communism was, in fact, a secularization of Calvinism, as it endorsed a predetermined, scientific future, paralleling in some ways the predestination doctrine of orthodox Calvinist theology.

Religious Culture in Communist Czechoslovakia

Traditionally, Czechoslovakia was a country with a split identity regarding religion. Many Czechs follow no church, considering themselves either atheist or agnostic. Belief in God is low among Czechs, and churches are held at an arms length, given the historical strife between Catholic and Protestant churches there. Religious skepticism has political antecedents as well, given the experience of fascism, the subsequent imposition of Stalinism after World War II, and the events of 1968. Slovakia, on the other hand, possesses a notably different character; trust in religious institutions is higher than in the Czech lands, and the Catholic Church exerts considerably more influence.

The treatment of religious belief and practice in Communist Czechoslovakia is a subject that, understandably, evokes strong feelings and memories. The official Communist Party perspective on religion during the 1950s was that belief signified class oppression and outmoded superstition. Policies were tempered in the 1960s and 1970s, and churches were not typically shut down. Still, one took risks if they attended church or were married in a religious ceremony.

Religious Orders in Czechoslovakia After World War II

The years immediately following the communist ascendency in 1948 were the most arduous for organized religion in Czechoslovakia. In 1950, ten members of various religious orders went on trial, trials roughly coinciding with the infamous Slánský political trials. The religious trials were followed by raids on the monasteries. On April 13, 14, and 15, 1950, units of the Peoples' Militia, along with local police, raided every monastery and religious school in the country. Even members of cloistered communities were removed to detention centers. The impetus for the raids was provided by the trials, which charged the ten religious figures with espionage and working towards the overthrow of the state by force. President Klement Gottwald supported the arrests and closures in 1950, stating that "reactionaries at home and abroad are in touch with the highest Catholic clergy and are preparing a struggle against our People's Democratic Republic."[6]

A movement to close down monasteries and convents commenced after World War II. In addition to charges of espionage, the monasteries were called "centers of Germanization," implying continued support for the now defunct Third Reich. Such claims stretched credulity, however, as many monks and other religious figures had suffered considerably under the Nazis, including leading Jesuits, Basilians, Salesians, and Premonsratensians, among others. In addition to the monasteries, the nation's convents were also closed down in 1950. Over 10,000 nuns were displaced or jailed, some serving as long as 16 years, many under conditions of hard labor. By the Prague Spring, their numbers had been reduced to less than 5,000.[7]

The removal operation was called "Action K," and was carried out by the Ministry of the Interior as a quasi-military maneuver. Many bishops, including Roman Catholic Bishop Stephen Cardinal Trochta of Litoměřice, and Greek Catholic Bishop Pavol Gojdič of Prešov, were rooted out and placed under house arrest. Some were given lengthy prison terms. According to a (opposition group) Charter 77 report, the crackdown on religious orders was a diversionary tactic used by the State to draw attention away from numerous domestic and economic problems, among these, shortages of consumer goods.[8]

State actions such as those of the early 1950s lessened with time—at least up to 1980. Police generally acted with greater caution. However, by the 1980s, police actions were ratcheted up. In March 1983, an attempt was made to wipe out the Franciscan order. Many were arrested and interrogated. Eventually, those charged or arrested were released without trial or were given suspended sentences. The next year, however, additional charges were brought against seven Franciscans in Liberec. During this round of arrests, charges made by police were typically vague, often falling under the general category of somehow "preventing the state's supervision of churches and religious societies." In fact, those arrested were typically not identified publically as religious persons. Such shielding may have been a tactic to promote the 1972 ideological statement from the periodical *Nová Mysl*: "On the whole it may be stated that the level of maturity achieved by our socialist society does not afford suitable conditions for the development of monastic life ... because today's young people are not interested in this way of life."[9]

This assertion was challenged by many who saw religious involvement, especially by young people, on the upswing since the events of the Prague Spring.

Official Policy on Religion

In spite of the arrests and show trials of the early 1950s—and later in the 1980s—the regime maintained an official position of religious tolerance in the Czechoslovakia. In 1977, an official pronouncement declared that religious freedom was guaranteed by the Czech constitution. Freedom of the religious press was assured and a statement issued that "no one has been harassed or persecuted" for participation in religious rites. Oppositional views, such as those put forth by Charter 77, were referred to as "slanderous." The statement read:

> Czechoslovakia is a country in which all working people, regardless of nationality, race, Weltanshauung, or religion, actively participate in building a developed socialist society.
>
> The Constitution and the laws in force in Czechoslovakia guarantee all basic human rights and liberties, including the freedom of religious belief.[10]

The statement went further, concluding that religious freedom was in line with Leninist principles, "which have been embodied in the Constitution ... that freedom of religion is guaranteed." As far as the State was concerned, the report declared that "authorities do not examine whether a citizen is without a religious belief or belongs to a certain church or community ... religion is a private affair, a free, personal, pure relation."[11] Statistics offered in the 1977 statement show 470 divinity students studying at six divinity schools; widespread publication of religious magazines and pamphlets, estimated at 250,000; and over 8,000 places of worship, including 195 in Prague alone. Western claims that Czechs are prohibited from attending church are called "nonsensical," as the social system and socialist society "do not require believers to abandon their faith." Further, any claim by opponents that human rights are not respected is dismissed as "distorted," and "harms the good name of Czechoslovakia ... and *has a disturbing effect on the Christian peace movement.*"[12]

The Czech lands tended to be non-religious or nominally Catholic, with small minorities of Evangelical Protestantism, while Slovakia was primarily Roman Catholic. Before World War II, Jews constituted about 150,000 persons in Czechoslovakia. Orthodox believers constituted a significant population as well, particularly in the East. Religious leaders were both controlled and paid by the state.[13] After the establishment of the communist regime, Catholic priests were allowed to say mass if they were deemed not to be religious "activists." The state would grant such formal status. Such permission often created a complicated relationship between priest, worshipper and the State, as priests were often expected to inform on their congregations to the authorities. In particular, pastors were expected to inform on any public servants or Party members who had attended a service.

Diocesan priests were required to register with the State. Such priests were permitted to say mass, and were generally left alone—particularly in villages. However, they were required to take loyalty oaths to the State. Since the demise of the communist system, the question has arisen about potential divisions between priests regarding those who took oaths and those who didn't. "It is a false dichotomy," says David, a church member. "All priests understood the reality of their options. No grudges are held against those who took oaths. Although some priests functioned as informants for authorities, the numbers were small." It was widely recognized that agents were present regularly in churches to monitor those attending[14]: "My problem was that I went to church, and somebody reported it at the hospital where I worked. Usually, I'd sit in the sacristy where there was a little stool prepared for me.... My boss called me into his office and inquired why it was necessary for me to go to church. And I told him, other people go to pubs and drink, and nobody harasses them about that."[15] Monitoring church attendance was particularly aggressive in the Czech lands, where the Party was much more aggressive towards the church than in predominantly Catholic Slovakia. In most localities, Sunday mass was permitted. Daily mass was more controlled and prohibited in some places. Interestingly, standing *choirs* were prohibited, as were religious clubs. No religious organizations with permanent members were allowed, although church music was permitted as long as it was not performed by a standing group.[16]

Religious people were "enemies of the society." Rita, a Slovak, recalls that those who worked in the civil service and in the public sector—or who had a role in youth education—were not permitted to attend religious services. If they did, they faced serious problems at work. Teachers in particular were seen as disseminators of Marxist–Leninist doctrine and the so-called "scientific" view of reality.[17]

Policy towards religion was anything but consistent, and the uncertainty accompanying religious practice was a sword that always hung over the population:

> The Czechs were not very religious, but Slovaks were often seen as "northern Hungarians" in their Catholicism. Within central/eastern Europe, there were profound differences in attitudes towards religion. The West, towards Austria, was largely Catholic and religious, while the East, into Ukraine, was typically atheist.
>
> The rule towards marriage was *not* to marry in a church. Party members and members of the military could have nothing to do with churchgoing. Teachers too. There were some exceptions, however. My grandmother was left alone by the 1980s to attend church as she pleased. Often the elderly were not bothered. In her case, however, the circumstances were more complicated. She had been a committed Communist. She had also been baptized, secretly, by a relative who was a fighter pilot in the military. The name of the priest was always kept a secret.[18]

A retrospective 1992 special edition of *The Vigil* offers a glimpse of church activity, from the politics of attendance and worship, to the role played by the priest both during and after services. Several lengthy sections are reproduced verbatim here:

> Students in the seminaries had as a compulsory subject a "Philosophy of Marxism–Leninism." All priests had to have a license from the State. Any priest who publicly

> spoke out (even in hints, for example, during his homily against all his oppression) had his license taken away. And if he then offered holy mass, they would put him straight in prison, for breaking the laws, dealing with state relations towards the Church.[19]

The account continues, referencing underground activity by clergy:

> Many priests then worked underground, educating young people and students—future secretly ordained priests. It was extremely difficult because they were followed by state police. They even had to go to work. To go to work was compulsory in communist countries. But in the references they had from their previous employers was written that they were priests and "problematic" citizens so everybody was afraid to employ them. But if they were not employed for some time—you had to have a stamp on your ID from your employer—they were put in prison for breaking the law of duty to work.[20]
>
> The same threats hung over laymen who were "too-active" working with youth, organizing pilgrimages, etc., or helping the priests or cooperating with "problematic" priests. Many lay people ended up in prison, too.
>
> Ordinary believers had to be careful as well. State police were photographing people coming out of church, recording everything at the pilgrimages, using camcorders, etc. People working for Public Services, The Ministries of Foreign Affairs, Internal Affairs, Correction Services, Education [e.g., teachers] were fired automatically if they publicly acknowledged they were believers. They then had great difficulties getting a proper job. Usually, they could not. Their children experienced psychological terror at schools, where the collaborating teachers checked how many children went to church, prayed before going to bed or believed in God. They also asked what children attended private religion lessons. That all had to be written in their Study Report.[21]

Marriage in Czechoslovakia was treated as a civil affair, to be performed at the city hall. Religious marriages were suspect and had to be conducted with discretion, especially for professionals, Party members, and teachers. Rita R. notes that only factory and agricultural workers and shop assistants wouldn't be prosecuted for their religion, and could be married safely in church. "We were both teachers when we got married—so we could not get married in a church. That is why we did it secretly in Hungary. My father's former classmate from secondary school was a priest [in eastern Hungary], so we trusted him."[22]

While religion was (however grudgingly) tolerated under the regime, State propaganda worked actively to discourage religious belief. For example, Ivana T. recalls that her grandmother read a State document in the early 1950s that implicated the Catholic Church in the Holocaust. This revelation caused her to leave the church, and to discourage her children from belief. The State also used other means to control religious expression—such as distraction. Ivana describes that

> we were sometimes told to come to school on Saturday. I found it odd and they always found some work for us to do like rake leaves in the school yard and similar activities—

> not like classes. It seemed strange to me as I sensed that it was almost like "pro forma" activity. At one point, I asked my mother why they wanted us to come to school on Saturday. I was told that on that day, there was a religious procession to [a nearby town] Levoča, and thus by being required to come to school on Saturday we were being prevented from potentially attending the procession. But I also remember that the rules were not so strict. If your parents wrote you a note for the teacher saying you were going somewhere for the weekend, it was ok. I didn't think at the time that any of my friends actually went to Levoča. However, it became clear to me after November, 1989, that some of my friends must have been [secretly] involved in the church. They had never spoken of it. I suppose that they had been instructed at home not to talk about it.[23]

Pilgrimages, an integral part of European religious tradition, were not prohibited under the Old Regime, but they were carefully monitored. Petr, from the central Slovak town of Huncove, recalls a regional pilgrimage to Levoča: "One year, the local football team offered the use of their bus for pilgrims who were making the three hour trip to Levoča. The authorities intervened, and claimed that such an arrangement was an inappropriate use of public funds for transportation."[24]

Although religious instruction was permitted, parents would have to sign documents confirming that their children were attending religious instruction. Often upon signing such documents parents and children alike would be warned of future repercussions, particularly with regard to educational opportunities.[25] But such threats could be arbitrary. Martina, from the copper producing town of Krompachy, explained that

> enforcement of religious rules could be quite selective. My father was a pediatrician and had status in the community. Therefore, he could not practice religion locally. He had to go to Košice [a larger city, 30 km away] to attend church. By doing this, he was basically left alone. But my sister was not so lucky. She was not permitted to attend university, because of her religious views. I was also limited in my choices of higher education, as I also held religious beliefs—but I was luckier. I was allowed entry to university in Svit [some distance away from Krompachy], but my sister was barred. One never knew exactly why some were treated in one way and others differently.[26]

One might speculate as to why, in a nominally atheist state, religious practice would be allowed at all. One possible explanation, says Petr, is that the "authorities didn't want any trouble."[27] Religious belief was not supported by the state, but its existence was, however, reluctantly acknowledged. The fear of local violent reaction to anti-religious state measures was always a concern. "The Communists in Czechoslovakia were smarter than their Russian counterparts," Petr continues: "In Russia they destroyed churches, but in Czechoslovakia they walked a more careful line, so as not to create major public disturbance. Religious practice could occur, but it needed to be discreet. For the majority of the population (who were not religious, or who didn't travel much), the regime and the standard of living could be excellent."[28]

Indeed, the trick was to remain off of the radar if one wished to practice religious faith. To an extent, the regime was willing to turn a blind eye to individuals although threats to their educational opportunities were sometimes made—and sometimes enforced, as noted above. Although individuals were not typically targeted for prosecution, they were frequently investigated for transgressions that could, the authorities hoped, lead to the uncovering of larger illicit networks. Investigations were shadowy affairs: they were not published, and the individual being investigated was not typically told what the inquiry was about. (However, State television often reported that certain persons were being sought—without mention of the alleged transgression they had committed.) Petr, who was never investigated himself, recalls the atmosphere of the time: "I studied in Košice and went to church regularly. I was also in the church choir. Some of us kept secret cassette recordings of religious sermons from a well-known priest who was followed by many in our community. However, I had one school mate who was a monk, and he was investigated. I recall that he never spoke about it."[29]

One of the religion-oriented issues facing the regime was the smuggling of illicit materials into Czechoslovakia, and religious materials comprised one of these controlled groups. Bibles were legal, but only the "State approved" version. Thus, the smuggling of bibles into the country was a common practice. Jaroslav, a librarian from Bratislava, recalls smuggling bibles and other literature from Yugoslavia:

> I was a Pioneer [scout], and I had never been stopped or questioned by the police. I had a clean record. In 1985, I became religious. I was converted by a friend. Typically the ŠTB (secret police) focused on priests, underground activities and activists, not average people. In the mid–1980s, a friend and I went for a trip to Yugoslavia. We took our passports with us, but authorities required us to leave our identity cards with them until we returned. I brought back three or four Bibles with me, and my friend managed eight to ten of them. Controls at the border were quite strict, and we were very nervous. I recall burying the bibles in a backpack, amidst other papers and books. Had we been caught, there certainly would have been an investigation.[30]

Petr concurs, as his mother was actually caught smuggling religious books into the country in 1980. She was subject to an immediate interrogation—who had given them to her, and who would she share them with. Her defiant response, when threatened with jail, was to tell the police "go ahead and throw me in jail. You and the State can take care of my six children." In the end, she was not placed in jail, but her materials were confiscated. In addition, a formal investigation was launched against her husband. In repeated interrogations (spanning many months), police demanded to know the family's connections to alleged underground religious networks.[31]

In spite of strictures upon religious behavior, overt displays of religious sentiment did exist, and even protests took place. On March 25, 1988, one such protest took place in the center of Bratislava. Participants (many of them school age) were warned by their teachers not to take part in the rally as it made its way through the streets of Bratislava. Helmeted police and dogs were brought out to monitor the group, which prayed the rosary as they marched. Jaroslav (who witnessed and supported the march), recounts that, at one point in the march, a woman was suddenly pushed into a police car, an event that disturbed him greatly as a young student: "If you had no strong religious views, you could live safely. The State would be little if any factor in your life. You just had to learn not to expect too much. But if you took part in a rally—even if you were not picked out and investigated, you could be watched."[32] Being watched was a peculiar state to find oneself in. Often, of course, one might have no knowledge of anything happening. More often, though a watched person could pick up clues that something *seemed* wrong. For example, people might sense that they were being followed after noticing a strange face that would appear twice in the same day walking on the street. Or, one could hear from friends, family members or an employer that they had been visited and that questions had been asked. Jaroslav recalls that such actions created their own social tensions among family members and between friends—as a questioned companion might resent being been placed at risk by the watched individual's alleged actions. It was not uncommon for watched people to be shunned by compatriots.[33]

Particular scrutiny was applied to teachers. Most were required to declare non-adherence to a religion, and attendance at church, if reported, could end a career: "At that time, it was impossible to be both a teacher and a church member, and this was exactly my case. This meant that I was in for it, and so were my colleagues. The principal was quite kind, and he spoke to us decently: 'Come on now, comrade, let's talk. What do you say? You yourself know you teach natural science, and there isn't any God.' What can I say? 'You graduated from a university. Why are you in that church? And why don't you leave it?'"[34]

Religion was far from a cut-and-dried ideological issue in Czechoslovakia during the later Cold War, and two distinct events drive the point home clearly. In both cases, the State intervened in local and religious culture—but also backed off from antagonizing local religious sentiments. One of these events took place in central Slovakia, in the city of Banská

Bystrica, center of the National Resistance of World War II; the other took place in the Czech lands, in the town of Most, in northern Bohemia.

Most: The Church That Moved

Considering the official state policies regarding religious practice, the story of Most, a city in the Czech lands, provides a more complex view of actual versus theoretical policy. Most (which means "bridge" in Czech) was an ancient town traditionally possessing a large German population, who called the town "Brüx." After World War II, many of the German territories of Czechoslovakia were emptied of their populations, based on the anti-collaborationist Beneš Decrees. Nearly three million Germans were expelled from the country. Cities like Most suffered huge population losses as 50,000 people of German descent left. But, by the late 1940s, a massive migration of Czechs and Roma had begun to repopulate Most.[35]

Energy production was a primary interest of the new communist regime in the late 1940s and early 1950s, particularly with regards to coal. The city of Most sat just on top of over 85 million tons of coal, which could be easily "surface mined." Before long, the argument was being made that "Old Most" was a mere "capitalist relic" of the past and could be leveled for its energy resources. (In fact, 116 Czechoslovak villages and towns were destroyed in the interest of coal mining from 1950 to 1980.) The decision was made in 1961 to "move" (that is, destroy) Most.[36]

Planners faced a serious problem, however, as the "move" went into effect in two stages from 1965 to 1967 and 1967 to 1970. What to do with the ancient Assumption of the Virgin Mary Catholic Church in the center of town? Was it to be torn down? By the early 1970s, the destruction of the town was near complete, and a huge mining pit had taken the place of the medieval town. Standing at the edge of this vast pit was the church. Officials made a decision not only to *not* destroy the ancient gothic structure but to *relocate* it some 840 meters away from its current foundation. The task would require a massive and sophisticated engineering effort. What followed was extraordinary. On the one hand, the State hailed the "new" Most, a collection of new State built apartments and buildings, as a "perfect fusion" of Socialist goals in the political, economic and social realms. On the other, local officials showed a remarkable tolerance for, and commitment to, the preservation of an ancient religious structure. The coal extracted from "old" Most yielded two billion Czech Crowns in profit. Former residents (who had a limited attachment to "old" Most, as many were new immigrants) applauded the modern housing they received, and the Church of the Assumption of the Virgin Mary was moved to safer ground and preserved.[37]

The Statue of Mary in Banská Bystrica

During World War II, no location in Czechoslovakia elicited more patriotic sentiment than Banská Bystrica located in central Slovakia, high in the mountains. It was from Banská that the Slovak National Uprising had its birth. A town with a history of copper production, Banská Bystrica was a "favored city" by Russia, as was neighboring Zvolen, for reasons both economic and historical. So special was Banská Bystrica to both Czechoslovakia and Russia that, in 1964, Nikita Khrushchev agreed to come to Banská to present a memorial to the 20th anniversary of the Slovak National Uprising. Mirka describes how the ceremony was to take place in the central square, where a significant political and cultural issue had to be addressed. In the center of the square sat a large statue to the Virgin Mary, which had been present in the square for several centuries. The Russian authorities deemed that it was impossible for Kruschev to appear in the square in front of a Roman Catholic statue, as this would send a confused message through the media covering the event.[38]

After some discussion, a decision was made to remove the statue from the main square for Khrushchev 's speech. This decision created a massive protest, as many locals demanded that the statue either be restored to its present position, or transferred to another suitable position. What followed were a series of candlelight processions and dedications of flowers to the (now removed) statue. As a compromise, the authorities agreed to place the St. Mary statue in the adjacent Kuria Park for the time being, where it stood for nearly 25 years. In 1989, the statue was finally replaced to its original position in the central square. In the minds of local residents, the protests against the removal of the Mary statue probably saved the monument from destruction.[39] Again, as with the policy of preservation in Most, local authorities bowed to popular sentiment in the protection of the religious symbol.

Raised as Catholic: "Two cripples"

Growing up with a strong religious background in an officially atheistic state could create unique stresses, both with the established authorities and with one's own family and compatriots. Such stresses are described by Jan C.:

> My parents were both quite committed to religious doctrine, but they expressed it in very different ways. My father was the son of a farmer, and possessed a talent for languages. He worked for a publishing house, as a literary chief, and had an enormous amount of control over what materials went to press. He also held a strong position in matters of strategy and tactics in publication decisions. On top of his responsibilities as a literary chief, he maintained an independent career as a scholar of the works of Franz Kafka.
>
> Although this reputation harmed him during the communist period, he was one of the "redeemed" scholars of the post-communist era.[40]
>
> My own upbringing was strict; it was not possible to question superiors. My mother's and father's parents had quite different opinions about raising children. My father's side of the family was strict, simply waiting "for children to grow up." Mom's side was different; they tended to have a more "open," more "emotional" take on the cultivation of childhood education. Their feeling was that faith should not be "beaten into" children, but, rather, discovered. I valued that perspective very much.[41]

Jan's maternal grandfather's father had been a Catholic literary critic early on in the communist regime and was caught up in the Show trials of 1951–52. He was sentenced to 20 years in prison, and he served ten of those years. The experience instilled a great sense of danger into Jan's grandfather—a fear that he passed on to Jan and the rest of the family. "In fact, the openness of my maternal influences freed me from doctrinal limitations and, ultimately, liberated me from the 'brainwork' of the other side of the family.[42] This often translated into a work ethic. We had a saying that (roughly) translates into Czech as 'no play on Saturday, as man is for Saturdays, not Saturdays for man.'"[43]

At home or in school, certain issues were not permitted for discussion. Sexuality was one of these:

> At school, it was very rare in the 1960s and 1970s to find fellow "believers." I found one; he was even more devout than I. His name was George, and he was interested in literature. We soon, at around the age of 10, found ourselves immersed in an "outer" world in which only we shared opinions. We had our own space, but it was a very private place. We saw the outside world as alien and hostile. But we occupied a very fragile territory.
>
> I remember, for example, one occasion, where I was humiliated—an experience that still haunts me today. At around age ten, our family was on our way to church, and, upon arriving, some of the family members began to sing a familiar religious song. Some of my classmates were nearby and started laughing at my family. I wanted, initially, to deny that I was part of my family—or of my religion—but I felt very torn. In the end, I did not reject the religious songs that we sang, or my stance, but it has haunted me ever since, even to today.[44] I found myself in a dilemma; I wanted to reject the "orthodox" aspects of my faith, with which I had issues. But, at the same time, I wanted to protect the faith from outside persecution. Big, social church—sponsored events

or protests were simply not a Czech tradition. Czechs tended to be more individual in their religious experience.

George came from an even more orthodox Catholic tradition than I. He was a self described "tough" Catholic; for example, when asked to join his friends at the playground, he would often be instructed by his parents to "pray, not play. Pray for your hour of death." We shared a sense of very high expectation on the parts of our respective families. Commensurately, we found ourselves, even at a very young age, sensing a gradual liberation—from what, exactly, I am not sure. Of course, George later looked at this "liberation" period a bit cynically. To him, later personal questioning of the church's teachings became the ultimate "true liberation." Perhaps significantly, he married a Protestant.

My ally in grade school has since gone on to become a psychiatrist. He no longer holds any strong Catholic religious beliefs. In fact, although he was never Communist, he has grown increasingly outspoken in recent years, against the "superstitions" of organized religion. I always think back to what he said about us as two kindred spirits against the system, back when we were kids. We would talk on the phone, on the playground at school, and in person, perhaps in the hallways of school or at home. He used to say that we were "two cripples leaning against each other, but falling without each other."[45]

Growing up Jewish: "Staying off the Radar"

Mirka and Alica grew up in Banská Bystrica in central Czechoslovakia, in a Jewish family. The family had lived in the country since long before World War II. Mirka recalls that while English was rarely spoken in Czechoslovakia prior to the 1960s, it became increasingly common after then. In Banská Bystrica, the historic second language had always been German. After World War II, the family name was changed—and Christianized. Her father was a furrier and hence was a "protected" Jew in the period just after the War. "Jews were not safe in Czechoslovakia right after the war, because many of the [fascist and anti–Semitic] Hlinka Guard members from the war period had switched sides and become functionaries in the new communist regime. Religion was forbidden, or at least strongly discouraged, from the 1950s to the 1970s, in Banská Bystrica. Individuals who wished to practice would have to go to small villages where they were not recognized."[46] The household was run with every effort to keep the Jewish identity private. Issues considered by the parents and grandparents too sensitive for the children's ears were uttered in German. This included matters of work and money, as well as religion. Many family members had left Czechoslovakia after World War II for Palestine/Israel and for Austria. From this time on, the extended family got together for a reunion only once; in the late 1980s, they all met up in Budapest for the first reunion since the 1930s.[47]

Mirka recounts that during the 1930s, the Jewish population of Banská Bystrica had been two thousand. When the Germans arrived (with help from local collaborator Slovak groups), the Jewish grandparents took the children to hide in the mountains, 20 km from their town. At the time, it was illegal to be found walking in the forest; one could be shot on sight. In the mountains, 12 people crammed into a small shelter and remained there for the duration of the war. Neighbors would bring them food, taking enormous risks in doing so. From October 1944 until June 1945, the whole group lived off of a single sack of potatoes in the mountains. During the war, the synagogue in Banská Bystrica was torn down—the closest one being in the neighboring city of Brezno.[48]

New Believers and the Moderation of Policy

By the 1980s, certain trends in Eastern Europe suggested a return to religious belief, or at least to a sense that one could express religious views openly without fear of recrimination. By the early 1980s, the New York Times was commenting on changing religious norms in Eastern Europe:

> Young people are converting, and others who were raised as Catholics are returning to the church. The young people are asking, "Why are we living?"
>
> "In Hungary, the Catholic bakers don't make bread just for the Catholics and the Communists don't just make bread for the Communists," said the Cardinal, 63 years old, in defending his philosophy of "small steps" during an interview at his stately residence at Esztergom near Budapest. "The Catholics and Communists together make Hungarian bread."[49]
>
> It is occurring in conditions of hardship and considerable church autonomy, and in Czechoslovakia, amid fierce state repression, particularly of the Roman Catholic Church. Activists often insist that their quest is spiritual, not political.[50]

In Czechoslovakia, the mood in the early 1980s had become an oppressive one; religion was often dealt with in a heavy handed manner. For example, priests were often rounded up and interrogated. Some were jailed. Many of the bishoprics remained unfilled as Czech Communist authorities refused to nominate candidates acceptable to the Vatican. Nevertheless, by the mid–1980s, believers were said to thrive in "clandestine cells," churning out at least three illegal mimeographed journals, suggesting membership of about 7,500 persons.

> "The underground has spread so widely that it could even be regarded as the mainstream," said Mr. Tomský, who noted that the movement was strongest in the Czech-speaking parts of the country rather than in traditionally Catholic Slovakia.[51]

Charter 77 and other opposition groups possessed strong backing throughout the 1970s and 1980s from organized religious groups. By 1989, these groups would coalesce in ways that discredited the old regime beyond repair. The development of these relationships continued well beyond the events of 1989.

Religion constituted an issue of multitudinous considerations for the Czechoslovak State. While anathema to official communist doctrine, religion had a long and diverse history in the country. Over time, a policy of official tolerance emerged, albeit with the caveat that covert police monitoring emerged as State policy. One could "stay off the radar" by practicing religious belief in neighboring towns or villages, but circumspection was the key. Priests as well as police informed. Border transit policies were established to control—but not ban—religious materials. At some level, experiences from the some of the world's most rigid communist regimes were, at least tacitly, acknowledged in policy. Maintaining the peace appears to have been the overriding concern, as evidenced by the extraordinary efforts of the State to save a medieval church in Most, or to avoid offending local sensibilities in Banská Bystrica during Nikita Khrushchev 's visit.

Like so many other policies and official pronouncements in Cold War Czechoslovakia, religion was a bugbear with which the ruling State became familiar; policy attempted to walk the fine line between overt State suppression of belief, and acceptance of religion as a legitimate social activity. Official pronouncements of materialism as the inevitable reality in modern society ran into centuries' old traditions of belief. The State, in turn, took a pragmatic stance on religion from the death of Stalin until the collapse of the Czechoslovak regime itself.

Chapter Nine

Roma Policy

Heard: A gypsy woman offers goods to a passerby, who decides to walk on without making a purchase. Gypsy woman: "Aww, geez, buy something because we all know what happened last time when you didn't!"

The "gypsy," or, more properly described contemporarily as "Roma," population in Czechoslovakia, is the subject of a long history of discrimination, caricature, stereotyping, jokes, and outright racism. Such traditions have accumulated antecedents that spanned hundreds of years, since the first arrival of the itinerant Roma in the Middle Ages from the Punjab region of Northwestern India.

Contemporary Roma History

Historically, the Roma population of Eastern Europe was part of a widely disseminated set of ethnic groups, making the term "nation state" a difficult one to fully realize, in any traditional sense, among the countries of the region. The 1920 Trianon Treaty, signed after the defeat and collapse of both the Ottoman and Austro-Hungarian empires after World War I, transferred large portions of these former empires to other states. Hungarian Transylvania, for example, was awarded to Romania. The new state of Czechoslovakia was awarded Hungarian territory as well. Slovakia, formerly under Hungarian control and possessing a sizeable Hungarian population, became the eastern third component of the new Czechoslovak state. The Roma population was also dispersed and absorbed into new states. As the Roma population was both visibly and culturally distinct from other ethnic groups in the region, they tended to bear the brunt of attacks, lack of opportunity, and general racism.[1] Roma were not classed as a "national minority" under the First Republic (1918–38). During this period, a special "traveling passport" was devised, based on a similar document used by the French government, to document their Roma population.[2]

Roma communities (in behavior that mirrored general Czechoslovak society during and after the communist period) tended to rely on private social networks to facilitate transactions. "Knowing the right people" was a superior strategy (compared to formal economic or political networks) as a means for obtaining goods, approving documents, or troubleshooting a problem. The lack of legitimate (or accessible) formal institutions, combined with regular shortages of material goods, served to perpetuate this mode of behavior. In Roma communities, the realities of discrimination and general alienation from the mainstream culture only exacerbated the need for informal power networks.[3]

The experiences of Czech and Slovak Gypsies during World War II differed significantly. Czech Roma were sent off to Treblinka or Auschwitz, and up to a million of them may have perished as a result. (In fact, the Czech region also had its own concentration camps, in which many Roma were exterminated.) The same was not true in the Nazi protectorate of Slovakia. Slovak Roma were, however, herded into forced labor camps by the collaborationist Slovak government, and subjected to constant harassment by the fascist Hlinka Guard militias. The Slovak regime used special identity cards to identify and regulate Roma.[4]

Post–World War II

Events in Czechoslovakia after the Second World War were immensely chaotic as significant and sizable population groups returned, while others were displaced. In the Sudetenland, the post War policy under President Edward Benes was to expel all collaborationist Germans from the Sudetenland region (about 90 percent). Exceptions were made to retain some German specialists needed to help build the postwar economy. The so-called "Wild Migration" of 1945 saw large numbers of Czechs, Slovaks, Magyars, and Roma from both the Czech and Slovak territories move into the heretofore German regions of Czechoslovakia. As homes and properties had been confiscated from Germans after the war, the acquisition of wealth was quite easy. In many cases, German families were forced out by angry Czech mobs even prior to being legally evicted. Tens of thousands of Roma, including 16,000 from Slovakia, were included in the rush to expropriate German property. However, the diversity and newness of the settlers made for a distinct lack of community and social cohesion: "This fluctuating ethnic diversity was a barrier to consolidation, particularly during the period of settlement from May 1945 to late 1946. There were also towns where a substantial minority of Germans remained not only until the end of the organized expulsions of 1946, but even into the 1950s and beyond. Some of these Germans had been deemed irreplaceable specialists and exempted from expulsion, while others were married to Czech spouses."[5]

Literature

In the modern, post-war world, one could look to a poem about Roma, "The Gypsy Whistle," dating from 1839, to glean a fairly accurate account of contemporary attitudes towards this sizeable minority population. In fact, "The Gypsy Whistle," penned by F. Ladislav, was used as standard text in the schoolbooks of the 1950s and 1960s:

> He could drink, he could play
> He worked lightly but slept hard
> And he knew how to shop for nice things
> With five fingers only
> Our daddy took very little care of us
> But he had the most amazing whistle
> When he whistled all roaches (*šváby*) ran from the house
> When he whistled in the villages and towns
> All of the German rats were on the road
> They had to roam, dance as he whistled
> And then they all had to jump into the lake.[6]

Significantly, although the above poem was widely read by 7th graders in Czech literature classes, it was perhaps the only mention of Roma culture whatsoever for post–World War II Czech students. The poem is telling in that the traditional stereotypical characterizations of Roma are present: musically talented, basically lazy, and thieving (shopping/stealing with "five fingers"). The *svab,* or cockroaches, most likely indicates a pejorative term for Germans often utilized in the Czech lands.

Gypsy themes often appeared in early 20th-century Czech literature. Jaroslav Hašek, the author of the famous work *The Good Soldier Švejk,* considered a classic illustration of Czech culture and mores, often included Gypsy characters in his works. In "The Gypsy Feast," he describes a pig thief who always denies responsibility for his crimes, even when caught red-handed. In "The End of a Monkey," Hašek describes a Gypsy circus family whose trained monkey dies. One day, after a long, protracted mourning period one day over the loss, the family happily devours the monkey for dinner.[7]

So too, did Gypsy myths and imagery appear in Czech music. Classical composer Leoš Janáček, in *Diary of One Who Disappeared,* describes a mixed-race relationship between a black (i.e., Roma) girl and a white boy. During the romance, the boy becomes swept away by the furious passion of the gypsy girl—so much so that he begins to lose his identity. In the end, he must join the Gypsy society as his partner, Zefka, is simply too passionate and mysterious for his world. In this work, the importance of mystery, myth, and magic Gypsy women is fully realized, and the themes of "wild" and "unrestrained" women are in full fruition. Writer Karel Čapek also explored mixed racial relations, drawing on the exoticism and mystery surrounding the "wandering" gypsy woman, whose close, almost animal connection with nature made her an object of danger for "civilized" men.[8]

Culture

The relationship between Roma and the white majority population was complex and certainly tinged with racism. However, it would be an oversimplification to state that the relationship was merely that of overt antagonism. In the white community, there was considerable admiration for "gypsy culture," especially with regard to art, music, and performance. Perhaps part of the appeal was a visceral appreciation of a perceived dynamic personal and social liberty among Roma, even within the midst of an oppressive state. Peter, a white Czech, describes an experience with a Roma community, one in which Roma cognizance of racial difference was explicitly acknowledged:

> Gypsies were considered to be excellent musicians even though they often did not know notes [possess formal training]. Their music is quick, rhythmic, and their performance temperamental. Here you feel FREEDOM. Their paintings were always full of color. They seemed to possess children's souls. If you show them respect, you will be accepted and treated with high honor.
>
> The father of a (white) colleague of mine accepted a gypsy family's invitation to be their child's godfather. He became a highly respected member of the entire gypsy community. What he said was, to them, like the word of God.
>
> One night, there was a conflict at a local tavern, with knives and axes. The gypsies there created a barricade in the tavern; they stopped their fighting until the godfather came. He was Chief Justice to them.[9]

The Communist Period

Many minority groups migrated from Czechoslovakia after World War II. For example, the post War population of Jews was about 15,000 (a mere 10 percent of the pre-war population), but many of these migrated, with about half leaving for Palestine. The new socialist government of 1948 attempted to integrate remaining minority groups into the new political order. There were many means by which this was attempted. In the first place, the use of *theater* was employed, in order to bring a basic understanding of socialist values to the countryside and to otherwise marginalized populations. Some strategies appealed to the "folk" culture, explaining socialism in simple terms that demonized bourgeois values while re-affirming local "traditional" mores. In some cases, even religious imagery was used (despite the official atheism of the Communist Party), such as the invocation of Jan Hus, an early Christian dissenter.[10]

From 1948 until 1989, the communist regime, like so many before them, attempted, in repeated "plans," to formulate a coherent *Roma* policy, with varying degrees of success. In many respects, they failed—as had numerous earlier attempts at reform. The post–War period unleashed energies that contributed to new social experiments, many of which affected Roma policy. A sustained program of "de–Nazification and de-racialization" was developed. Assisting this transformation in ethnic, class, and overall social relations was a longstanding tradition of civic education in both Czechoslovakia and the Soviet Union.

By 1950, a new program was announced for the benefit of national minorities and introduced in the southern Bohemian village of Soběslav, in July. The main thrust of the plan was to integrate the goals of collective rural education with that of collective political education. Agriculture was to be increasingly collectivized, and national minority groups were to be integrated into the process, through *osvěta* (mass education). The program was to be run by the Ministry of Information, which, under director Kopecký, became known as the "long arm of the Party."[11]

Roma Policy During the Early Communist Period, 1948–1958

The Communist Party changed their Roma policy on numerous occasions from 1948 to 1989. Initially, activists who were to work on behalf of the Roma population were trained by the State. Elena Lacková of Prešov, and Karol Holubec were two of these activists. (Notably, however, Roma activism was accompanied by the violent collectivization of rural agriculture.)[12] Even during the initial post–War relaxation of social strictures against Roma, historic sentiments prevailed as Roma continued to be seen as outsiders. A commonly held belief was that 80 percent of all Roma carry venereal disease, and that they "are not Czechs." Ideas of nationalism, paternalism, and social Darwinism were still prevalent, in spite of official communist policy statements to the contrary.[13]

Adding to the volatility of post-war Roma policy was the influx of new Roma, displaced by post-war events, into Czechoslovakia, along with an annual population growth rate of 5 percent. Meanwhile, the new communist authorities were more concerned with consolidating their power base and stamping out vestiges of the previous regime. Hence, energies were devoted towards eliminating political opponents, churches, ex-capitalists, and others deemed a threat to the new state apparatus. Roma policy was given a comparatively low priority, at least initially. In fact, the evident passivity of the communist authorities may have, in fact, been rooted in ideological assumptions that readily accepted racism.

From the 1950s, Roma policy often took two tracks; one was of continued, traditional racism and intolerance, enforced by state strictures and limitations on mobility and lifestyle. The other was an effort to assimilate a traditional "out" group into the mainstream of the Czechoslovak state. In the early 1950s, for example, brutal programs of agricultural collectivization (often hitting rural Roma populations particularly hard) existed side by side with state-sponsored programs to train Roma activists.[14]

Overall, in the 1950s, Roma policy reflected an effort to correct the wrongs of the past, and "de–Nazification" and "de-racialization" formed the core of state action. Roma had been mistreated severely during the Second World War; fascist militias attacked them in the Czech lands, and the Hlinka Guard fascist units held them in check in the Slovak territories. With the end of the capitalist system, the Roma population was considered by Communist Party chiefs to have been at last liberated. Socialism and equality would trump the "vestiges of capitalism" that kept the Roma poor.[15]

Roma Policy 1958–1965

Some scholars have referred to the first ten years of the communist regime as a "no policy" or "lost decade" period with regard to Czechoslovak Roma. The second phase, roughly from 1958 to 1965, is sometimes characterized as a "wrong policy" period. However, the prevailing passivity and inactivity of government policy towards Roma in the immediate aftermath of World War II seemed to give way to a more proactive stance. In 1958, the Central Committee of the Communist Party issued a resolution demanding a solution to the Gypsy question. The issue was tackled on several fronts. Special commissions were established for information that would be disseminated to both white and Roma populations. Restrictions were introduced on Roma travel, both within and without the territory of Czechoslovakia. "Nomadism" would now constitute a crime.[16] The government organized a special police action, which took place during the winter. Peter describes how Roma were herded into tilt cars to various villages, where they were deposited. Here, they were given permanent addresses, certificates of birth, I.D. cards and so forth. The village was then required to provide their new residents with a flat, and with a job.[17] The regime proclaimed: "Resolution of the Party and the Government: to solve the Gypsy problem by 1970. Zdravotnícke noviny, 15 April 1961. Activists from among the citizens of Gypsy origin expressed during discussion their gratitude to the Communist Party of Czechoslovakia and the Government for the concern with the dignified life of Gypsy citizens and accelerated removal of all injustices of the capitalist era. Ľud, 31 January 1959."[18]

The new policy rested on several assumptions, each of which was guided by ideology. In the first place, treatment of Roma as a separate "category" of population found little favor with the Party. Roma did not satisfy prevailing norms for "nationhood," as they did not possess claim to a particular territory. They were not suitable as either a nation state or ethnic group, because they were deemed not to maintain a unified and unique cultural identity. Even Roma language was considered more akin to dialect, thus further invalidating any claim to nationhood and separate identity. Following the logic of assimilation, Roma were instead categorized into one of three groups: the *Olah,* or nomads, considered the most primitive and least assimilated population; the *Semi-nomads,* many of whom were seasonal workers in both the Czech and Slovak territories, and a group comprised of settled, established, "domesticated" gypsies. Of these, the second group was deemed the most numerous. The Act on Permanent Settlement of Nomadic People, enacted on October 17, 1958, read as follows:

> Section 1: People's Committees shall furnish to individuals maintaining a nomadic way of life manifold assistance enabling them to adopt a settled way of life; in particular they are obligated to assist such individuals in securing suitable employment and housing, and to exert, through educational means, pressure towards the goal of their

> becoming orderly, toiling citizens. Section 2: A person leading a nomadic way of life is one who, in groups or individually, wanders from place to place, shuns honest work or obtains his livelihood by iniquitous means even though he may be registered in some community as its permanent resident. Section 3: He who persists in maintaining a nomadic way of life, despite the assistance offered to him towards permanent settlement, shall be punished.[19]

The 1958 law was intended to curb itinerant populations; nomads would henceforth register with the State, and their movement would be discouraged. Further, a punitive element was included in the law, as communist authorities had to contend with a backlash of anti–Roma sentiment, along with charges of favoritism, from the general population. Complaints were numerous and disparate:

> Present court practice shows that the investigation of Gypsies' criminal activities and their punishment is much more lenient than in the case of other citizens. The offenders know very well that there are certain "extenuating circumstances"—illiteracy, low cultural standards, etc.—and that in fact there is actually a "justification" for sexual abuse and parasitism. And they take advantage of it.
>
> It is indisputable that because of some hypersensitive sentiments (so that we would not be accused of racism) we managed to turn the population of Gypsy origin into a special caste, a privileged group which recognized only their rights but no duties. A different yardstick is applied to a person of Gypsy origin than to a normal [*sic*] citizen.[20]

The early communist period was often characterized by "crash course" social engineering schemes—many of which failed outright. The 1958 Roma policy was not successful; after the strictures on nomadism, many Roma attempted to establish more permanent living standards. However, communities often drove off Roma as they approached; in effect, many Roma were forced to continue roaming, despite official policy. Many of these "forced wanderers" found their way into wretched gypsy hamlets in the eastern portion of the country. "Peoples' Committees" and other advocacy groups began to focus on the second group—seasonal nomads. The key word at the time was *indoctrination*, as both whites and Roma were to participate in the process of integration. This program had many components—public service, student staffing of schools, literacy, mixed housing—but mainly failed, as most Roma tended not to participate.[21]

The post–1958 period tended to harden attitudes towards Roma, who were seen increasingly as "parasites" in the state, abusing state welfare benefits through large families and scheming. A summary is provided by a Czech with some familiarity of Roma culture and norms: "The criminality of Gypsies is twice that of the whites and in certain felonies even ten times higher. The state, though, is far more worried about the Gypsies' harvesting of undeserved advantages. The man exploited in the past became the exploiter. It is stated bluntly that for a Gypsy honest work is a necessary evil, and the statistics to a considerable extent support this contention."[22]

A second, academic account of Roma culture reveals some contemporary employment statistics, as well as tales of health benefit abuse, deemed by some apocryphal, but taken as folk wisdom by many others: "Thus, in a state where employment is both a duty and a norm, among the 70,000 Gypsies in Eastern Slovakia only 16,000 hold permanent jobs. In Slovakia as a whole, 34% of Gypsies of working age have their livelihood secured by the so-called invalid's pension. Incidents of self-mutilation are frequent. Cases of Gypsies with active tuberculosis were reported as spitting—upon request—in the mouth of their healthy brethren so that they too could profit from the illness. Lung disease means a pension and it is then left to physicians to despair about these patients avoiding cure."[23]

Roma Policy After 1965

In 1965, the government made an about-face and announced a new set of policies on the "gypsy question." During the 1958–65 period large amounts of demographic data was collected on the Roma population; in 1965, a "universal, long-range assimilation plan" was announced, radically changing Roma policy. Part of the formal presentation of new policy included a bit of ideological revisionism, as previous policies were condemned as erroneous. Instead of assimilation, new policy would place stress on the *economic* and *social* roots of discrimination and exclusion. In addition to providing an economic model for ameliorating the condition of Roma, the general public would also be "educated" as to the reality of the situation of the Roma. Mass media would be used to reverse racist tendencies in the country; Roma policy would place stress on employment, training, and dispersal. That is, all able-bodied Roma would be provided with work opportunities, Gypsy hamlets would be razed, and the Roma populations would be spread through and integrated with the white populations throughout Czechoslovakia.[24] Gypsy population groups in industrial areas (generally in Bohemia and Moravia) would not be the focus of resettlement; rather, rural hamlets (typically in Slovakia) would be the targeted areas.

> At the time, of the 153,000 Gypsies in Slovakia, 103,000 (i.e., 67.3%), lived in such settlements "under conditions which are not fit for human living." Some fresh data were offered: on average a single hut was inhabited by two families with six to seven

members each. Living space per person was 1 5 square meters. In eastern Slovakia, of 56,000 Gypsies only 2.2% lived on premises with an adequate water supply. The proposed 1965 improvement was disappointingly modest. Of the estimated 300 Gypsy hamlets "at least"—i.e., "only"—435, totaling 4,409 families with 27,000 persons, were to be liquidated. (Another source indicated the abolition of 200 settlements as a target for 1970.) To make things worse, these plans, inadequate as they were, were not met. Thus the 1966 target of moving 512 families to Czech provinces was 20% fulfilled. In 1967 only 58 hamlets of a planned 155 were abolished. The resettlement program was severely handicapped by insufficient money.[25]

The resettlement program faced multiple difficulties, including lack of popular support and charges of "favoritism" towards Roma who were compensated for their makeshift homes and offered new accommodations. Stories abounded:

1. The districts of Šumperk [Moravia] and Michalovce [Slovakia] concluded an agreement on resettlement of six families. The Gypsies received for their expropriated huts from 6,000 to 8,000 crowns each [a rather generous price]. They moved at the expense of the state, and obtained in the Šumperk area both housing and employment. Within two weeks they were joined by 120 other Gypsies for whom Šumperk had neither accommodation nor jobs. These 120 people moved in with the six families and a new Gypsy camp was thus born. From the District of Rožňava two families moved into the village of Rybníčky in the Olomouc area. This transfer cost the state 70,000 crowns. Within three months these two families, without any ado, returned to Slovakia.... There was such a commotion in the village that the officials of the local People's Committee, in fear of a pogrom, in no time forced out and sent back to Rybníčky both the Gypsies and their belongings....

2. It might well happen that the pogrom temper could spill over from eastern Slovakia into other regions and, as is usually the case with unleashed passions, could affect the innocent—perhaps just those Gypsies who live and work properly. The first such sign, at which one's heart almost stops beating, was reported from Sokolov [a mining town in Bohemia].

3. In a residential area, it was reported that the children walked in public a Gypsy child on a chain, like a trained monkey. On his back he carried a sign—"Gypsy." The adults looked on but did not intervene. Are we in Texas, or in a country which considers racism of any sort to be a crime? This incident is all the more tragic in that it happened to a child of an honest man.[26]

Assimilation was an ideological issue as well as a cultural one. Orthodox communist ideology did not recognize racial or ethnic differences as truly significant in the class struggle paradigm that it promoted. The socialist economic social model was one of unity; racial difference and cultural hierarchy conflicted head-on with this ideal, at least officially. As a result, the "Gypsy anti-hero" in Czechoslovakia folk mythology—the brave and uncompromising individualist—was gradually subjected to laws that attempted to limit "Gypsy" behavior, in the interest of full assimilation. In fact, the "assimilationist" policies of the 1970s hid other realities of social policy. Population in the 1970s and 1980s was on the decline; abortion had been legal since 1957 (in contrast to Romania, where abortion was prohibited in 1966) as part of a "pro-natalist" program, combined with improved maternity privileges for women in the early 1960s. In 1972, a *sterilization* law was passed. Designed as a "protective" measure (presumably against the rapid population growth of certain minority groups), the law was, in fact, ethnically neutral. However, social workers were offered financial incentives to encourage Roma to undergo sterilization procedures, for which participants were offered lucrative financial incentives of 2,000–10,000 kr. White Czech women were discouraged from the procedure, and Roma women were often misled as to exactly what they were getting into. In the end, between 21 percent and 36 percent of all women who underwent sterilization in Czechoslovakia were Roma. In fact, the sterilization program continued beyond the Velvet Revolution of 1989 and continued even into the 1990s.[27]

"Revisiting" the City of Most: Environmental Concerns and Forced Relocation

One of the sure measures of racial attitudes in Czechoslovakia after World War II involved examining parts of the homeland considered fair game for destruction. Leading the pack was the town of Most. Coal mining needs caused the destruction of 116 villages between 1950 and 1980. But the city of Most was no village. It was a town of 28,000 inhabitants and had served as a center for gas production (through forced labor) during World War II. The town had a history that stretched to the Middle Ages. Its crime was that it stood upon nearly 100 million tons of near-surface coal. The town of Most suffered from other strategic problems, as well. In the first place, it had, historically, been a "German" Czech town. The original German name for Most had been Brüx. With the expulsion of Sudeten Germans (more than 50,000 from the Most region alone) after World War II, Most lost two thirds of its pre-war population.[28]

Second, the post-war dislocations had not only caused a significant departure of German-Czech inhabitants, but had encouraged a significant influx of Czech and Slovak Roma into the region, particularly from 1945 until the early 1950s. The Roma settlers remained in Most, even after the city was set for destruction. In fact, Roma were the last to leave as the town was torn down, even until the late 1970s. The official government policy for the re-location of Roma to other regions was, ominously, named *Likvidace* or the "liquidation" of Roma from urban areas into modern housing projects.[29] Workers had little loyalty for the Most region, in part, perhaps, because of sheer racism, but also because northern Bohemian workers had little interest in historical justice.

The decision to move Most was made in 1961. The population, most of which was new to the city after World War II, was vacated by 1970. The evacuation process took three phases: Phase I was from 1965 to 1967, Phase II from 1967 to 1970, and Phase III from 1970 to 1977, when the final evacuations were ordered.[30]

Recollections

Roma poet and journalist Jan Horváth recalls that he learned nothing about his own culture from schoolbooks or lessons; in fact, the only mention of Roma at all was through commonly used expressions like "being as dirty as a Gypsy." He does recall, however, that he was subjected to a wide range of abuse at school in the early 1970s. Students would cuss at him, calling him a "dirty Gypsy," or would tell us to "stop talking in Gypsy language." "There is no way that those thoughts came from the children themselves," he would write later; "they learned those things from their parents."[31]

Štefan Mika recalls that, as a child, he was quite content and happy—until he entered school. At that time, he was told that he was a Gypsy and that the term was not flattering. Roma students, many (if not most) of whom were enrolled in remedial, or "special" schools, received little if any training about their own culture and thus had few if any role models to follow. Non-Roma Czech students, on the other hand, were given *no* training whatsoever in Roma culture and, in fact, were educated in a manner that, for all intents and purposes, denied the very existence of Roma.[32]

After the communist ascendency in 1948, Roma policy shifted, at least officially, to move towards an assimilation stance. The traditional notion of the Roma as "outsiders" was well established long before World War II.

Stereotypes of Roma as over-sexualized, under-civilized "non–Czechs" were widespread. But Czech Roma had been largely shipped off to Nazi concentration camps during World War II. Slovak Roma had not—and this development led to accusations of conspiracy by many Czechs. The theory held that Slovaks, with their large eastern Roma population, had used the chaos of the post-war period to expel their Roma population to the Czech lands.

In addition to widespread conspiracy fears was a widely held view that the social pluralism and diversity in Czech society was not healthy for the body politic. Hence, communist authorities pushed for a policy of assimilation, emphasizing class over race as a social signifier. Gypsies, henceforth, would be "culturally re-educated."[33]

Eastern Czechoslovakia—the Slovak territories—possessed the largest groups of Romani. Tomáš K. grew up in this region, near the major city Prešov in eastern Slovakia. His comments reflect both the communist period and the post–1989 changes:

> As I recall, there were always problems with the Roma population. I lived my whole life two km from Ostrovany and five km from Jarovnice. Both villages have a very high population of Roma. Some say that Jarovnice has the highest per capita population of Roma in Slovakia. In my own village, there was a small Roma population ... mostly stealing, robbing or physical attacks. [For example] Roma stole my dog ... he was an expensive pedigree ... and was sold for food to another Roma. (Fortunately) we got him back.
>
> I was robbed by older Roma in the village when I was seven or eight. We were attacked at school with "karate kicks" by some Roma at school when I was ten.
>
> Roma stealing was quite a typical issue here ... various stuff around the house, in gardens, outside cottages, etc. But the situation before 1989 was not as bad as it is now.[34]

In the period before the changes of 1989, there were, arguably, reasons why "Roma" relations were mitigated. One was that the society was a sort of "totalitarian" construct in which societal order was highly valued. Second, work was compulsory. One could say people had "less time to steal" from one another. People were much more afraid of the police than they are today. Streets tended to be empty during the day, as everyone was at work. One saw mainly "mothers and pensioners" on the street. People had some money, and this included Roma.[35]

The State was much more generous to Roma prior to 1989 than after. This was particularly salient in housing. Roma who "behaved correctly" could be provided with decent, low income housing, for a very reasonable rent. This policy was sometimes called "positive discrimination," as it was a State attempt to elevate the status of a particular minority group. Oddly, during the pre–1989 period, one could often find Roma occupying housing in the center of cities. The reasons for this were historical. After the communist takeover in 1948, many "central" properties were nationalized, among them the historical centers of towns—and, subsequently, these "old" (historical) properties were turned over to needy minority populations, such as Roma.[36] "With compulsory work, people had less opportunity to steal. Before 1989, one could find Roma living in the very center of some Slovak towns, such as Sabinov, Košice, and Prešov. They were moved to the center of town, where the properties had been confiscated after 1948. These areas were often dangerous to walk in before 1989, as one might be robbed. My grandmother had one of these houses in Prešov—on the main street—and our family was able to recover it by 1992."

Another recollection comes from Petra, who recalls growing up in the town of Košice:

> I remember one of my first English classes, in Košice. The language school, had an arrangement to use the space of a "special education school" or "Osobitná škola" after official study hours. So in the late afternoon/evening, language classes were taking place there. Many of them [Roma] were however placed into a special education school because they came from families where they had difficulty studying (no conditions to do so, no support of parents) so their results in school were bad and therefore they were just placed into special education schools. Some appeared to have mental handicaps, and many did not seem prepared to be in school. The State seemed to pay little attention to this.
>
> As a child (in the small town of Jelšava), we had gypsies as neighbors. They had a reputation for stealing furniture, and we had a hard time holding them accountable. However, I would say that the "Roma issue" was not really a racial matter; rather, it was a social and cultural one. There was even a "hierarchy" in popular conceptions of Roma. At the top were the *olásky cigáni*, or "white" Roma. These were aspiring gypsies, and they aspired to become integrated into the general society. Many did, in fact, integrate.[37]

Conversely, there were the "other" Roma, who were infamous for stealing crops, robbing unsuspecting people, nomadism, and "living in nature." Some efforts were made during the communist period to integrate these Roma into general society—but, as housing projects, such as the infamous Luník IX in the eastern city of Košice illustrated, such efforts often failed. Petra adds that "Some had horses in their apartments. Others tore up the (brand new) floors, and built fires with the boards. The dirt and mess was hard to compare—even with the *Olásky* gypsies."[38]

Petra recounts a story of attempted robbery that seems to have gone astray: "I had an incident in Košice when I was young. Some gypsy kids 'attacked' me when I was coming home from school, and pulled my hair. They stole nothing from me. I think they just wanted to scare me."[39]

Lucia recounts village life in the Czech town of Tanvald, where the local Roma population lived close to the train station: "My parents and their neighbors were quite affected by the local Roma population. There was a separation, but the media didn't report the differences as much as they do now. There was a problem at the time, and unfortunately it remains unresolved to the present day."[40]

Similar sentiments are expressed by Jakub, who compares the pre–1989 period with the present: "There is no real difference between Roma policy then and now. The regime *controlled* the problem during the communist period but they didn't fix it. Human rights are more carefully considered today, but the right wing is also stronger. Not much has been resolved. Assimilation for Roma used to be talked about but not now."[41]

Contemporary human rights concerns about Roma also factor into present day treatment and protections: "Today they [Roma] are much more aware of their rights. Sometimes, flats are rented to Roma because they are considered a safer bet. The state will guarantee the rent."[42]

Racism

Many Czechs and Slovaks note that negative interactions with Roma were common both during and after the communist period. Incidences of stealing, violence and even murder were well known within the white population. One statistic stands out prior to 1989; the prison population in the eastern city of Prešov was 80 percent Roma, and this continued after 1989. It bears noting that the Roma population of the Slovak region of Czechoslovakia was no more than 10–15 percent of the general population. Many believed that crime, not race, was behind anti–Roma sentiment: "People were just angry about those who were behind the crimes. On the other hand, it was also true that crimes involving Roma were called 'Roma' crimes [with a racial reference], whereas those involving white people were not identified by race."[43]

When Roma were accused of crimes, the description was often racially tinged with references to "dirty" Roma. (It is useful to note that Roma themselves made a racial distinction between themselves and "whites," referring to them as *gadžo*.)

"White" Czechs and Slovaks are often torn on the historical aspect of racism. On the one hand, many of them lived among large, impoverished Roma populations. Sometimes they were preyed upon by these Roma—but in other, perhaps more typical cases, they worked and played alongside this very Roma population, as Petra did: "In my town there were some Roma families who were okay and most of them were very friendly. I also had some Roma friends and schoolmates. It is true that many, if not most of them, had trouble at school, but there was never any sign of overt hostility between us."[44]

After 1989, policy towards Roma changed, and many of the state subsidies disappeared. The Roma standard of living decreased, and Roma crime (often violent) increased. Racism towards Roma increased commensurately. After the changes of 1989, many became wary of Roma—farmers refused to plant crops for fear of theft, and overt racist acts became more common—which continues to this day.[45]

Education Policy

By the 1970s, education had been adopted by the communist regime as the de facto assimilationist policy. The state made a concerted effort to "combat backwardness" through a process of "re-rearing" (socializing) the Roma population, a policy know as *prevýchova.* During this period, teachers of Roma were often held up by authorities as national heroes. The policy faced opposition, however, by those who believed that the Roma suffered from "Nomadism," a condition related to perpetual movement that some perceived as a genetic affliction. Often heard were the charges that "a Gypsy may not be a Czech" and that "blood is blood."[46]

The 1970s introduced a range of attitudes towards Roma. Czech writer Karel Čapek sought to explain gypsy behavior in terms of "exoticism" and mystery. Gypsies possessed a unique and secret lifestyle, he argued, that could not be fathomed by the white population. During the same period, the Czech film industry produced numerous films that depicted the "gypsy condition," often in stereotypical ways. Roma were often portrayed as unstable, passionate, and thieving.[47]

Roma Sterilization Policy

In 1972, a new Sterilization Law was introduced as a means to protect citizens from unwanted or arbitrary sterilization procedures. The law described specific procedural norms that would have to be followed in order for a sterilization procedure to be implemented on any citizen. The law was ethnically neutral and was intended to cover all citizens, regardless of ethnic background. In addition, no mention was made of compensation to individuals for having the procedure performed. However, between 1972 and 1990 (*after* the end of the communist regime), Romani women were sterilized at a rate grossly disproportionate to their population numbers. Additionally, many Roma were given financial inducements to have the procedure performed. In the end, while comprising less than two percent of the overall population, Romani women comprised between 21 percent and 36 percent of all sterilization procedures in Czechoslovakia.[48]

The question then arises about the rationale and means for the implementation of a policy that clearly was not spelled out in the letter of the law. Evidence suggests that the sterilization policy was privately and surreptitiously adopted, with a wink and a nod from the authorities above. The logic for such a program may have stemmed from historically low birthrates in Czechoslovakia by the late 1960s—at least among the "white" population. This pattern was reflected in most of the Eastern Bloc, leading in at least one case (Romania, 1966) to a law banning abortion in the interest of population growth.[49]

In Czechoslovakia, "pro-natalist" policies of the 1960s included increased periods of maternity leave, increasingly generous allowances from the State to families with children, and even preferential treatment in housing to larger families. Lurking behind each of these incentives was the commonly held concern that "white" Czechoslovakia was not reproducing itself, while the Roma continued to reproduce at high rates, despite widespread poverty. Indeed, during the "Normalization" period following the 1968 Prague Spring, population policy began a subtle shift from the quantitative to the qualitative. The Roma population was seen increasingly as polluting the national gene pool while siphoning off resources to an unproductive, damaged, deviant population. Indeed, by 1970, the State was devoting 11 percent of its budget to family allowances and other pro-natalist policies. The shift in policy emphasis was most clearly evident in the 1970 National Demographic Conference. Parenting, social deviance, quality of children, and respectability were leading concerns of the campaign. While the family state allowance was adjusted upwards to three children, the allowance for large families was actually trimmed.[50] Again, while no *explicit* mention of Roma appeared in the policy shift, the implications were clear; "undesirable" populations were being targeted.

In 1968, the Governmental Commission for the Gypsy Population went so far as to recommend an exemption to privately paid birth control, to encourage groups with limited monetary power to access free birth control. Concern that the Roma population was growing at an exponentially faster rate than that of whites was borne out by statistics showing a Romani birthrate more than double that of the general, white population.[51]

In addition to the fears of a Romani population explosion, many stereotypes about Romani reproductive behavior were pervasive in Czechoslovakia. Prominent in these was the notion that Romani women were promiscuous. Even medical personnel often fell prey to the idea that the better part of Romani women had regular sex with multiple partners, without regard for consequences. A leading urban legend of the late communist period was that a Romani couple had been seen copulating in front of an elevator shortly after the woman had given birth. Far into the 1990s, such stories were still used as justification for discriminatory treatment to Roma.[52]

In maternity matters, Romani have experienced recent mistreatment in very specific forms. Given that the Roma population after World War II was concentrated in eastern Slovakia, much of the data is drawn from that region. For example, maternity and gynecological wards have often been separated into "white" and "Gypsy" sectors, where bathrooms and toilets are separated, as are dining and TV rooms. Some medical personnel have claimed that such separation is necessary in order to accommodate white women, who do not wish to be situated in close proximity with Roma, nor to have their privacy violated. Such institutionalized segregation has been documented in the eastern cities of Prešov, Košice, Gelnica, and Krompachy, among others.[53]

Moreover, accounts of verbal and mental abuse against pregnant Roma women have been recorded, with accounts of Roma women having been referred to as "stinking gypsies," "stupid Gypsies" and "young whores" accused of having too many children. Many Roma women have complained of having been slapped or otherwise abused during childbirth on account of their being Roma.[54]

The Sterilization Law Revisited

A 2008 report documented statistics that, during the 1970s and 1980s, Roma women constituted a special target for sterilization, often through the use of financial inducements. In 1986–87, for example, 60 percent of all sterilization operations performed in the eastern city of Prešov, were performed on Roma women, who constituted only 7 percent of the female population in the district. Another study claims that, in 1983, about 26 percent of all sterilized women in eastern Slovakia were of Roma origin. This figure was said to have risen by 1987 to 36.6 percent.[55]

Financial incentives for sterilizations were abolished after the end of the communist regime, but little if any research has been done on how policy changed as a result. Regardless, it is known that, post–1990, Romani women continued to be sterilized at hospitals. For example, in 1999, a group of Finnish nurses working in Roma refugee centers told researchers from Amnesty International that they noticed a high incidence of ovary removal and sterilization among Romani asylum seekers from eastern Slovakia.[56]

By 2004, the Slovak government had provided certain protective procedures against gender and racial discrimination. These protections were adopted in 2004. However, racial discrimination against Roma in eastern Slovakia was rampant in the post-communist era. These attitudes have been passed on throughout many generations.

The 1972 law was, on the surface, intended to prevent "arbitrary and ill informed" sterilization of Czech women, as endorsed by the Health Ministries of both federal republics of Czechoslovakia. We know now, however, that Romani women in Czechoslovakia were sterilized at a rate that was astonishing, compared to the general population. What is most fascinating about the 1972 law is not only that it seeks, ostensibly, to "promote reproductive health," but that it is, on paper, strictly ethnically neutral. "Gypsies," "Roma," or other minority groups simply don't appear in the words of the legislation.[57]

However, research has demonstrated that, beneath the claims of "ethnic neutrality," a concerted (if unstated) policy of ethnic population control was underway under the 1972 law. Many testimonies from local doctors, Roma, and social workers have suggested that the impetus to sterilization typically came from *local* officials, who used the 1972 law as a mandate to carry out implicit sterilization orders from above.

This interpretation sheds much light on Eastern European Communist systems, as it flies in the face of the "top down," command economy understanding of political decision making. Instead, this interpretation suggests that the proclamations of the national Communist Party were less significant than the actions undertaken by local functionaries, who interpreted laws (and were allowed to do so) as they saw fit. Czechoslovak Communism may have presented a uniform face to the outside world, but, internally, many divergent forces were at work. The data suggests that, while "racial bias" was prohibited under the laws of the regime, "unofficial" racial bias was, in fact, the norm through much of Czechoslovakia. The ethnic target of the sterilization policy was never fully enunciated from above, nor fully institutionalized, but was always understood to refer to

Romani women by local practitioners, who inhabited a "dual world" between the "official discourse" and unofficial racial bias, and thus who were unable to perceive the racially charged nature of their actions.[58]

"Racial bias" was no accident in the Czechoslovakia of the 1970s and 1980s. Among white citizens, birth rates were dropping at a precipitous rate. This trend was, in fact, true for the entire Eastern European theatre, which experienced some of the lowest fertility rates in the world. By 1968, for example, Czechoslovakia had fertility rates commensurate with those of the 1930s.[59]

Abortion was legalized in the Soviet Union in 1955, and Czechoslovakia followed suit in 1957. The 1972 law was intended to provide a comprehensive, "pro-natalist" policy, and, in fact, even some Western demographers considered the law to be the "most comprehensive pronatalist population policy in the developed world."[60] By 1964, the regime had introduced longer maternity leaves and increased allowances for families with multiple children. Housing was also allotted based on family size, and mothers were afforded the opportunity of early retirement—for each child raised, a woman could retire one year earlier than the mandatory age of 60. (The regime in the 1960s and 1970s showed tendencies both towards sexism and towards a progressive ethic towards women's emancipation.)[61]

Policies towards Roma in the communist era could perhaps best be described as erratic, from time to time ideologically based, but, in the end, unenlightened—perhaps with the best intentions but lacking in addressing the core issues of this beleaguered, poor population—with ramifications that extend to the present.

Chapter Ten

Examining Memory

Is it true that the Czech patriots appealed to the Red Army for help?
Yes, it is true, but they appealed in 1939, and help arrived only in 1968.

How do the Czechs know that the Earth is round?
In 1945, the imperialists were driven out to the West, and in 1968 they returned from the East.

In 2003, a Czech band, *Chinaski*, produced a song titled "1970." In the song, the band referenced what it called "Husák's Kids," the generation of children born during the post–1968 "Baby Boom" years. The song elicited considerable controversy as many considered the Husák regime to be the most oppressive of the modern period in Czechoslovak history. One well placed commentator dismissed the expression "Husáks kids" as simplifying the issues of an era that drew from multiple causes. "Neither Husák nor another politician of that period's governing guard should be linked directly to the baby-boom. That [was] not being about the people, it's not the point, families to support...."[1]

The normalization period after the events of 1968 has been interpreted in many ways; an overall consensus, however, exists regarding the predominant trends of the post 1968 invasion period. One widely accepted thesis is that society turned inward and that private life, withdrawal, and alienation prevailed. During this period, the revisionist government of Husák attempted to provide a material level of comfort in society that would stave off further efforts at social and political change. A discouraged, passive, and alienated populace would assist this process, as private consumers could ease comfortably into their private lives, with the willing approval of state authorities. The second notion, widely held, was that the

Husák government represented a departure from the values of political pluralism and economic openness. Indeed, the "new order" represented a return to Stalinist centralization, lack of government accountability, and a loss of political voice and input from the general population.

Nevertheless, the recollections of many of the "Husák's Kids" create a collage of images that render the language and symbols of the Cold War sterile. They recall a time that was very different from today; they remember their childhoods, not just the regime in power during that period. What is remembered are relationships, and perhaps more importantly, the recollection of a collective zeitgeist. Petra S., a Prague resident, reacts to the moniker "Husák's Kids" by noting that "it is not really appropriate. It merely denotes a specific era, where a certain person represents culture and government. (To me) the term is not offensive, but I don't embrace it either. What is remembered are childhood experiences, such as the 'civil defense exercises,' where children were expected to run through the parks, wearing plastic bags on their hands and feet, and gas masks on their heads. For some, the exercises were fun; for others, they represented an inconvenience."[2]

Another interviewee explains the overall feel of the culture at the time: "It is true that colors tended to be gray, as I was 16 years old in 1968. Our private lives were not affected that much."[3]

One often hears that childhood and young adulthood were "influenced" by the political regime but were not necessarily directly affected, either positively or negatively. "My childhood was touched by the political situation," Petra continues, "but not in any concrete way." She was able to participate in many activities, both in and out of school, to join the scouts, and to attend music school. "Families tended to hold together tight," she adds, either as dissident cells or simply by virtue of the fact that opportunities were limited. "I personally looked at the fact that I could experience a 'taste' of a totalitarian regime, without ultimately having to live in that ... could widen my horizons."[4]

Childhood memories often had overtly political images. Petra F. recalls that the yearly May Day parades often utilized the Pioneer scouts to "guard" the Panzer tanks on display. "I remember being terribly cold as we watched those tanks," she says. "There was more general societal respect in those days. In general, the kids had more respect for teachers than kids today." Memories of hysterical parents attempting to procure tangerines and bananas just before Christmas, trying to obtain copies of *Čtyřlístek*, a popular, hard-to-obtain comic book, leads Martin F. to conclude that "I am really glad about these experiences. I have learnt from others that when you want something, you have to fight for it. As for the generation that hasn't lived in this period, I often have the feeling that it considers many things as given for granted and automatic—and that they are not willing to do something in exchange [for what they want]."[5]

One hears repeatedly the recollections of need, but not desperation, along with the knowledge that things could be obtained with the proper connections. This knowledge led to societal cooperation, however surreptitious. "We managed to get by with less," is a common refrain from Czechs and Slovaks during this period. However, the conclusion that is often drawn is positive; relative deprivation and deemphasized materialism led to a positive result. In the mind of Katka C. "Our education and self awareness was formed very differently from our contemporaries in the West, and, as a result, certain things were withheld from us (such as) books, trips and undistorted history.... We were maybe more curious and hungrier about information."[6]

When comparing the "old regime" to the present day, one cannot help but observe in those, like Katka who lived through the period, a brief hesitancy. The communist era was a dysfunctional and difficult time in many respects, but it also produced (whether by design or chance) a quality of life that is, in diverse respects, fondly remembered. "My mother always said—even today—that the socialist era was a peaceful period; workers got off work at 3 or 4 p.m., leaving them time to spend with their children—not like today. There was no fear of crime ... a four- or five-year-old could wander at will on the city street. It was very safe, and there wasn't much traffic or noise." It was true, her mother argues, that there was more economic equality at that time, and that social security (such as pensions) was stronger. "I admit," says Katka, "that people may have been a bit lazier at that time, because of the policy of full employment and the social security that everyone enjoyed. One of the problems with socialism was that it didn't think enough about the future. They planned economics, but not politics."[7]

Sense of community could assume many manifestations under the old regime. Opposition to the regime created alliances and loyalties. Katka continues: "My brother and sister were denied entry to university because of their (and my) parents' religious activity. They could go to church in the next town, but sometimes they were reported, if seen. In the end, however, the old times under the socialist government made us stronger in our faith—and possibly in our social structure—because of the *shared risk* that we all accepted. In many respects, this ethic has carried on today."[8]

Few would disagree that, in both the Czech Republic and in Slovakia, the post-communist period has experienced a sharp rise in violence, crime, drugs, pornography, and materialism. The Communists are often credited with having kept "popular morality" in check and maintaining social and political stability, however paternalistic the system might have been. Katka comments:

> Socialism had two faces; it did not represent freedom but it did provide some social and material benefit. The key was to learn to live "under the radar," where one could actually benefit from the system. Those who didn't experienced considerable problems.
>
> There was also a certain degree of "fakery" that had to be internalized; May Day parades, filled with smiling politicians and obedient Pioneers were "pure charades," but playing along with the charade was a vital part of sustaining oneself in the system. "People were not allowed to show their actual personalities," and exceptionalism was discouraged. Equality was the universally accepted goal.[9]
>
> We never talked about politics. We only learned later about our parents and their experiences in 1968. Before 1968, we were taught to enjoy stale bread with a little bit of milk and sugar. It was considered a "treat." We never felt that we were poor or needy.[10]

Egalitarianism has given way to a more market-oriented individualistic ethic since 1989. Although few would argue whether freedom of speech and movement has created new opportunities, there has also been a lingering sense that much of the new wealth has been gained illicitly. Much wealth was gained shortly after the ending of the old regime, often through privatization schemes that benefited a few well-placed individuals disproportionately. The political and economic culture has changed; poverty exists where none did before. Class distinctions have increased, and social guarantees have been scaled back. In some circles this has led to resentment and accusations of unfair advantage: "Those who got rich so quickly have frustrated the hopes of the 1989 generation. They're guilty of a second normalization, and they've degraded work to begging; they must be punished. Human rights without social freedoms are worthless. If you don't have a job, if you don't have anything to eat or anywhere to live, you couldn't care less that you can fly to the Canary Islands, vote for one bastard after another in the elections, or feel free to cuss out the government in the bar over your overpriced beer."[11]

One hears repeatedly a form of grudging acknowledgment that, in spite of its limitations, the old regime had its merits, at least in the economic and social realms. What appears is a duality of memory; recollections like Beáta's, of a period where political rights were suppressed, and opportunities limited: "I guess there are basically two types of the answer—that it was a horrible time, no freedom, no rights, etc."[12] At the same time even strong opponents of the communist system admit that certain benefits accrued: "The other group [others] would remember that it was time with social security, everybody had a job, safe passivity, no responsibility."[13]

In the end, comparisons typically emerge, comparing the present market-oriented system to the communist model. While some sympathy (especially in distant retrospect) can be discerned for the "old days," final judgment tends, overall, to favor the post-communist developments: "I think, for example, that most of my high schoolmates appreciate the current system; they wouldn't have achieved positions they have now, traveled ... their children can study abroad, etc. When we occasionally meet (today) we usually make fun of those stupid rules, books we had to read and memorize, music ... we couldn't believe how that system could work."[14]

The Nature of Memory

The means by which a culture holds on to the past, by which it recollects shared experience, is a complicated and controversial process. Czechoslovakia provides an interesting example of "memory in process," as the events both before and after 1968 provide ample data for how the old regime was conceptualized, experienced and, ultimately, remembered.

In the case of Czechoslovakia, the past may well be colored by the present. Lucia notes that "When abroad, we avoid Czechs even today. The reason is that we see ourselves in them. The lack of self-confidence that was indoctrinated during the communist period is alive today. Many are 'frozen' in that time and mentality."[15] She continues: "Even in the best of times, Czechs (and Slovaks) can be very hard on each other. We are a very envious society. Even during the communist period, the idea of equality and equal disbursement gave way to envy over who was able to bribe or otherwise procure something that you did not have. Today, we like to meet our fellow countrymen and women abroad only for the purpose of complaining."[16]

Renewed nationalism from the post-communist period has also fostered an opportunity to settle old scores and prejudices. Lívia, a Hungarian, remarks:

> Since the end of the communist period, Slovaks and others have been "paying back" others with retribution. I was heard speaking Hungarian in the High [Slovak] Tatra mountains in 1990, and was refused service in a restaurant. These feelings go back to 1968 and even as far as the Austro-Hungarian period.
>
> It seems also that many in the East are of the belief that the EU is a good thing in that even if defeated countries can't get territories back, they *can* win their people back,

> through nationalist or ethnic appeals. One can see this, for example, in Slovak or Romanian ethnic Hungarians and other cross-border ethnicities.
>
> Memory has not changed much since 1989. It has stayed constant. We had no power—we were oppressed. We couldn't travel. We had an expression for an emergency—that "the Russians were in the pantry." This was our feeling much of the time. However, we don't like to talk about this period because of the shame that we feel for participating in the 1968 invasion, and because of the low self-esteem that the period inflicted upon us.[17]

Oral History and Collective Memory

Since the revolutions of 1989, the focus of Western scholarship has tended towards institutional change, the development of markets and the transition from a planned economy to a market—driven one. As a result, the *language* of collectivism in Czechoslovakia has given way to a new, individualist rhetoric. An effect of this paradigm shift is an alteration in the way people articulate the past. Although considerable research has yet to be performed on the subject of Czechoslovak memory and ideology, much work points towards the likely role of pervasive cognitive dissonance in examining memory. This is true especially in light of certain assumed Western "truths" regarding the Cold War narrative.

Some oral history accounts from the communist era seem to suggest that terminology depicting the past may be more fluid and fungible than had been previously assumed. On the one hand, interviewed individuals often recount having experienced a degree of self reliance under the old regime, meaning that they could typically exert adequate control over their activities. However, self—determination, as it were, was often a mechanism of survival and adaptation to need, often resembling a type of cultural barter system:

> Outside of the *nomenklatúra*, people of all social classes had to develop adaptive strategies—to shortages, decrees and prohibitions—whether or not their strategies were active forms of opposition to the State. According to a survey conducted in April 1988 by the Economic Research Institute in Prague, and reported in January 1989, 75 percent of respondents in Czechoslovakia had used bribery, gifts, additional payments, or reciprocal services in purchasing retail goods; 49.5 percent in obtaining health care; 44.5 per cent in obtaining repairs and other tradesmen's work, and 37.5 per cent in the purchase and repair of automobiles.[18]

At the same time, other evidence suggests that many experienced the post–1989 period as having represented a loss of rights and privileges from the earlier era. Further complicating matters is the subsequent transition from a political and cultural ideology of collective action and social construction to one of individual self interest and market relations.[19]

Generational perspective may also play a part in collective memory. Younger individuals may assume certain social and economic freedoms enjoyed after 1989, while older citizens may fear the uncertainty of social security guarantees as they approach retirement age. Many feel that capitalism is concerned only with profit; thus, while appreciative of "individual liberty," many fear the unknown future, with the result that some become attracted to extremist political parties with anti-foreigner and often racist agendas.[20] Although often overlooked, autonomous individual-driven activity working both within as well as around the system, as such, was, arguably, healthy and vibrant during the communist period.

Nostalgia

Without question, large numbers look back upon the old regime and see themselves neither as active participants nor as opponents of the regime. Many of them may have joined the Party for the many social and economic benefits that might be assured, while privately hoping to extend as little positive support as they could get away with. A considerable amount of these very people maintain certain nostalgia for the past. They do not see themselves as an exploited, "lost" generation. Rather, they typically enjoyed their previous lives under the Party. The communist period, whatever its flaws, was a time of peace, social harmony and relative equality.

The standard of living, while short of affluent, was livable and acceptable. Crime was low and most people felt safe. They see, in the modern world, abuse and exploitation, privatization schemes that benefit a few, and growing inequality and social isolation. Western narratives that developed during and after the Cold War often ignore perspectives of the past that diverge from the "official narrative," but those perspectives exist and thrive nonetheless: "People still grumble a lot, but they've never been so well off ... only there are bad things in politics ... prices are rising, we're having a hard time with unemployment, and everybody will tell you that there is a lot of injustice. And it'll get worse: there'll be millionaires and paupers."[21]

Some of the ambivalence is expressed by J. Čapek, who calls attention to the growing corporate material model ascendant in the modern Czech and Slovak Republics: "So there's freedom: people can travel and I can say what I want, write what I want, you see? But in terms of, say, the economy

... five textile companies have disappeared, and there's not one left. You see? Do we really need four Kaufland hypermarkets?"[22] Such views cut across the grain of the dominant Cold War narrative of totalitarianism and oppression. Many others see the post 1989 period as replete with economic and social freedoms, as well as freedom to travel, and to speak freely.

Assessing Blame for the Past

Václav Havel, later elected the first President to post–Communist Czechoslovakia, wrote extensively on the nature of memory. In his view, one must "live within the truth" as the means by which one recovers their true humanity and sense of responsibility. This task was hard, and not all were up to it. Therefore, Havel tended to see complicity in all sectors of society towards the old regime, even among well intended, "innocent" citizens. Therefore, in the 1990s, he opposed efforts to try to prevent a South African–style "truth commission," whereby leading figures of the communist period would be brought to justice. In his view, the entire society—not just leading figures—bore collective responsibility for the past; singling out scapegoats would be "unproductive," he said.[23]

Building on Havel's argument against a "reckoning" is the added dimension of the tension between the Czech and Slovak nations, leading to the eventual split in 1993, "distracted" attention from the process of internal cleansing of the old regime. This, in turn, may have had (at least for a time) a profound effect on the tone and narrative of collective memory from the communist era.[24]

The dominant narrative of the old regime—and one that served the Communist Party well for decades—was that they represented liberation from Nazi oppression. The communist narrative was also directly associated with the liberating forces of the Soviet army at the close of World War II. Those who lived through the War were generally receptive to the language of liberation, even years after the post-war glow had faded.[25]

Two perhaps related themes have appeared repeatedly in my own research. One is the notion that "we didn't know what freedom was—we thought we were free," a sentiment echoed in several interviews regarding the communist period. The other is that, after 1989, "we were *too* free." In the first statement, the implication is that of a doctored and manipulated social, economic and political narrative that swayed the better part of the population into acquiescence. The second theme is an indication of frustration, a feeling that the post–1989 changes produced a form of "democracy" in which "the sense of human decency has been totally lost." In this sense, "democracy" and "freedom" mean little more than licentiousness, selfishness and an abandonment of the social contract. Such claims are not benign; the absence of social cohesion creates fertile soil for the development of racist and exclusionary ideas—and Roma and other minorities have borne the brunt of such thoughts. Thus, the perception of the past is a multi-layered and culturally specific phenomenon, one that is filtered not only though politics and history, but through social encounter and personal recollection.[26]

Shared Memory

The research presented in this manuscript is focused primarily on the stories of the communist era in Czechoslovakia, recounted as oral histories by individuals who lived through that period. Establishing an elaborate societal theory of societal memory is a topic for another book. However, it is useful to at least touch upon recent scholarship on memory and its applicability to Czech and Slovak history.

The work of French sociologist Maurice Halbwachs distinguishes between different modes of memory, the individual, or "autobiographical" memory; the collective, or "group" memory; and the phenomenon of history itself. Autobiographical memory is *individual*, drawing on the experiences of the singular actor. The individual, however, is influenced by the collective in his or her recollection. Thus the *collective* memory involves a group recollection that is separate from, but also informing to the individual. Finally, there is the process of history itself, which, Halbwachs argues, exists as a separate sphere of neutral events and facts. History is, in essence the recounting of events after all witnesses to those events no longer exist; the historian is viewed by Halbwachs as a neutral and disinterested observer who attempts to interpret and report the events transpiring from the past.[27] Halbwachs examines the means by which "shared remembering" occurs over time. Personal recollections are seen as existing in a sphere separate from, but informing to—a collective sense of memory that is socially constructed and, ultimately, informs private memory[28]: "Halbwachs distinguishes between the individual, or 'autobiographical' memory, the collective, or 'group' memory, and history itself. Halbwachs accords the two memory modalities different functions, while at the same time acknowledging that they complement one another. Personal recollections, perceived as private and unique, are positioned against the backdrop of the whole collectivity that is specific to a particular group. For Halbwachs, collective memory is socially mediated, and informs the patterns of individual memory."[29]

History and social memory is summed up thusly: "According to Halbwachs' model of memory, individuals exist between the tripartite poles of history, personal memory and collective memory. Individual recollection is determined by the relation to the shared stories of one or more collectives as well as recorded history."[30]

Post-Memory

Marianne Hirsch has developed a theory of *post-memory* as a means to better understanding intergenerational recollections of events. Post-memory is a concept useful in understanding societally or culturally traumatic experiences and has been used as a model for understanding both the Holocaust of World War II, and the events in Czechoslovakia of 1968. Hirsch writes: "In my reading, post-memory is distinguished from memory by generational distance and from history by deep personal connection. Post-memory is a powerful form of memory because its connection to its object or source is mediated not through recollection, but through an imaginative investment and creation.... Post-memory characterizes the experience of those who grow up dominated by narratives that preceded their birth, whose own belated stories are evacuated by the stories of the previous generation shaped by traumatic events that can be neither understood nor recreated."[31] Post-memory, therefore, involves an *inter-generational* experience (and conflict) of memory, in which specific recollections of experiences and events may be realized and altered through storytelling and shared recollection.

Space and Memory

Place factors importantly into memory, as do the relations that people forge with their surroundings, which comprise the product of their own historical narratives. In Czechoslovakia, for example, a central place of modern memory is Wenceslas Square. Here, the Czechoslovak Radio Broadcast, a leading source of information to residents during the Soviet invasion, was, after unsuccessful efforts to jam its transmission, violently seized by the Soviet military several days after the invasion. The resistance of Czechoslovak Broadcast (which continued for a week after the invasion) to the invaders continues to be a source of pride. During the invasion, for example, many Czechs printed slogans (in multiple languages, including Russian) on street signs, buildings, and markers. Further, some of the most famous images of the 1968 invasion include two individuals in Wenceslas Square with signs on their backs reading (in Russian) "why are you shooting at us?" This image mocks the official line that the Soviets were "called in" to quell civic disturbance, at the request of the Czechoslovak authorities.[32]

Milan Kundera, in his 1979 work *The Book of Laughing and Forgetting*, depicts the process of "official" memory in Czechoslovakia, when he describes a famous photograph of V. Clementis (a victim of the early 1950s purges) standing next to K. Gottwald. In the years that followed the purge, Clementis was literally "erased" from the picture (as was the photographer who took it). In other words, society was guided through a process of officially forgetting the past.[33]

Another theme that emerges from interviews with Czechs and Slovaks regarding the nature of remembering the communist period is that "one learned to stay off the radar, and by doing so, remained safe."[34] As discussed previously, Václav Havel's position on memory was comprehensive and personal. In numerous essays, he argued against living as a hypocrite instead waging all-out opposition and resistance:

> In the Czech Republic, Václav Havel has suffered an assault on his principled stance on remembering. Havel's essays, most pointedly the classic "Power of the Powerless," unsparingly exposed *the compromises of everyday life* ("living the lie") and proposed a way out through "living in truth," refusing the co-optations of the system.
>
> This was a rather Kundera-like strategy of *absolute resistance* together with a Konrád-like understanding of the reality of collaboration. He continued to confront uncomfortable memories, whether of participation in the communist system or of Czech treatment of Sudeten Germans after 1945. But with the complete failure at the polls in 1992 of his former dissident intellectual colleagues, he was left a lonely voice in the wilderness, plaintively repeating his call for "morality in politics...." Meanwhile, the dissident narrative focused on 1968, and the Soviet suppression no longer seems to evoke the slightest public interest.[35]

Monuments are another means by which spatial memory is evoked and preserved. The question is often raised regarding edifices from oppressive or discredited regimes. Should these tangible sentinels of the past be permitted to stand, should they be destroyed and erased from memory, or should they be "refitted" to society, as was the Sculpture Park outside of Budapest, Hungary, where old communist era statues have been preserved and resettled. The spatial memory of street names are more historically malleable, as Kundera discusses a boulevard in Prague, and the placement of communist monuments in Budapest:

> Kundera goes on to cite the five different names in this century—before 1989—of a single street in Prague: "They just kept changing its name, trying to lobotomize it."
> In the debate that raged over the fate of the [Budapest] monuments, some called for them to be "wiped off the face of the earth"; others argued that they had become part of the city's landscape, part of an undeniable lived past, and as such should be allowed to stand.[36]

Of course, such accounts represent the most lurid and sensational of Cold War stereotypes. Looked at from a post–1989 perspective, there is little that appears definitive. Previous descriptions of totalitarianism and planned economy gave way to the language of capitalism and markets. Over time, the distinction between these seemingly opposing ideologies is rendered less and less clear.[37]

One can perceive repeatedly that the anticipation of the end of communist rule was followed by a sense of freedom, but one that failed to signify a break with the past; "We have the same kind of freedom that we always had. You can complain but it doesn't do any good if you don't have enough money or the right connections. And it is very hard to get any justice." Similarly, interviewees express deep reservations about journalism and journalist, often opining that true media independence was never achieved, and that journalists merely switched hats, leaving their official government sponsors for the deep pockets of private interest. "Unfortunately, the Czech media has become a kind of mouthpiece for the interests of their owners and have given up any kind of journalistic ethics and independence."[38]

Balancing the Old and the New

Memory in the post–Communist Czechoslovak milieu is very subjective, at best. In the first place, memory is not a static phenomenon, and the memories of childhood—or of the early post-communist period—are likely to be quite different from, say, later reflections from 1995 or 2005 or 2015.[39] One is left with an evolving series of impressions about change, improvement, decay, or stasis. Nonetheless, impressions count for something, and they may convey a sense of the *gestalt* of the period during which they are collected. The following section is devoted to those subjective impressions.

Many distinct memories are positive—particularly towards the period prior to 1948. "My family had a much better status after 1945," says Juraj; "the older ones, especially. The old capitalist system was unfair, and the poor were treated unfairly, as were the ethnic minorities—the Ruthenians, for example." However, Juraj himself, a strong anti-communist from an early age, now thinks that he misjudged ethnic and senior groups in their 1990s-era nostalgia. "I thought that they lacked perspective," which, he says, he doesn't believe anymore. "In fact, Marx was on to something. He saw the deficiencies of capitalism." Within those views are the competing contemporary conceptions of social life in the Czech and Slovak Republics today. Two models are often referred to—the Catholic or conservative model, which holds that the family is the basic unit of society, and the modern perspective which, though differentiated, often holds that the family *impedes* gender equality, and that the family ensures the continuance of this inequality.[40]

Juraj describes himself as "more sober" in his assessment of the Old Regime, but he also acknowledges that societies shift values and policies slowly. "Flipping a society [from capitalist to Communist] 180 degrees doesn't work. The media plays an enormous role in what people think, and connects the past to the present, but one cannot change their views overnight."[41]

Questions of *redistribution* also factor in. To what degree, if any, Juraj asks, should the State intervene to create better equality through inheritance laws, redistribution of taxes, and other means?[42]

It is often argued that 1989 was, in essence, about the lack of efficiency in society; collectivism in economy and politics was held up as the central sin. New ideas were introduced at that time, as were money—making schemes. Juraj explains:

> The problem was that there was no distinguishing between good and bad ideas. Everyone was out for a buck. We used the term "civic society" as the means to further our money making schemes, but, in fact, it was just a buzzword. The real concept at work at the time was wild, rampant capitalism. Now, in Slovakia, at least, after a period of [autocratic ruler] Mečiar and [populist] Fico, not to mention V. Klaus in the Czech Republic, people see that oversight of public funds and investments is a good idea. We have come, however gradually, to see the usefulness of the concept of the *public good*, in the modern, liberal sense of the public sphere.[43]

After the end of communism, a sort of primitive, "buchaneer" capitalism pervaded in Czechoslovakia. "Macro and Micro economics were confused in the early years," says Juraj. He continues, on the topic of post–1989 economic reform:

> We were driven (in 1989) by the economic idea of the *Slušovice*.[44] This concept referred to the *collective* idea, to the "agrocombinat," the combined intelligence and ingenuity of a group towards the interests of a collective good. We were told in 1989 that our mission was to create, out of the ashes of communism, a *Slušovice* in the

> interest of a collective economic success. In fact, we were lied to. Those who succeeded after 1989 tended to be those who possessed hidden information. There was no system of competition, and these individuals benefitted well from such a system.
>
> After 1990, market principles dominated our "privatization" schemes, and, in the end, efficiency triumphed over equality. During communism, it was always the other way around. Now, we lack balance. The key event in our experience was 1968, when we learned how the world actually worked, and we developed, for better or for worse, a critical perspective.[45]

In assessing the past against the present, another perspective concurs that "nothing was changed." The only variable in play was that we now "recognize certain positive aspects of the communist era. The past has shown us that history may not be evaluated only in black and white. I cannot name it nostalgia ... as negative aspects of memory prevail."[46]

How, then, is communism remembered today? "[We had a] low standard of living ... we were not hungry, but certain types of food were simply too expensive, or were inaccessible. This was true, for example, of bananas and oranges—except at certain times of the year, around the Christmas holidays."[47]

Many young people were fairly aware, even in grade school, that they did not live in a "free" society. Tomas K. describes realizing this fact as a child of 10, by the daily experiences that he faced. In his school, every grade school class had its *Pioneer* chairman. These people were selected before the votes were held for their positions, but the process by which they were chosen was always murky. After all of the pomp and circumstance, a *Pioneer* leader would, invariably, be chosen. An election within the *Pioneers*, he recalls, proceeded thusly:

> The act of election was formal and public. There were three "pro forma" questions, for the voters: who is for, who is against, and who abstains. One of my schoolmates "abstained" from the vote (I know that it was for fun). You should see what happened next: The election was stopped. The adult members of the Pioneer organization asked the abstainer to come before the entire auditorium. There, they (some 300 persons) asked him publically what he had against the proposed, "official" candidate. The "act" of elections was, of course, public. My friend was so scared at this point that he could not say a word. After this public humiliation, they sent him back to his position, and the election was repeated. This time, the result was unanimous.[48]

Sometimes, memories revolved around incidents that were slower to evolve: Tomáš describes a later period in the 1980s, when he faced some big trouble. The problem was a high level of bribery in some university programs: "The standard cost was 10,000 crowns. This was four months salary for my father, and for admission to the law school at Košice [in eastern Slovakia], the price was 100,000 crowns. Well—connected people could pay these bribes—butchers, shop directors, and car sellers ... people who were responsible for 'social capital.' Anyone who worked with goods in shortage was in a position of power, as were higher ranking administrators."[49]

Recent Reassessments

How is the communist period understood today, in all of its complexity and contradictions? Petra J. offers some insights, ranging from work performance and travel to cultural intelligence, censorship and entertainment:

> I would like to connect with the question of what worked well in the past. It was a regime for average people ... it was not a regime which promoted personal initiative, personal opinion or critical thinking. One was to be "average." But people existed during that regime with much better "anchors of certainty," as activities were typically state sponsored. One didn't have to follow along; there was a joke that everyone had a low but substantial standard of living but at least this was certain. Another significant observation follows: people were required to be smarter.
>
> There were very strict regulations in the culture. Censorship required many authors to hide certain anti-regime meanings between the lines. Many entertainers became famous as a result of their ability to "speak between the lines," and these included Werich, Lasica, Satinský, Horníček, and others. A common theme heard about the post–1989 period is "we didn't know what to do with our freedom."[50]

In other words, how were the (suddenly) revolutionary forces to deal with profound social, political, and economic transformation? No answer was readily apparent, even among the opposition leadership, and the general population knew it well. Petra admits, "We were free to travel, but we weren't quite sure where to go. Even experimentally—we didn't quite know what to do at first. We had to evaluate new freedoms and the presumed social and certain economic costs that they would impose upon us. That took some time."[51]

Scholarship published after the 20th anniversary of the Velvet Revolution suggests that the dominant narrative in both the Czech and Slovak Republics is that the non-violent approach to change was both desirable and effective. The Velvet Revolution is closely correlated with the fall of communism—and is typically seen as an integral element of the fall of the regime. However, the peaceful creation of a market economy and liberal democracy has been interpreted by some as a capitulation, a show of weakness against a fight for real, substantive economic reform—even an indication of passivity, with precedents in 1938, 1948, and 1968.[52]

Academic tracking of popular sentiment for the 10th, 15th and 20th anniversaries of the Fall of Communism in Czechoslovakia has consistently shown recurring themes of pessimism and frustration, even disillusionment with reforms or changes that were promised but never fulfilled. The banking crisis of the 1990s tended to stoke nostalgia for the Old Regime and cause more to remember fondly the communist past. This trend was exacerbated during a series of political scandals in 1997–98. In polling data over time, respondents with a more left wing interpretation of politics have tended to support the idea that the Velvet Revolution or the Fall of Communism (the two events are closely equated in the popular mind) was more of an economic adjustment supported by the people. Those of a more right-wing perspective tend to believe that the events of 1989–1993 were more political in nature and led by an elite.[53]

One mass survey, performed with over 1,000 participants in 2008, found that the dominant memory of goals in 1989 was revolution, according to 59 percent of respondents. Reform was suggested by a mere 15 percent, and 58 percent supported the idea that the major change was political, rather than economic. Finally, 25 percent believed that dissidents (such as V. Havel) instigated change, whereas over one-third of respondents had no opinion at all. Older residents tend to believe that the events of 1989 and the Velvet Revolution "manipulated the people" and "destabilized" the status quo. Interestingly, "the top 10 percentile of educated individuals polled," tended to support the notion that the events of 1989 were more about market capitalism than about democracy.[54]

As one can ascertain from the results, there was widespread perception of major political change, limited economic change, and significant evidence of passivity. The dominant negative views tended towards that of social uncertainty, and were emphasized by older segments of the population. In conclusion, the study suggests no clear consensus on the meaning of the events of 1989.

Selective Memory and Narrative

A 2005 study by scholar Haldis Haukanes draws on data collected from the Czech Republic in the early 1990s when the communist period and questions of national identity were being hotly debated. This account emphasizes the perceptual void between "official" memory, that of institutions, dissidents and national events, and of the "private" memory of individual recollection.

Haukanes' research focuses primarily on memories of south Moravian and south Bohemian peasants and working-class individuals. Questions were posed about the post–World War II period onward. Almost none of those questioned drew attention to the events of 1948 (the communist "coup," as it was sometimes called). Even the events of 1968 were largely vacant from the interviewees' accounts. Instead, general comments about the pleasures and stability of the simple life proliferated. The exception to this trend to remove national events from memory regards the revolutionary year 1989, which is mentioned frequently.[55]

In these interviews, subjects might, the author suggests, be engaging in defining their own *genre* of storytelling, one that does not emphasize the national and dramatic, but rather the local and personal. While events of, say, 1948 or 1968 might be profoundly experienced by local communities, they might nonetheless be relegated to lesser status in personal recollections of the period. To put it another way, sordid tales of military service and "grand dramas" are found to give way to personal and family/community events such as marriage, family and local community or working careers when individuals are asked to frame their experiences. One aspect of memory that proved salient was the widely held belief that "people stuck together more" during the communist period. "Nowadays, everyone just sits in front of their own television."[56]

Additionally, while respondents often spoke of their relationship to the Communist Party, rarely if ever did they delve beyond their individual experiences into more general statements for or against the organization. This was true also of the government. While interviewees spoke of relations with government officials, more often they were referring not to the national or regional governmental functions, but rather to the local functionaries who held considerably more influence over the day-to-day events of their lives. "Macro" accounts, such as descriptions of Russian tanks moving through streets, rarely found a voice in the research.[57]

Respondents showed a shrewdness when addressing their relationship to the Old Regime; this is certainly not surprising, as, by the early 1990s when this research was conducted, the present and future role of the communist ideology and past proponents and opponents was at yet uncertain. In the end, respondents did not engage in the "grand narratives" of their country's history. Haukanes chose to interpret these results as intentional, a process by which individuals "protected their dignity and integrity from official versions of history," both past *and* present.[58] The data here could be interpreted as a resistance to historical narratives "from above," a reaction to experiences with communist censorship, or perhaps a more general distrust by a people long conditioned to political disturbance and uncertainty.

By contrast, Czechoslovak scholar Revan Schendler writes of a mill that was nationalized in 1948 and then returned to private ownership in 1990. None of the employees there would "dismiss the socialist experiment as a failure," he writes. "They accept the idea that the State should ensure everyone has a place to live and enough to eat and free schooling and health care." Blame for oppression is placed at the feet of individuals, not at the hands of the state or of socialism generally.[59]

But others view the communist period as having inflicted certain systemic damage to the general culture, as the state assumed responsibilities and individual initiative was suppressed, creating over time a sense of entitlement and dependency: "Even today when we travel abroad, we often avoid interacting with Czechs and Slovaks. In a sense, we look down on them, as lacking confidence. These feelings of inferiority and envy were nurtured in the communist period, as individual initiative was not encouraged. Many Czechs are today 'frozen in the communist times' when they travel. We see ourselves negatively in our countrymen as if we are looking into a mirror."[60]

The issue of societal and individual memory is and will continue to be a dynamic phenomenon, shifting over time and reflecting contemporaneous events as much or more than the past itself. Scholarly research and the unsealing of confidential documents will too exert influence over how the past is perceived. Sympathetic accounts of the "good old days" may wrap communism less in the garb of ideology and more as a symbol of stability and safety. In a current age where social dislocation worldwide often leads to renewed tribalism and nationalism, communism could well be seen as the system that "maintained order" and reduced violence and criminality. Finally, politicians will undoubtedly use popular attitudes towards the past to fine tune their present-day messages. Twenty-eight years on from the revolutionary events of 1989, the reckoning with the past remains a work in progress.

Conclusion

A standard post–1989 central European narrative has been recounted many times; there was initial optimism for change which faded over time to disappointment with the transition to a market economy seen increasingly over time as corrupt, favoring inside groups, and ultimately (as one of my interviewees commented) "giving rise to a new set of elites to replace the communist elites that we had displaced."[1] For those old enough to remember the events of 1968, the political domination of that era, coupled with the Warsaw Pact invasion, was being reinvented with economic exploitation imported from the West, and, to add insult to injury, was being manipulated by many of the same indigenous malefactors of the old regime.

Although this may come as a surprise to many Western readers, the evidence through the research in this and some other narrative based books on Communist-era Czechoslovakia suggests that a significant majority portion of the population did not consider "communism" as such to be manifestly unjust and devoid of legitimacy. To put it another way, communism was not perceived by Czechoslovaks by and large to be a system judged by one prevailing moral, political or economic criterion. Rather, policy and ideology divergence, though present in the general population, was typically piecemeal rather than systemic. If one looks closely, one can perceive—even among opponents of the regime—that there were things that worked, policies that helped people, laws that protected workers rights and guaranteed child care, initiatives that were indeed forward thinking and innovative. Add to that that the model of the West was hardly a shining success story. Flaws with Western-style democracy were well known, ranging from wealth inequality and poverty to the Vietnam war and the endemic racism in Civil Rights–era America.

In Communist Czechoslovakia, grievances amongst the populace were often specific: travel was too difficult, church attendance was awkward and monitored, and consumer goods were reserved for the well connected. There were indeed ideological opponents of the regime but even many of these found, in the reforms of 1968, a means that might mitigate the excesses of both market-based capitalism and Stalinist-styled Communism. The system had flaws, but that fact in itself was hardly remarkable. The successes of and support for the old regime in Czechoslovakia ebbed and flowed from 1948 to 1989, but there was always faith that a "middle way" could be found. Alexander Dubček tried the political route to this result; his successors, under normalization, attempted the same under an economic and consumer mantle. Until the late 1980s, at least, support for the Party was consistent enough to justify its existence.

Of course, the revolutionary events from 1989 in Czechoslovakia did not take place in a vacuum; the West pounced on the Velvet Revolution as a vindication of capitalism and all things Western. In fact, Czechoslovakia represented to many in the West a mere extension of Soviet influence and policy in the larger, late Cold War struggle between the United States and Russia. To the Western popular mind in 1989, whatever was wrong with Russia was equally wrong with Czechoslovakia, *as they were widely perceived as the "same" ideologically*—and, by some extension, culturally. Regarding Western popular perceptions of the East, I recall the Western-oriented, English-language newspapers that began to crop up in the former Czechoslovakia in the 1990s. Although ostensibly dedicated to local news in English, they seemed to serve a much more insidious purpose—to open new vistas to investor money. For example, in Slovakia under Vladimír Mečiar in the late 1990s, Western English-language papers made use of "human rights" and "democratic" rhetoric to criticize old, "atrophied" governmental structures; 20 years hence, with the retrogressive Mečiar regime long gone, the "English news" looks less human rights-oriented and more a tool of new market players, interested in discrediting the recent past, and paving the way for new (often foreign) players in government and civil society. And, perhaps to no-one's surprise, any detailed evaluation of the old regime is entirely suppressed, other than to note that Western-style economics had emerged triumphant.

In basic political and economic terms, the transition from a command socialist economy to a market-based one has certainly been successful; travel is no longer centrally and politically controlled, and unbridled consumerism abounds. Amazon operates a distribution center from the Czech Republic. Opportunities exist where they did not previously. But material prosperity has not brought with it increased happiness and satisfaction. Far from it; market economics has created significant and salient economic imbalances within society. Additionally, the social security brought about by the previous, communist social contract, has been largely abandoned.

What emerges in the interview data is a sense of longing for elements of a previous time, but this is not to say that people are nostalgic. Most recall the shortcomings and inefficiencies of the previous order. Thus, a view of the past that tries to simply compare or superimpose past and present falls short. On the other hand, 50 years on from the Prague Spring, there is a strong sense of unease about the present—a sense that something has been lost, something very difficult to articulate. The past may be a memory, but it continues to hang heavily over the experience of the present. This is understandable: While it may not seem efficacious to dwell in the past, one can certainly possess empathy for someone who has lived and endured a committed life under a previous regime, experiencing successes and failures within the rubrics of that culture and system, comprehended within the parameters of possibility under that rule. To disparage such a life is both cruel and unrealistic, as is to negate, suppress or culturally expunge those memories and experiences. The process of retrieving those impressions and memoires from those who lived through the experiences creates disturbance, as the recollections churn and collide within the channels (both official and unofficial) of memory and narrative.

A recurrent theme within the communist era narratives is that of *community*. The term is a vague one, suggesting, in some general sense, levels of social interaction and cooperation. Reading between the lines of the interviews, "community" seems to imply several things. First, it suggests an inclusive localism, free from a specifically religious, ethnic or regional tag. From an early age, youth were nurtured and indoctrinated into the Pioneer scouts, local sports, folk groups, international socialist campaigns, scholarly clubs and later to the collective efforts of the Brigáda workers and Party candidacy. To see these as merely compulsory or ideological (and many were) is to miss the point. They were opportunities for young people to meet, interact, and to enjoy nature, community service—and even to poke fun at the authorities who were dragging them from school to perform these "patriotic" tasks. There was freedom in community—even subversion. One could look forward to a free education, a good career and even an apartment if they navigated successfully the prevailing ideological and social minefields. Further, regardless of whether one was within or outside of the Party infrastructure, one could find time to withdraw from official life to the private sphere, to the *chata*, to the family. After 1968, of course, support for such a retreat into the complacency and consumerism of the private sphere was promoted as official state policy.

A common lament heard amongst interviewees is that "we didn't know that we were not free." While it may be true that the closed nature of the communist system, bolstered by omnipresent propaganda, might have had a chilling effect on ones world perspective, "might it" also be supposed that, in some ways, Czechoslovaks didn't appreciate *how free they were* in other respects, such as the relatively moderate influence of the problems associated with industrialization on culture (particularly in Slovakia), the closeness to nature, the freedom from the iron hand of the market, and the overall simplicity of a non-monetary based community. Many of these habits were deeply inculcated. I recall, even in the late 1990s, that my Czech and Slovak students rarely went out to dinner, to a movie, or to other "external" entertainment venues. They formed communities and made their own entertainment. Music, bonfires in the woods, or drinks at a friend's apartment all were part of the self creative impulse towards entertainment. In a very real sense, they remained free from not only market forces and influence, but from reliance on money itself.

One of the many surprises that I encountered while researching this manuscript was that virtually none of the interviewees were concerned about shielding their identities, although that option was available to all who participated. (In the end, I elected in most cases to use only first names and surname initials.) Quite the contrary; most participants wanted to be heard. Their stories were of no vital political import at present, but they did convey information about a recent past that disappeared abruptly and ignominiously—a past complicated and contradictory, a past in danger of being buried in an avalanche of historical Western triumphalism after the termination of the Cold War.

This is not to suggest that interviewee perspectives were in any way congruent—they were not. A whole host of attitudes, ideologies and cultural perspectives emerged from the interviews that I conducted for this book. Differences emerged and were regional, national (Czech and Slovak), historical (based on World War II remembrances—or those of 1968), class driven and religiously diverse. All of these criteria were filtered through a historical framework that, until recently, had not encouraged the expression of memory, of storytelling for the communist period. As one interviewee stated: "We never really learned how to talk about politics or controversy. We were taught obedience, and this often made it hard for us to 'sell' ourselves or our opinions to others later on. We learned not to trust and not to speak out and to openly question."[2] Internalized insecurity, shame and a culturally induced lack of self confidence are often cited as reasons for remaining reticent on the communist past. However, many interviewees expressed great satisfaction once an interview was under way. Memories would return and the discussion of past days often led to insight, recollection and catharsis.

Most requests for interviews were accepted. A few requests, primarily of older (World War II) era individuals, were refused. My interviews initially imposed little structure. I was interested in talking about the issues that mattered to my interviewees, while minimizing my own role. In fact, their responses and topical references ultimately shaped the chapters of the book. I had, more or less, devised a series of topics that interested me—or that I thought might interest others—but this plan eventually gave way to the stories that I collected. Thus, the interviews "drove" the research. After a point, I devised more pointed questions in interviews, but even these were drawn by some topical lacunae that developed from previous and free-form interviews.

To be sure, there is a decided Slovak "tilt" to my research. I lived and taught university in Slovakia for nearly three years, I have greater familiarity with Slovakia than the Czech Republic, and my understanding of Slovak language is better than my knowledge of Czech. However, I found numerous Czechs willing to commit to this project; I interviewed them in Brussels, Prague, Luxembourg, Brno, Bratislava, Heidelberg, and online. I am eternally grateful to them.

Western readers of these interviews may be influenced (if not prejudiced) by the leading narratives of the post–Cold War Western world. Democracy won, oppression lost. How one accepts those narratives can influence our historical perspective as well as our sense of the present. Residents of Czechoslovakia from the Second World War era experienced a different narrative. They lived through the events of 1939 when the West seemingly abandoned a "backwater of Europe" to the greater goals of appeasement with Nazi Germany. Rarely does the West acknowledge the deep and lasting effect of this profound event. Second, in 1956, Hungary was all but abandoned to Russia when the Nagy regime attempted modest reforms within the communist rubric. Where was America in 1956? Where was the West? Americans and Western Europeans may choose to forget these inconvenient events, but, do so at their own peril. Easterners remember the 1948 "coup" in Czechoslovakia when the Communists seized power. But they also remember that, at the time, the Communists were the most popular party in the country. They also recall 1968 when the aspirations of reform communism were stamped out by diktat from Moscow, supported by most of their neighbors, and totally unassisted by allies in the West.

The "dirty little secret" about Communism in Czechoslovakia is that, at least for a time in the 1960s and early 1970s, it delivered the goods economically and even socially. Doubtless, there was corruption, unfairness, and sham "democratic" institutions. But if one asks whether the standard of living was acceptable for the major part of the population, one would have to respond in the affirmative. There is a second point—that Eastern European history has not been a linear phenomenon. Although this point may be stating the obvious to historians, central Eastern Europe experienced in relatively short order invasion, repeated occupation both during and after World War II, the extreme ideologies of fascism and communism, followed by a harsh and rapid transition to a market economy. Third, it is simply a logical error to assess Eastern Europe as a monolith. Tempting though it might be from the decades old narratives from the West, "Eastern Europe" never really existed as such. Czechoslovakia must be seen through the lens of its own history, culture, and relations with its neighbors. On specific policy or social issues, Czechs and Slovaks live in their own narrative, one not readily familiar to a Western audience. Czechoslovakia was a mid-sized, land locked new country, created after World War I, but with a high degree of industrialization, particularly in the Czech territories. Modern democratic principles were established from 1918, but the experience of historical hostility and domination by neighboring powers was and remains today part of the collective DNA.

Work was a central function of Czechoslovak life—in both practical and ideological terms. Everyone worked, and unemployment was unknown. Goods were priced to be affordable, and gender policies were generally progressive—albeit with numerous inconsistencies. Money was less of a factor than stability. Cash was non-convertible, and major purchases were determined more typically by who one knew and what they could barter. The black market, whether accessed through Tuzeks or by individual connections with a local merchant, was the way things were done, and everyone knew it. A timely hospital surgery was typically planned through a significant "gift" to the surgeon, and to others who could "grease the wheels" of a dysfunctional, lopsided, corrupted system that was, technically, designed to serve all equally.

Czechoslovakia maintained, by world standards, a high standard of living throughout the post-war period. In fact, by the 1970s, official policy was to "placate" the private sphere with material comfort, while maintaining a rigid political regime. For a time, it worked. In fact, the high material comfort that Czechs experienced was a source of displeasure for none other than Václav Havel, who saw the population being "bought off" with crass materialism, at the price of increased obedience to the status quo.

Although it might be tempting to see Communist Czechoslovakia as a culture deeply tinged with cynicism, it is probably more accurate to see social and economic life as a series of pragmatic concessions to a system that was accepted for what it was, rather than what it *said* it was. Czechs and Slovaks were conditioned from an early age to understand society and government as a series of layers of interpretation—some real, some rhetorical. As noted by several interviewees, this "adaptive" strategy had the advantage of creating smart citizens who could "see between the lines" of proclamation and effect. Given that truth is the first casualty of war and politics, a culture of healthy skepticism might have functioned as a positive attribute.

More important was what the system *did* than what it called itself. Economics might have been the Party's strong suit, but when political and social freedoms were demanded, the system responded. Moscow, in what might be seen as a reassertion of its historical sphere of influence prerogatives, threw down the gauntlet and re-established its authority. But look carefully at how they did what they did in 1968: there existed little overt Russian presence on the streets, and respect for local authority was encouraged. The Czechs too, avoided violent confrontation with Russian troops, viewing them more as victims than as aggressors. Perhaps most difficult for Western audiences to fathom is the sense of betrayal that Czechs felt towards the Russians. Russia was held in high esteem by many Czechs. Russians were not the bogeymen from the East, but were the historical protectors of the Czech lands, the liberators from fascism, and they had now transformed into conquerors.

It would be a serious mistake to consign the Communist Party and the phenomenon of communism to the historical dustbin, particularly with regard to the Czech Republic. Unlike its neighbors Poland, Hungary, and Slovakia, the Czech Communist Party has maintained a stable foundation since 1990 and has remained a presence in the lower house for the entire period. Further, as recently as 2004, the Communist Party won 20 percent of the national vote.[3]

The Czechoslovak Communist Party was not outlawed after the revolution of 1989. In fact, there was a consensus, voiced by many, including Václav Havel, that the Party should be permitted a continued existence, based on the belief at the time that it would wither and die on its own within a few elections. This did not happen. The Party has continued to influence contemporary politics even though membership numbers are closer to 50,000 today—a far cry from the 1.5 million members in the late 1980s. (At that time, the Party comprised a staggering 10 percent of the entire population of Czechoslovakia.) A Prague radio broadcast from 2015 looks back at the Party in a 26-year anniversary retrospective:

> Many Party members held out hope in 1989 that their time would return in the future, but others held a more pessimistic perspective. There were people who left the Party in 1989 and 1990 because they wanted to follow their careers and spat in their own faces.
>
> There were others who left the Party because they were frustrated. But there were others who understood that this was not the end of history.[4]

The present-day Party is described as both conservative and elitist, insofar as it references the system of an earlier period: "They are not a genuine workers' party, they are not linked to the lower classes of society.... It is more of a party of former bureaucrats and pensioners."[5] The contemporary Czech Communist Party has been described as both nationalist and self-centered. Some consider it to be a last remaining vestige of pan–Slavism and pro–Russian sentiment.

The research presented here allows for a glimpse into the complexities associated with experience and memory in the former Czechoslovakia. Traditional Western efforts to paint the Warsaw Pact nations with a common brush must continue to give way to a more complex, nuanced understanding of internal tensions within communist regimes—as well as the evolution of those regimes into more progressive or reactionary entities. As the historical place assigned to communism continues to evolve, it is hoped that continued research will shed light into an increasing number of past phenomena associated with that old regime.

Finally, both traditional and contemporary support for the communist project, or for some limited aspects of it, should never be underestimated. A certain core has remained faithful to the legacy of the Communists, both in the Czech Republic and in Slovakia, although they have been manifested in somewhat different ways. Support continues for the Party through 2017, commensurate with the new pressures and disunities within the EU regarding immigration policy and rising nationalism. The persistent, lingering sentimentality for the old order, or at least elements of it, suggests that a continued examination of the communist era will prove invaluable in informing both the present and the future.

Chapter Notes

Introduction

1. In fact, Red-baiting in American politics long predated the Cold War. But the exigencies of the post-war world generated an urgency and a new power to the rhetoric and themes.

2. Slavenka Drakulić, *Café Europa: Life After Communism* (New York: Penguin, 1996), and *How We Survived Communism and Even Laughed* (New York: W.W. Norton, 1991).

3. James Krapfl, *Revolution with a Human Face: Politics, Culture and Community in Czechoslovakia 1989–1992* (Ithaca: Cornell University Press, 2013).

4. Padraic Kenney, *A Carnival of Revolution: Central Europe 1989* (Princeton: Princeton University Press, 2003).

5. Mary Heimann, *Czechoslovakia: The State That Failed* (New Haven: Yale University Press, 2009).

6. Kevin McDermott, *Communist Czechoslovakia, 1945–89: A Political and Social History* (Basingstoke: Palgrave Macmillan, 2015).

7. Jana Hensel, *After the Wall* (New York: Public Affairs Press, 2004), p. 90.

8. Staughton Lynd, "Oral History from Below," *Oral History Review* 21, no. 1 (Spring 1993), p. 6.

9. *Ibid.*

10. Bradley Adams, *The Struggle for the Soul of the Nation* (Lanham, MD: Rowman & Littlefield, 2004).

11. Paulina Bren, *The Greengrocer and His TV: The Culture of Communism After the 1968 Prague Spring* (Ithaca: Cornell University Press, 2010); Paulina Bren and Mary Neuberger, *Communism Unwrapped* (Oxford: Oxford University Press, 2012); John Connelly, *Captive University: The Sovietization of East German, Czech, and Polish Higher Education, 1945–1956* (Chapel Hill: University of North Carolina Press, 2000).

12. Miroslav Vaněk, *Velvet Revolutions: An Oral History of Czech Society* (Oxford: Oxford University Press, 2016).

13. John Mueller, "What Was the Cold War About? Evidence from Its Ending," *Political Science Quarterly* (Winter 2004), 1–3.

14. "The Cold War Historiography," 1–2. Accessed January 3, 2010, http://www.spiritus-emporis.com/cold-war/historiography.html.

15. William H. Kautt, "Communism After WWII," *History in Dispute*, p. 3. Accessed September 1, 2006, http://galenet.galegroup.comeproxy.umuc.edu.

16. Slavenka Drakulić, *How We Survived Communism and Even Laughed* (New York: W.W. Norton, 1992), and *Café Europa* (New York: Penguin, 1996).

17. Gil Eyal, "Identity and Trauma: Two Forms of the Will to Memory," *History and Memory* 16, no. 1 (2004), p. 5.

18. Greg Barrow, "South Africans Rec-

onciled?" BBC News, Friday, 30 October 1998. http://news.bbc.co.uk/2/hi/special_report/1998/10/98/truth_and_reconcilia tion/142673.stm.

Chapter One

1. Daniel Kubát, "Social Mobility in Czechoslovakia," *American Sociological Review* 28, no. 2 (April 1963), pp. 203–212. Published by American Sociological Association, stable URL: http://www.jstor.org/stable/2090607, pp. 203–207.

2. *Ibid.*, p. 206.

3. A few words on extant Cold War Czech labor law helps to place the reality of the workplace into proper perspective: On June 16, 1965, the National Assembly passed Law No. 65, the new labor code, which unified the "socialist" labor relations of the country. Many diverse laws and regulations from the previous two decades were brought into one uniform system. The new code improved job security by enumerating the specific reasons that an employer might terminate an employee; the 1945 presidential decree on obligatory labor was laid to rest—this measure was a post–World War II effort to prevent employees from "endangering national security" by changing jobs without going through proper channels, such as obtaining the permission of the manpower department of the district national committee. Vacation time was increased under the 1965 law by one week. Apprentices would received four calendar weeks of vacation, and "apprentices working underground" would receive five weeks. Trade unions, however, found that by agreeing to the new labor code, that they forfeited certain previously-held rights. For example, they would give up their right to have a say in the hiring of new employees. They would retain the right to prior approval over dismissals. In the case of contested dismissals, however, unions would no longer act as an arbitration board, as all cases would be referred directly to the courts. (Czechoslovakia had no purely "labor" courts at this time.) Further, the new legislation would limit the amount of overtime work by an employee in a year to 150 hours—down from 240—unless a trade union applied for an exception. Finally, the new legislation would better police unexcused work absences by cutting accrued leave by up to three days for every work day missed.

"The Czechoslovak Labor Code" (Open Society Archives, Radio Free Europe Research, Country Series, 10/15/65), pp. 1–2.

4. Frank Pohl, "Environmental Deterioration in Czechoslovakia" (Open Society Archives, Radio Free Europe Research, 5/6/83), p. 1.

5. *Ibid.*, pp. 3, 4, 5. The first of these measures was Law No. 20, passed in March of 1966, concerned with the "People's Health." The legislation required all places of employment to take measures to provide a healthy and safe work environment for its employees. Punitive sanctions were set up to punish transgressors; superior agencies would be charged with implementing the law. Managers and "leading workers" would bear *personal* responsibility for enforcement of the legal provisions in the field. Following Law 20 were a trio of "special" laws passed between April 1967 and October 1977. Law No. 35 dealt with the quality and purity of air and replaced an earlier law from 1960. Employers who polluted the air beyond certain strict limits would be subjected to fines. (Oddly, factories with high smokestacks were exempt from the provisions, ignoring their impact on populations outside of the immediate areas.) The second reform law, Law No. 138 of October 1973, focused on water quality. This legislation was significant, as Czechoslovakia lay on the European water divide, and most waters flowed out of the country; sanctions were stipulated for violations against surface or subterranean water violations. The third of the laws, No. 6, from October 1977, was concerned with the protection of forests. It eclipsed a previous law from 1960; gas and solid emissions would be controlled so as to protect forested areas; restoration of affected areas was also a feature of this legislation.

6. *Životní Prostředí* 6 (November–December 1982), p. 332.

7. Pohl, *Environmental Deterioration in Czechoslovakia*, p. 2. Law No. 35 of 1967

established a state regulatory agency called the Technical Inspectorate Against Air Pollution, which had the power to levy fines against violations. However, in the first ten years of the agency's existence, a mere 55 million Czech crowns were collected as fines. Factories came to realize that it was cheaper to pay fines than to abide by regulations and invest in pollution controls.

8. *Ibid.*, p. 3.

9. *Ibid.*, pp. 4, 5, 6. Approximately ⅔ of Czechoslovakia's power, by 1983, was provided by coal mined from northern Bohemia. Trees also weakened from airborne chemicals in significant numbers through the late 1970s and early 1980s, to the point that spraying from airplanes had to be employed (popularly called "chemistry versus chemistry") to stem the problem.

10. Sonia Winter, "The Sovietization of Czechoslovakia: 1968–1983" (Open Society Archives, Radio Free Europe Research, 8/16/83), p. 4.

11. Interview with Pavol F., May 24, 2010, Košice.

12. Interview with Zora V. and Diana S., June 20, 2009, Bratislava.

13. Interview with Beáta, Banská Bystrica, October 21, 2010.

14. *Ibid.*

15. *Ibid.*

16. Interview with Tomáš K., Prešov, Slovakia, May 23, 2010.

17. *Ibid.*

18. *Ibid.* In one earlier instance, Tomáš was asked to give approval to a batch of medicine that was known to be slightly defective, which he refused to do. A colleague, however, who was willing to grant such approval, later spent two years in prison after having been exposed.

19. Winter, *The Sovietization of Czechoslovakia*, p. 3.

20. Interview with Pavol V., Brussels, Belgium, July 6, 2009.

21. *Ibid.*

22. *Ibid.*

23. *Ibid.*

24. *Ibid.*

25. Interview with Lucia, Brussels, Belgium, May 12, 2017.

26. Interview with Jakub, Brussels, Belgium, May 12, 2017.

27. Mita Kastle-Kanerová and Alena Valterová, "Interview with Elena Valterová, Founder of the Women and Mothers Party," *Feminist Review* 39 (Autumn 1991), pp. 161–165.

28. *Ibid.*

29. *Ibid.*, pp. 162–164.

30. Interview with Dano, Prešov, October 24, 2010.

31. Interview with Suzanna, Bratislava, June 20, 2009.

32. Interview with Július R., Košice, October 22, 2010.

33. Interview with Ela K., Casteau, Belgium, June 18, 2008.

34. Interview with Soňa C., Prešov, October 23, 2010.

35. H.P. Kolár, "Some Problems Confronting Czechoslovakia's Youth" (Radio Free Europe Evaluation and Analysis Department, Czechoslovak Unit, 1960), p. 1.

36. *Ibid.*

37. *Ibid.*, p. 2.

38. Interview with Vierka S., January 23, 2012, Bratislava.

39. *Ibid.*

40. *Ibid.*

41. *Ibid.*

42. *Ibid.*

43. *Ibid.* Vierka mentions that the dominant school of psychiatry in Slovakia during the 1970s and 1980s was classical German theory, with less emphasis on Freud, Jung and psychodynamic theory. Budapest, she notes, was a center of psychodynamic thought, as well as some of the larger Czech cities—but less so in Bratislava, where she practiced.

Chapter Two

1. Joseph Hraba, Rehan Mullick, Frederick O. Lorenz, Jiří Večerník, Allan McCutcheon, "Education and Support for the Czech Reforms," *Sociology of Education* 75, no. 2 (April 2002), pp. 150–151.

2. *Ibid.*

3. The author.

4. *Ibid.*

5. Interview with Luba S., Brussels, Belgium, April 5, 2009.

6. Interview with Zora V., Bratislava, June 20, 2009.

7. *Ibid.*
8. Interview with Vierka S., January 23, 2012, Bratislava, Slovakia.
9. *Ibid.*
10. Martin Kreidl, "Politics and Secondary School Tracking in Socialist Czechoslovakia,1948–1989," *European Sociological Review* 20, no. 21 (April 2004), pp. 123–139. DOI: 10.1093/esr/jch008, available online at www.esr.oupjournals.org.
11. *Ibid.*, p. 127.
12. *Ibid.*
13. The author.
14. *Ibid.*
15. Interview with Jana K., Banská Bystrica, Slovakia, May 2010, and Petra K., Prešov, Slovakia, May 1999.
16. Interview with Beáta, October 21, 2010, Banská Bystrica.
17. Interview with Jaro, Prešov, October 24, 2010.
18. Interview with Patricia L., Luxembourg, October 14, 2013.
19. Interview with Jaro T., Bratislava, December 2014.
20. Interview with Zuzana P., Bratislava, June 20, 2009.
21. John Connelly, *Captive University: The Sovietization of East German, Czech and Polish Higher Education, 1945–1956* (Chapel Hill: University of North Carolina Press, 2000).
22. Author's note: Friends, peers and colleagues recounted stories of hidden cameras in offices as well as assumed identities, i.e., "undercover" names for informers. These were said to be most common in English language departments and the social sciences, particularly government and political theory.
23. Interview with J.S., Prešov, Slovakia, September 1997.
24. Christopher P. Loss, "Party School: Education, Political Ideology and the Cold War," *Journal of Policy History* 16, no. 1 (2004), pp. 5–6.
25. *Ibid.*, 6.
26. History Resources Center, "Soviet Troops Withdraw from Czechoslovakia, February 26, 1990." Accessed September 1, 2006, p.1. http://galenet.galegroup.com.ezproxy.umuc.edu/servlet/History/hits?r=d&origSearch=fa.
27. Interview with Jiří B., Heidelberg, August 1, 2009.
28. Interview with Beáta, Banská Bystrica, October 21, 2010.
29. Interview with Ela K., Casteau, Belgium, June 18, 2008.
30. Interview with Pavol V., Brussels, Belgium, July 6, 2009.
31. Interview with Zuzana P., Bratislava, June 20, 2009.
32. Interview with Tomas K., Šarišské Michal'any, May 23, 2010.
33. *Ibid.*
34. Interview with Sylvia, Bratislava, June 19, 2009.
35. H.P. Kolár, "The Problem of 'Academic Mortality' in Czechoslovakia's Universities" (Radio Free Europe Evaluation and Analysis Department, 12/21/60), p. 1.
36. *Ibid.*
37. *Ibid.*, p. 2.
38. *Ibid.*, p. 4.
39. *Ibid.*, p. 3.
40. *Ibid.*, p. 4.
41. Jindra Kulich, "Adult Education in Czechoslovakia 1948–1965," *Comparative Education Review* 11, no 2 (January 1967), pp. 235–240.
42. Martin Kriedal, "Politics and Secondary School Tracking in Socialist Czechoslovakia 1948–1989," *European Sociological Review*, Vol. 20, no 2, (April 2004), p. 137.
43. *Ibid.*

Chapter Three

1. In fact, the folk movement would seem to run counter to the Communist ideological project regarding—among other things—modern social class consciousness.
2. This organization was a rough equivalent to the Boy Scouts and Girl Scouts and will be described in greater detail later.
3. Anna K., interview April 11, 2013, by phone, from Aviano, Italy.
4. Cris T., interview September 9, 2009, Leuven, Belgium.
5. Mila, interview in Brussels, Belgium, September 16, 2011.
6. Miroslav Vaněk, *Velvet Revolutions:*

An Oral History of Czech Society (Oxford: Oxford University Press, 2016), pp. 47–48.

7. *Ibid.*, pp. 47–50.

8. *Ibid.*, pp. 45–50.

9. Rita R., interview in Prešov, Slovakia, 2010.

10. Thomas Land, "Coping with Communism's Grim Legacy of High Rise Buildings," *Contemporary Review* 280, no. 1637 (June 2002), p. 355.

11. *Ibid.*, pp. 356–357.

12. *Ibid.* Two hundred thousand of these high rise units exist in Budapest, and more than 280,000 in Berlin. (Note: While I was writing this manuscript, the aged mother of a friend jumped to her death in Petržalka, in 2010.)

13. L'uba S., interviewed May 3, 2009, Brussels, Belgium.

14. Beáta, interview in Banská Bystrica, Slovakia, October 21, 2010.

15. Paul V., interview July 11, 2009, Brussels, Belgium

16. Paul V., interview July 6, 2009, Brussels, Belgium.

17. Paul V., interview July 11, 2009, Brussels, Belgium.

18. *Ibid.*

19. John M. Kramer, "Drug Abuse in Eastern Europe: An Emerging Issue of Public Policy," *Slavic Review* 49, no. 1 (Spring 1990), pp. 20–21.

20. *Ibid.*

21. Paul V., interview July 11, 2009, Brussels, Belgium.

22. *Ibid.*

23. *Ibid.*

24. "Trial of Czechoslovak Jazz Section Imminent" (Open Society Archives, Radio Free Europe Research, Country Series, 12/22/86), p. 1.

25. *Ibid.*, p. 2

26. *Ibid.*, pp. 2–3.

27. *Ibid.*, pp. 1–2.

28. Vierka S., interview Bratislava, January 23, 2012.

29. *Ibid.*

30. *Ibid.*

31. *Ibid.*

32. "The New Czech Dramatic Avant-Garde" (Open Society Archives, Radio Free Europe Research, 2/17/65), pp. 1–3.

33. *Ibid.*, p. 4.

34. *Ibid.*, p. 5.

35. *Ibid.*, pp. 4–9

36. *Ibid.*, p. 9.

37. *Ibid.*, p. 10.

38. *Ibid.*

39. Paula Bren, *The Greengrocer and His TV* (Ithaca: Cornell University Press, 2010), pp. 12–17.

40. *Ibid.*, pp. 15–17.

41. This is a tradition that has continued to this day in parts of the former Czechoslovakia.

42. Interview with Miloš Forman, January 18, 1997, Episode 14, *Red Spring*, Alexander Street Press, alexanderstreet.com, 2009, p. 6.

43. *Ibid.*

44. *Ibid.*, p. 2.

45. *Ibid.*, p. 3.

46. *Ibid.*, pp. 3–4.

47. Richard Porton, "Porn Again: The People vs. Larry Flynt: An Interview with Miloš Forman on Censorship and his Years in Stalinist Czechoslovakia," *Cineaste* 22, no. 4 (March 1997), pp. 1–2.

48. Sheila Johnston, interview with Jiří Menzel, *Sight and Sound* 18, no. 6 (June 2008), pp. 1–2.

49. *Ibid.*

50. Peter Hames, "Down from the Mountain," interview with Juraj Jakubisko, *Sight and Sound* 14, no. 3 (March 2004), pp. 1–2.

51. *Ibid.*, pp. 2–3.

52. *Ibid.*

53. Michael Brooke, Video Recording Review, *Sight and Sound* 16 (June 2006), p. 88.

54. Interview with Ivana T., Iowa City, IA, December 2014.

55. Andrew Lass, "The King of May: A Conversation Between Allen Ginsberg and Andrew Lass, March 23, 1986," *Massachusetts Review* 39, no. 2 (Summer 1998), p. 169. It is interesting to note that Cuban laws limiting local national access to foreigners was couched in protective language; Cubans were not permitted to "bother" foreigners while they visited Cuba.

56. *Ibid.*, pp. 171–173.

57. *Ibid.*, pp. 172–173.

58. *Ibid.*

59. *Ibid.*, pp. 176–179.

Chapter Four

1. Miroslav Vaněk, *Velvet Revolutions: An Oral History of Czech Society* (Oxford: Oxford University Press, 2016), pp. 185–187. Interview with Jana L.

2. *Ibid.*, p. 189.

3. Interview with Juraj K., Prešov, Slovakia, November 30, 2014.

4. Interview with Pavol S., Prešov, Slovakia, November 23, 2010.

5. Paula Bren and Mary Neuburger, eds., *Communism Unwrapped* (Oxford: Oxford University Press, 2012), pp. 27–30.

6. *Ibid.*, pp. 28–36.

7. Interview with Zora V., June 20, 2009, Bratislava, Slovakia, and June 25, 2010, Prague, Czech Republic.

8. Interview with Lucia, Brussels, Belgium, May 12, 2017.

9. *Známosti* was the term used for "connections" to items through a friendly intermediary.

10. Pavol V. interviewed in Brussels, Belgium, July 6, 2009.

11. Zora V. interviewed in Bratislava, Slovakia, June 20, 2009.

12. Online interview with Peter D., March 14, 2015.

13. Interview with Mirka and Alica, Banská Bystrica, Slovakia, October 21, 2011.

14. *Ibid.*

15. Online interview with Peter D., March 14, 2015.

16. *Slovak Publicist Speaks up for the Consumer by Trend* (Open Society Archives, Background Report, 5/28/65), p. 1.

17. *Ibid.*, p. 2.

18. *Ibid.*, pp. 2–3. "Return to Economic 'Normalcy' in Czechoslovakia" (Open Society Archives, Radio Free Europe Research, 6/22/70), p. 5.

19. "The Problem of Excess Purchasing Power in Czechoslovakia" (Open Society Archives, Radio Free Europe Research, 8/3/65), pp. 1–2.

20. "Novotny on Economic Reforms" (Open Society Archives, Radio Free Europe Research, 1965), pp. 1–2.

21. "Implementation of Czechoslovak Economic Reforms" (Open Society Archives, Radio Free Europe Research, 11/11/65), pp. 1–2.

22. Zora V., June 20, 2009.

23. *Ibid.*

24. *Ibid.*

25. *Ibid.*, p. 191.

26. *Ibid.*, pp. 192–93.

27. *Ibid.*, p. 200.

28. *Ibid.*

29. *Ibid.*, pp. 203–204.

30. *Ibid.*, p. 207.

31. *Ibid.*, p. 21.

32. Miroslav Vaněk, *Velvet Revolutions: An Oral History of Czech Society*, Oxford Oral History Series (Oxford: Oxford University Press, 2016), Kindle, p. 163, interview with O.O.

33. Open Society Archives, *Lidová demokracie, 24 August, 1967.*

34. *Ibid.* Overseas visits by Czechs and Slovaks increased by nearly 25 percent between 1965 and 1967, with a modest increase toward capitalist countries.

35. Dorina, interviewed in Bratislava, Slovakia, June 20, 2009.

36. Juraj K, interviewed in Prešov, Slovakia, November 20, 2014.

37. Zora V, interviewed in Bratislava, June 20, 2009.

38. Juraj K, interviewed in Prešov, Slovakia, November 30, 2014.

39. *Ibid.*

40. Patrícia L, interviewed October 14, 2013, Luxembourg City, Luxembourg.

41. Mirka and Alica, interviewed in Banksá Bystrica, Slovakia, October 21, 2011.

42. *Ibid.*

43. *Ibid.*

44. *Ibid.*

45. *Ibid.*

46. *Ibid.*

47. *Ibid.*

48. Jana T, interviewed December 2014, Iowa City, IA.

49. Peter Bischoff, "Limonadovy Joe; or the Western in Czechoslovakia," *Journal of Popular Culture* 27, no. 1 (1993), pp. 23–24.

50. *Ibid.*, p. 26.

51. Paulina Bren, *Closely Watched Screens: Ideology and Everyday Life in Czechoslovakia after the Prague Spring*, dissertation, New York University, 2002, pp. 171–172.

52. Paula Bren, *The Greengrocer and*

His TV (Ithaca: Cornell University Press, 2010), pp. 109–111. Bren's account draws extensively from serials, documentaries, and other presentations in the late socialist period.

53. *Ibid.*, pp. 7–9.

54. *Ibid.*, pp. 114–120.

55. *Ibid.*, pp. 263, 176.

56. *Ibid.*, p. 184.

57. However, the one company that produced television antennae for such purposes (a Pilsen firm) was, for reasons unknown shut down in the 1970s after an "anti-aerial" campaign, which asked people to voluntarily refrain from watching Western programming and turn in their aerial antennas.

58. Bren, *The Greengrocer*, pp. 261–267.

59. *Ibid.*, 262.

60. *Ibid.*, p. 269.

61. Beáta, interviewed in Banská Bystrica, November 27, 2014.

Chapter Five

1. Ela K., interviewed in Casteau, Belgium, June 2008.

2. Phone interview with Peter D., March 14, 2015.

3. *Ibid.*

4. Jana T., interviewed December 2014, Iowa City, IA.

5. Zora V. interviewed in Bratislava, June 20, 2009.

6. Online Interview with Ivana T., June 10, 2017.

7. Pavol, interviewed in Bratislava, October 23, 2010.

8. *Ibid.*

9. Zora V., interviewed in Prague, June 20, 2009.

10. Soňa C., interviewed in Prešov, October 23, 2010.

11. *Ibid.*

12. Patricia L., interviewed October 13, 2014, Luxembourg City, Luxembourg.

13. Janka T., interview December 2014, Iowa City, IA.

14. Beáta, interviewed at Banská Bystrica, November 27, 2014.

15. *Ibid.*

16. Juraj K, interviewed November 30, 2014, Prešov.

17. *Ibid.*

18. Institute of Marxism–Leninism of the CPCz and Institute of Marxist–Leninism of the CPS CC, *An Outline of the History of the CPCz* (Prague: Orbis Press Agency, 1985), p. 393.

19. *Ibid.*

20. *Ibid.*, p. 394.

21. *Ibid.*, p. 395.

22. *Ibid.*

23. *Ibid.*, pp. 297–298, 300.

24. *Ibid.*, p. 304.

25. *Ibid.*, p. 396.

26. Vladimir Macura, *The Mystifications of a Nation* (Madison: University of Wisconsin Press, 2010), p. 53.

27. *Ibid.*, p. 56.

28. *Ibid.*, pp. 57–58.

29. Jiří Kubka, "*Americký brouk*," *Lidové noviny* 58, no. 161 (July 12, 1950), 3, in V. Macura, *The Mystification of a Nation*, p. 56.

30. Interview with Soňa C., October 23, 2010.

31. Macura, *Mystifications*, p. 59.

32. Sabrina Ramet, "UFOs over Eastern Europe and Russia," *Journal of Popular Culture* 32 (1998), p. 3. *Paranoia* is one of several recurrent themes represented in both Eastern and Western recollections of the Cold War.

33. *Ibid.*

34. Macura, *Mystifications*, p. 62.

35. *Ibid.*, p. 65.

36. Ibid., p. 66.

37. *Ibid.*, p. 67.

38. Interview with Pavol, Prešov, 2010.

39. *Ibid.* Interestingly, although this was, in fact, a kindergarten joke told by teachers to students, and by students to each other, Pavol was forbidden to tell this joke at home or to friends by his father.

40. *Ibid.*

41. Vladimír V. Kusín, "The Seven Wonders for Communism" (Radio Free Europe Background Report, 12/12/85).

42. Jan C., interviewed in Praha, January 27, 2012.

43. Miroslav Vaněk, *Velvet Revolutions: An Oral History of Czech Society* (Oxford: Oxford University Press, 2016), p. 177. Interview with Jan H.

44. *Ibid.*, pp. 179–182.

45. Online interview with Jana T., October 2014, describing stories of her mother.

46. Interview with Soňa C, October 23, 2010.
47. Interview with Petra K, Tienen, Belgium, 2008.
48. Interview with Ivana T., June 10, 2017.
49. Interview with Jan C., Praha, January 27, 2012.
50. *Ibid.*
51. *Ibid.*

Chapter Six

1. Heda Margolius Kovaly, *Under a Cruel Star: Life in Prague 1941–68* (New York: Holmes and Meier, 1986), p. 158.
2. Matthew Frost, "Czech Republic: A Chronology of Events Leading to the 1968 Invasion" (Radio Free Europe, Radio Liberty, 8/9/98). Accessed 2/27/11, http://www.rferl. org/content/article/1089303.html.
3. *Ibid.*
4. *Ibid.*
5. Ithiel De Sola Pool, "Public Opinion in Czechoslovakia," *The Public Opinion Quarterly* 34, no. 1 (Spring 1970), p. 24.
6. *Ibid.*, 11, 20.
7. Pat Lyons, *Mass and Elite Attitudes During the Prague Spring Era: Importance and Legacy* (Prague: Institute of Sociology AV CR, 2009). Reviewed in *Sociologický časopis/Czech Sociological Review* 47, no. 6 (2011), pp. 1230–1231.
8. *Ibid.*, pp. 1231–1232.
9. *Ibid.*, pp. 1230–1232.
10. Matthew Frost, "Czech Republic: A Chronology of Events Leading to the 1968 Invasion" (Radio Free Europe, Radio Liberty, 8/9/98). Accessed 2/27/11, http://www.rferl. org/content/article/1089303.html.
11. *Ibid.*
12. Julia Friday, *Czechoslovakia from the Prague Spring to the Velvet Revolution: The Composition of Memory, Public Record and Archive*, Dissertation, State University of New York, Binghamton, 2010, pp. 138, 139. Slogans included "Occupants—What Did Lenin Teach You?"; "Only with You, Traitors Beware"; "Long Live Dubček."
13. *Ibid.*, pp. 140–141.
14. *Ibid.*
15. *Ibid.*
16. Paulina Bren, *The Greengrocer and His TV* (Ithaca: Cornell University Press, 2010), p. 25.
17. Interview with Vladimír, Košice, May 24, 2010.
18. *Ibid.*
19. Interview with Jan G., October 20, 2011, Bratislava.
20. Miroslav Vaněk, *Velvet Revolutions: An Oral History of Czech Society* (Oxford: Oxford University Press, 2016), p. 11.
21. *Ibid.*
22. Friday, *Czechoslovakia from the Prague Spring*, p. 137.
23. Interview with Beáta, Banská Bystrica, October 21, 2010.
24. Interview with Soňa C, October 23, 2010, Prešov.
25. Interview with Július, Košice, October 22, 2010.
26. Online interview with Ivana T., March 16, 2015.
27. Interview with Ela, Casteau, Belgium, June 18, 2008.
28. Interview with Zuzana, June 20, 2009, Bratislava.
29. Interview with Tomáš K, Šarišské Michel′any, May 23, 2010.
30. *Ibid.*
31. Miroslav Vaněk, *Velvet Revolutions: An Oral History of Czech Society* (Oxford: Oxford University Press, 2016), p. 25.
32. Interview with Lívia, June 2, 2017, Brussels, Belgium.
33. Paulina Bren, *The Greengrocer and His TV* (Ithaca: Cornell University Press, 2010), p. 29.
34. Ján G., interviewed in Bratislava, October 20, 2011.
35. Friday, *Czechoslovakia from the Prague Spring*, p. 125.
36. *Ibid.*
37. *Ibid.*, p. 126.
38. Noam Chomsky, *Understanding Power: The Indispensable Chomsky* (New York: New Press, 2001). "Brainwashing" was a widely accepted concept throughout the west by the mid–1950s. FBI Director J. Edgar Hoover penned a book in 1958 detailing the methods and results of Communist conspirators both domestically and abroad. Hoover described the "soulless social cog" created by Communist indoctrination, discipline, and education,

and his work topped the *New York Times* non-fiction best seller list. Hoover's conceptions of Communism were significant, as they pointed to a threat that was more profound than mere ideology—in fact, the fate of humanity was at stake. The cultural resonance to such concerns was pronounced, and fear of the "loss of the national soul" was particularly significant in evangelical communities, launching the careers of such preachers as Billy Graham, Carl McIntire, and Billy James Hargis. Numerous religious leaders, as well as secularists, believed that the West was engaged in a global holy war.

39. Jiří B., interviewed in Heidelberg, Germany, August 1, 2009.

40. *Ibid.*

41. David R, interviewed November 27, 2014, Bratislava.

42. Jana T., interviewed in Iowa City, IA, December 2014.

43. Melissa Harris, "Invasion 68: Prague by Joseph Koudelka, Interview with Melissa Harris," *Aperture* 192 (Fall 2008), pp. 22–27.

44. *Ibid.*

45. *Ibid.*

46. *Ibid.*

47. *Ibid.*

Chapter Seven

1. Zvi Gitelman, "The Politics of Socialist Restoration in Hungary and Czechoslovakia," *Comparative Politics* 13, no. 2 (January 1981), p. 189.

2. *Ibid.*

3. Fred H. Eidlin, "'Capitulation,' 'Resistance' and the Framework of Normalization: The August 1968 Invasion of Czechoslovakia and the Czechoslovak Response," *Journal of Peace Research* 18, no. 4 (1981), pp. 320–321.

4. *Ibid.*, p. 322.

5. *Ibid.*, p. 326.

6. *Ibid.*, p. 330.

7. Paulina Bren, *Closely Watched Screens: Ideology and Everyday Life in Czechoslovakia after the Prague Spring*, Dissertation, New York University, 2002, p. 200.

8. Zvi Gitelman, "The Politics of Socialist Restoration in Hungary and Czechoslovakia," *Comparative Politics* 13, no. 2 (January 1981), p. 191.

9. Interview with Jan G., Bratislava, October 21, 2011. Both G. Husák and L. Svoboda had been imprisoned earlier in the Czechoslovak Communist regime for alleged crimes against the party.

10. Paulina Bren, *The Greengrocer and His TV* (Ithaca: Cornell University Press, 2010), p. 33.

11. Antonín Kratochvil, "The Cultural Scene in Czechoslovakia" (Open Society Archives, Radio Free Europe Research, 2/3/70), pp. 1–2.

12. Interview with L'udmila M., in Miroslav Vaněk, *Velvet Revolutions: An Oral History of Czech Society* (Oxford: Oxford University 2010).

13. *Ibid.*, p. 12., interview with Iva K.

14. *Ibid.*, pp. 2, 3.

15. *Ibid.*

16. *Ibid.*, p. 5.

17. *Ibid.*, p. 6.

18. S.A. Winter, "The Sovietization of Czechoslovakia: 1968–1983" (Open Society Archives, Radio Free Europe Research, 8/16/83), pp. 1–2.

19. *Ibid.*, pp. 1, 2.

20. *Ibid.*, p. 3.

21. Mary Heimann, *Czechoslovakia: The State That Failed* (New Haven: Yale University Press, 2011), Kindle, location 7190–7197.

22. *Ibid.*, location 7490–7517.

23. Michael T. Kaufman, "Good Times Help Czechs Subdue Trauma of '68," Special to *the New York Times*, February 10, 1986: A-1.

24. *Ibid.*

25. Miroslav Vaněk, *Velvet Revolutions: An Oral History of Czech Society* (Oxford: Oxford University Press, 2016), pp. 19–20, interview with H.D.

26. *Ibid.*, pp. 57–58.

27. Miloš Jůzl, "Totalitarian Regimes in Czechoslovakia," *International Review of Aesthetics and Sociology of Music* 27, no. 1 (June 1996), pp. 46, 45.

28. *Ibid.*, p. 49.

29. *Ibid.*, p. 47.

30. *Ibid.*, p. 48.

31. Interview with Vladimír, Košice, May 24, 2010.

32. *Ibid.*

33. Interview with Beáta, Banská Bystrica, October 21, 2010.
34. *Ibid.*
35. Interview with Jan G., Bratislava, October 20, 2011.
36. *Ibid.*
37. *Ibid.*
38. *Ibid.*
39. *Ibid.*
40. *Ibid.*
41. *Ibid.*
42. Hanus Hájek, "Who Invited the Invaders?" (Open Society Archives, Radio Free Europe Research, 12/31/70), pp. 1–2.
43. *Ibid.*, p. 2. The Soviets, sensing widespread popular opposition to the invasion, immediately cancelled plans to install a collaborator government from the start.
44. *Ibid.*, p. 3.
45. *Ibid.*
46. Mary Heimann, *Czechoslovakia: The State That Failed* (New Haven: Yale University Press, 2010), Kindle, location 6255–6261.
47. *Ibid.*
48. *Ibid.*, p. 6.
49. Ladislav Nižňanský, "A Move to Destroy the Dubček Legend" (Radio Free Europe, 7/21/70), p. 1.
50. *Ibid.*, p. 4.
51. *Ibid.*, pp. 2–3.
52. *Ibid.*, p. 4.
53. *Ibid.*, p. 5.
54. Paulina Bren, *The Greengrocer and His TV* (Ithaca: Cornell University Press, 2010), pp. 64–67.
55. Kevin Devlin, "Exiles Look Back at Prague Spring 20 Years Later" (Open Society Archives, Radio Free Europe Research, 5/11/88), p. 1.
56. *Ibid.*, pp. 1–2.
57. *Ibid.*, p. 3.
58. Miroslav Vaněk, *Velvet Revolutions: An Oral History of Czech Society* (Oxford: Oxford University Press, 2016), p. 11.
59. Barbara Donovan, "The GDR Sides with Czechoslovakia in a Dispute Over Dubcek's Interview" (Open Society Archives, Radio Free Europe Research, 5/2/89), p. 1.
60. *Ibid.*

Chapter Eight

1. Jonathan Herzog, *The Hammer and the Cross: America's Holy War Against Communism*, Dissertation, Stanford University, 2008, 74–75.
2. *Ibid.*, 75.
3. Henry Black, "Religion and Communism—A Parallel," *Christian Century*, June 27, 1934, pp. 861–862.
4. *Ibid.*
5. Nicholas Berdyaev, "Russian Religious Psychology and Communistic Atheism," in Carl Schmitt, et al., eds., *Vital Realities* (New York: Macmillan, 1932), pp. 149–186.
6. Antonín Kratochvíl, "The History of the Abolition of Religious Orders in Czechoslovakia" (Open Society Archives, 9/4/85), pp. 1–2.
7. *Ibid.*
8. *Ibid.*
9. *Ibid.*, p. 4.
10. "Regime's Account of Religious Freedom in Czechoslovakia" (Radio Free Europe Research, Open Society Archives, 6/21/77), p. 1.
11. *Ibid.*
12. *Ibid.*, p. 2.
13. Pavol, interviewed in Bratislava, October 19, 2011.
14. Interview with David R., November 27, 2014, Bratislava.
15. Miroslav Vaněk, *Velvet Revolutions: An Oral History of Czech Society* (Oxford: Oxford University Press, 2016), p. 36, interview with Ž.M.
16. *Ibid.*
17. Interview with Rita R., February 7, 2011, Prešov.
18. Interview with Lívia., June 2, 2017, Brussels, Belgium.
19. *The Vigil,* special issue, 1992, p. 1, St. Michael's Garbandal Center for Our Lady of Carmel. Accessed March 9, 2015, http://www.garabandal.org/vigil/communism.shtml.
20. *Ibid.*
21. *Ibid.*
22. Interview with Rita R., February 7, 2010.
23. Ivana T., interviewed December 2014, online, from Iowa City, IA.

24. Interview with David R., November 27, 2014, Bratislava.

25. *Ibid.*

26. Interview with Martina, Bratislava, October 20, 2011.

27. Interview with Pavol, Bratislava, October 19, 2011.

28. *Ibid.*

29. *Ibid.*

30. Interview with Jaroslav, Bratislava, October 20, 2011.

31. Interview with Petr, Bratislava, October 19, 2011.

32. Interview with Jaroslav, October 20, 2011, Bratislava.

33. *Ibid.*

34. Dana Moree, *Učitelé na vlnách transformace. Kultura školy před rokem 1989 a po něm* (Prague: Karolinum, 2013), 78, in Vaněk, Miroslav, *Velvet Revolutions: An Oral History of Czech Society*, Oxford Oral History Series (Oxford: Oxford University Press, 2016), Kindle, p. 224. Miroslav Vaněk, *Velvet Revolutions: An Oral History of Czech Society* (Oxford: Oxford University Press, 2016), pp. 36–37.

35. Eagle Glassheim, "Most, the Town That Moved: Coal, Communists and the 'Gypsy Question' in Post-War Czechoslovakia," *Environment and History* 13, no. 4 (November 2007), p. 449.

36. *Ibid.*, pp. 455–465.

37. *Ibid.*, pp. 449–468.

38. Interview with Mirka, October 20, 2011, Banská Bystrica.

39. *Ibid.*

40. Interview with Jan C., January 23, 2012, Praha.

41. *Ibid.*

42. *Ibid.*

43. *Ibid.*

44. *Ibid.*

45. *Ibid.*

46. Interview with Mirka and Alica, Banská Bystrica, October 21, 2011.

47. *Ibid.*

48. *Ibid.*

49. James M. Markham, "Young People in East Europe Turn Increasingly to Church," Special to the *New York Times*, 23 January 1984: A1.

50. *Ibid.*

51. *Ibid.*

Chapter Nine

1. Sherrill Stroscheim, "Strategies for Roma and Hungarian Minorities in Central Europe," *Voluntas: International Journal of Voluntary and Nonprofit Organizations* 13, no. 1 (2002), p. 4.

2. Celia Donert, "The Struggle for the Soul of the Gypsies: Marginality and Mass Mobilization in Stalinist Czechoslovakia," *Social History* 33, no. 2 (March 2008), p. 126.

3. *Ibid.*, p. 4–5.

4. *Ibid.*, pp. 126–128.

5. Eagle Glassheim, "Ethnic Cleansing, Communism, and Environmental Devastation in Czechoslovakia's Borderlands, 1945–1989," *The Journal of Modern History* 78, no. 1 (March 2006), pp. 88–92.

6. František Ladislav Čelakovský, "*Cikánova píšťalka—Čítanky pro 7. ročník*," accessed in Vera Sokolová, *Racism, Gender and Social Deviance in the Politics of the "Gypsy Question" in Communist Czechoslovakia 1945–1989*, pp. 132–35.

7. Sokolová, "A Matter of Speaking," p. 136.

8. *Ibid.*, p. 137.

9. Interview with Peter D., March 14, 2015.

10. Sokolová, pp. 16, 128, 129, 132, 133.

11. *Ibid.*, pp. 133–136.

12. *Ibid.*, p. 124.

13. Sokolová, "A Matter of Speaking," pp. 90–95.

14. Celia Donert, "The Struggle for the Soul of the Gypsy," *Social History* 33, no. 2 (March 2008), pp. 123–124.

15. Otto Ulc, "Communist National Minority Policy: The Case of Gypsies in Czechoslovakia," *Soviet Studies* 20, no. 4 (April 1969), p. 423.

16. *Ibid.*, pp. 425–426.

17. Online interview with Peter D., March 14, 2015.

18. Ulc, "Communist National Minority Policy, pp. 423–427.

19. *Ibid.*, p. 426.

20. *Ibid.*, pp. 426–427.

21. *Ibid.*, p. 427.

22. Interview with Tomáš K., Prešov, 2010.

23. Ulc, "Communist National Minority Policy," p. 429.

24. *Ibid.*, p. 432.
25. *Ibid.*, p. 432.
26. *Ibid.*, pp. 433–434.
27. *Ibid.*, p. 139.
28. Glassheim, "Most, the Town that Moved," pp. 447–450.
29. *Ibid.*, p. 449.
30. *Ibid.*, 455, 465.
31. Milena Hübschmannová, *Šaj pes dovakeras*—Můžeme se domluvit, 88. 4. nezm. vyd. Olomouc: Univerzita Palackého, 2002.
32. *Ibid.*, pp. 89–93.
33. *Ibid.*, pp. 97–98.
34. Interview with Tomáš K., online, April 5, 2015.
35. *Ibid.*
36. *Ibid.*
37. Phone interview with Petra J., April 8, 2015, Aviano, Italy.
38. *Ibid.*
39. *Ibid.*
40. Interview with Lucia, May 12, 2017, Brussels, Belgium.
41. Interview with Jakub, May 12, 2017, Brussels, Belgium.
42. Interview with Lucia, May 12, 2017, Brussels, Belgium.
43. *Ibid.*
44. *Ibid.*
45. *Ibid.*
46. Sokolová, *Matter of Speaking*, pp. 247–252.
47. *Ibid.*, pp. 137, 138.
48. Vera Sokolová, "Planned Parenthood Behind the Curtain: Population Policy and Sterilization of Romani Women in Communist Czechoslovakia, 1972–1989," *The Anthropology of East Europe Review*, 2005, p. 1.
49. *Ibid.*, p. 2.
50. *Ibid.*, p. 4.
51. *Ibid.*, p. 5.
52. *Comments to the Fourth Periodic Report of the Slovak Republic on Performance of the Obligations Arising from the Convention on the Elimination of all forms of Violence Against Women*, June–July 2008, Centre for Civil and Human Rights, p. 3.
53. *Ibid.*, p. 4.
54. *Ibid.*
55. *Ibid.*
56. *Ibid.*
57. Sokolová, "Planned Parenthood Behind the Curtain," pp. 1–3.
58. *Ibid.*, p. 3.
59. *Ibid.*
60. *Ibid.*, p. 4.
61. *Ibid.* The Czechoslovak Civil Law, based on the 1960 Constitution, considered the family and the raising of children to be the "purpose of marriage."

Chapter Ten

1. Von Ivan Dramlitsch, "Generation Husák," *Prager Zeitung*, December 2, 2009, p. 1–23. Comments were from Marie Černáková, Director of the Institute of Sociology of the Czech Academy of Science.
2. *Ibid.*, p. 2.
3. Interview with Jakub, Brussels, Belgium, May 12, 2017.
4. *Ibid.*
5. *Ibid.*, p. 3. Such comments echo the sentiments of the economist mentioned in the chapter on the events of 1968, who suggested that the "deceits" of 1968 made the population smarter and less likely to be fooled by official state propaganda.
6. *Ibid.*, p. 4. Katka C. comments on the cultural subject of making more with less: In school cafeterias there were "these nasty fellow students [girls] who would control you with their eagle eyes if you [failed to] leave a plate empty."
7. Interview with Katka C., Bratislava, Slovakia, January 24, 2012.
8. *Ibid.*
9. *Ibid.*
10. Interview with Lucia, Brussels, Belgium, May 12, 2017.
11. Miroslav Vaněk, *Velvet Revolutions: An Oral History of Czech Society*, Oxford Oral History Series (Oxford: Oxford University Press, 2016), Kindle, pp. 40–41, interview with Jaroslav S.
12. Online interview with Beáta, March 15, 2015.
13. *Ibid.*
14. *Ibid.*
15. Interview with Lucia, May 12, 2017, Brussels, Belgium.
16. *Ibid.*
17. Interview with Lívia, June 2, 2017, Brussels, Belgium
18. Revan Schendler, "They Made Free-

dom for Themselves: Popular Interpretations of Post-Communist Discourse in the Czech Republic," *Oral History*, Autumn 2001, p. 79.

19. *Ibid.*, pp. 73–76.

20. *Ibid.*, p. 78.

21. Miroslav Vaněk, *Velvet Revolutions: An Oral History of Czech Society*, Oxford Oral History Series (Oxford: Oxford University Press, 2016), Kindle, p. 170, interview with Konrád N.

22. *Ibid.*

23. *Ibid.*

24. John Borneman, *Settling Accounts: Violence, Justice and Accountability in Post-Socialist Europe* (Princeton: Princeton University Press, 1997).

25. Schendler, "They Made the Freedom for Themselves," p. 80.

26. *Ibid.*, p. 81.

27. Maurice Halbwachs, *The Collective Memory* (New York: Harper & Row, 1980), 52.

28. Julia Friday, *Czechoslovakia from the Prague Spring to the Velvet Revolution: The Composition of Memory, Public Records and Archive*, Dissertation, State University of New York, Binghampton, 2010, pp. 14–30.

29. *Ibid.*

30. *Ibid.*, pp. 19–27.

31. Marianne Hirsch, *Family Frames: Photography, Narrative, and Post-Memory* (Cambridge: Harvard University Press, 1997), 22.

32. Friday, *Czechoslovakia from the Prague Spring*, pp. 123, 126.

33. Milan Kundera, *The Book of Laughing and Forgetting* (1979), accessed through Wikipedia, 3/4/13.

34. Interview with Mila, Brussels, Belgium, September 16, 2011.

35. Richard S. Esbenshade, "Remembering to Forget: Memory, History, National Identity in Postwar East-Central Europe," *Representations* 49, Special Issue: "Identifying Histories: Eastern Europe Before and After 1989" (Winter 1995), pp. 80–81.

36. *Ibid.*, p. 72.

37. Miroslav Vaněk, *Velvet Revolutions: An Oral History of Czech Society*, Oxford Oral History Series (Oxford: Oxford University Press, 2016), p. 7.

38. *Ibid.*, p. 34.

39. *Ibid.*

40. Interview with Juraj K., Prešov, Slovakia, November 30, 2014.

41. *Ibid.*

42. *Ibid.*

43. *Ibid.*

44. This term meant several things. It was an agricultural cooperative farm producing bumper crops; it often referred also to biochemical production and electronics. In fact it offered some of the first computers available in the country.

45. *Ibid.*

46. Online interview with Tomáš Kosiak, April 4, 2015.

47. *Ibid.*

48. *Ibid.*

49. Online interview with Tomáš K, April 4, 2015.

50. Online interview with Petra, April 4, 2015.

51. *Ibid.*

52. Pat Lyons and Alžběta Bernardyová, "Satisfied, Sceptical or Simply Indifferent? Current Public Opinions towards the fall of Communism in the Czech Republic," *Europe-Asia Studies* 63, no. 9 (November 2011), pp. 1719–21.

53. *Ibid.*, pp. 1724–25.

54. *Ibid.*, p. 1737.

55. Haldis Haukanes, "Telling Lives: Autobiography and History After Socialism," *The Anthropology of East Europe Review* 23, no. 1 (2005), pp. 160–161.

56. *Ibid.*, pp. 162–163.

57. *Ibid.*, pp. 165–166. However, respondents were certainly influenced by communist renderings of history, which tended to be both formal and formulaic, stressing the Marxist faith in the emergence of a new future from a deterministic historical process.

58. *Ibid.*, pp. 160–166.

59. Revan Schendler, "Spinning Yarns," *Columbia University* 29, Winter 1997-98, pp. 46, 56.

60. Interview with Jakub, Brussels, Belgium, May 12, 2017.

Conclusion

1. Interview with Juraj, in Prešov, November 2014.

2. Interview with Lucia, Brussels, Belgium, May 12, 2017.

3. Jan Richter, Český rozhlas 7-Radio Praha Broadcast, "Twenty-Six Years After Velvet Revolution, Czech Communists Say History's Still in Their Favor," 11/17/15, p. 1–3.

4. *Ibid.*, p. 2.

5. *Ibid.*

Bibliography

Adams, Bradley. *The Struggle for the Soul of the Nation*. Lanham, MD: Rowman & Littlefield, 2004.

Baldwin, Hanson W. "The Road to Total War." *New York Times*, September 13, 1953.

Barrow, Greg. "South Africans Reconciled?" BBC News, Friday, October 30, 1998.

Berdyaev, Nicholas. "*Russian Religious Psychology and Communistic Atheism*," in Carl Schmitt, et al., eds., *Vital Realities*. New York: Macmillan, 1932.

Bischoff, Peter. "Lemonadovy Joe; or, the Western in Czechoslovakia." *Journal of Popular Culture* 27, no. 1 (1993).

Black, Henry. "Religion and Communism—A Parallel." *Christian Century*, June 27, 1934.

Borneman, John. *Settling Accounts: Violence, Justice and Accountability in Post-Socialist Europe*. Princeton: Princeton University Press, 1997.

Bren, Paulina. *Closely Watched Screens: Ideology and Everyday Life in Czechoslovakia After the Prague Spring*. Dissertation, New York University, 2002.

_____. *The Greengrocer and His TV: The Culture of Communism After the 1968 Prague Spring*. Ithaca: Cornell University Press, 2010.

_____, and Mary Neuburger. *Communism Uwrapped*. Oxford: Oxford University Press, 2012.

Brooke, Michael. Video Recording Review. *Sight and Sound* 16 (June 2006).

Byrne, Richard. "Understanding the Gap Between Eastern and Western Europe." *The Chronicle of Higher Education* 50, no. 5 (2003).

Čelakovský, František Ladislav. "Cikanovka Pistalku in Citak Pro 7," in Vera Sokolova, *Racism, Gender and Social Deviance in the Politics of the "Gypsy Question" in Communist Czechoslovakia 1945–1989*. Dissertation, University of Washington, 2002.

Chomsky, Noam. *Understanding Power: The Indispensable Chomsky*. New York: New Press, 2001.

Comments to the Fourth Periodic Report of the Slovak Republic on Performance of the Obligations Arising from the Convention on the Elimination of all forms of Violence Against Women. June–July 2008, Centre for Civil and Human Rights.

Condon, Richard. *The Manchurian Candidate*. New York: Pocketstar, 2003.

Connelly, John. *Captive University: The Sovietization of East German, Czech and Polish Education, 1945–1956*. Chapel Hill: University of North Carolina Press, 2000.

"The Czechoslovak Labor Code." Open Society Archives, Radio Free Europe Research, Country Series, 10/15/65.

Darden, Keith, and Anna Grzymała-Busse.

"The Great Divide: Literacy, Nationalism and the Communist Collapse." *World Politics* 59 (2006).

Devlin, Kevin. "Exiles Look Back at Prague Spring 20 Years Later." Open Society Archives, Radio Free Europe Research, 5/11/88.

Dittner, Lowell. "Political Culture and Political Symbolism: Towards a Theoretical Synthesis." *World Politics* 29, no. 4 (July 1977).

Donert, Cecilia. "The Struggle for the Soul of the Gypsies: Marginality and Mass Mobilization in Stalinist Czechoslovakia." *Social History* 33, no. 2 (March 2008).

Donovan, Barbara. "The GDR Sides with Czechoslovakia in a Dispute Over Dubcek's Interview." Open Society Archives, Radio Free Europe Research, 5/2/89.

Drakulić, Slavenka. *Café Europa: Life After Communism.* New York: Penguin. 1996.

_____. *How We Survived Communism and Even Laughed.* New York: W.W. Norton, 1991.

Dramlitsch, Von Ivan. "Generation Husák." *Prager Zeitung,* December 2, 2009.

Dunne, Matthew. *A Cold War State of Mind: Cultural Conditionings of Brainwashing in the 1950s.* Dissertation, Brown University, 2008.

Eidlin, Fred H. "Capitulation, Resistance and the Framework of Normalization: The August 1968 Invasion of Czechoslovakia and the Czechoslovak Response." *Journal of Peace Research* 18, no. 4 (1981).

Esbenshade, Richard S. "Remembering to Forget: Memory, History, National Identity in Postwar East-Central Europe." *Representations* 49, Special Issue: "Identifying Histories: Eastern Europe Before and After 1989" (Winter 1995).

Eyal, Gil. "Identity and Trauma: Two Forms of the Will to Memory." *History and Memory* 16, no. 1 (2004).

Forman, Milos. Interview with Milos Forman. January 18, 1997, Episode 14, *Red Spring,* Alexander Street Press, alexanderstreet.com, 2009.

Friday, Julia. *Czechoslovakia from the Prague Spring to the Velvet Revolution: The Composition of Memory, Public Records and Archive.* Dissertation, SUNY-Binghampton, 2010.

Frost, Matthew. "Czech Republic: A Chronology of Events Leading to the 1968 Invasion." Radio Free Europe, Radio Liberty, 8/9/98. Accessed 2/27/11, http://www.rferl.org/ content/article/1089303.html.

Gitelman, Zvi. "The Politics of Socialist Restoration in Hungary and Czechoslovakia." *Comparative Politics* 13, no. 2 (1981).

Glassheim, Eagle. "Ethnic Cleansing, Communism and Environmental Devastation in Czechoslovakia's Borderlands, 1945–1989." *Journal of Modern History* 78, no. 1 (March 2006).

_____. "Most, the Town That Moved: Coal, Communists and the 'Gypsy Question' in Post-War Czechoslovakia." *Environment and History* 13, no. 4 (November 2007).

Gömöri, George. "The Satellites in Eastern Europe." *Annals of the American Academy of Political and Social Science* 317 (May 1958).

Hájek, Hanus. "Who Invited the Invaders?" Open Society Archives, Radio Free Europe Research, 12/31/70.

Halbwachs, Maurice. *The Collective Memory.* New York: Harper & Row, 1980.

Hames, Peter. "Down from the Mountain." Interview with Juraj Jakubisko. *Sight and Sound* 14, no. 3 (March 2004).

Haukanes, Haldis. "Telling Lives: Autobiography and History after Socialism." *The Anthropology of East Europe Review* 23, no. 1 (2005).

Harris, Melissa. "Invasion 68: Prague by Joseph Koudelka." Interview with Melissa Harris. *Aperture* (Fall 2008).

Haynes, John Earl. "The Cold War Debate Continues: A Traditional View of Historical Writings on Domestic Communism and Anti-Communism." *Journal of Cold War Studies* 2, no. 1 (2000).

Heimann, Mary. *Czechoslovakia: The State That Failed.* New Haven: Yale University Press, 2009.

Hensel, Jana. *After the Wall.* New York: Public Affairs Press, 2004.

Herman, Edward S. *The Banality of Evil.* Accessed 4/02, http://www.informationclearinghouse.info/article7278.htm.

Herzog, Jonathan. *The Hammer and the Cross: America's Holy War Against Com-*

munism. Dissertation, Stanford University, 2008.

Hirsch, Marianne. *Family Frames: Photography, Narrative and Post-Memory.* Cambridge: Harvard University Press, 1997.

History Resources Center. "Soviet Troops Withdraw from Czechoslovakia February 26, 1990." http://galenet.galegroup.comezproxy.umuc.edu/servlet/History/hits?r=d&origSearch=fa.

Hoffman, David L. "Was There a Great Retreat from Soviet Socialism?" *Kritika: Explorations in Russian and European History* 5, no. 4 (Fall 2004).

Horvath, Jan. Milena Hubschmannová, *Saj Pes dovakeras.*

Hraba, Joseph, Rehan Mullick, Frederick O. Lorenz, Jiří Večerník, and Allan McCutcheon. "Education and the Support for the Czech Reforms." *Sociology of Education* 75, no. 2 (2002).

Hunter, Edward. *Brainwashing in Red China.* New York: Vanguard Press, 1951.

"Implementation of Czechoslovak Economic Reforms." Open Society Archives, Radio Free Europe Research, 11/11/65).

Institute of Marxism–Leninism of the CPCz and Institute of Marxism–Leninism of the CPS CC. *An Outline of the History of the CPCz.* Prague: Orbis Press Agency, 1985.

Johnston, Sheila. "Interview with Jiri Menzel." *Sight and Sound* 18, no. 6 (June 2008).

Jůzl, Miloš. "Totalitarian Regimes in Czechoslovakia." *International Review of Aesthetics and Sociology of Music* 27, no. 1 (June 1996).

Kanerová -Kastle, Mita, and Alena Valterová. "Interview with Elena Valterova, Founder of the Women and Mothers Party." *Feminist Review* 39 (Autumn 1991).

Kaufman, Michael T. "Good Times Help Czechs Subdue Traumas of '68." Special to the *New York Times,* February 10, 1986.

Kautt, William H. "Communism After WWII." *History in Dispute.* http://galenet.galegroup.comeproxy.umuc.edu.

Kenney, Padraic. *A Carnival of Revolution: Central Europe 1989.* Princeton: Princeton University Press, 2003.

Kohn, Jerome. *Totalitarianism: The Inversion of Politics.* Hannah Arendt Center, New School University. http://www.memory.loc.gov/ammem/arendthtml/essayb5.html.

Kolár, H.P. "The Problem of 'Academic Mortality' in Czechoslovakia's Universities." Radio Free Europe Evaluation and Analysis Department, 12/21/60.

_____. "Some Problems Confronting Czechoslovakia's Youth." Radio Free Europe Evaluation and Analysis Department, Czechoslovak Unit, 1960.

Kovaly, Heda M. *Under a Cruel Star: Life in Prague 1941–68.* New York: Holmes and Meier, 1986.

Kramer, John M. "Drug Abuse in Eastern Europe: An Emerging Issue of Public Policy." *Slavic Review* 49, no. 1 (Spring 1990).

Krapfl, James. *Revolution with a Human Face.* Ithaca: Cornell University Press, 2013.

Kratochvil, Antonín. "The Cultural Scene in Czechoslovakia." Open Society Archives, Radio Free Europe Research, 2/3/70.

_____. "The History of the Abolition of Religious Orders in Czechoslovakia." Open Society Archives, Radio Free Europe Research, 4/85.

Kreidl, Martin. "Politics and Secondary School Tracking in Socialist Czechoslovakia 1948–1989." *European Sociological Review* 20, no. 21 (April 2004).

Kubát, Daniel. "Social Mobility in Czechoslovakia." *American Sociological Review* 28, no. 2 (April 1963).

Kubka, Jiří. "*Americký brouk.*" *Lidové noviny* 58, no. 161 (July 12, 1950).

Kundera, Milan. *The Book of Laughing and Forgetting.* New York: Harper Perennial Modern Classics, 1999.

Kusín, Vladimír V. "The Seven Wonders for Communism." Radio Free Europe Background Report, 12/12/85.

Land, Thomas. "Coping with Communism's Grim Legacy of High Rise Buildings." *Contemporary Review* (June 2002).

Laski, Harold. *Communism.* New York. Henry Holt, 1927.

Loss, Andrew. "The King of May: A Conversation Between Allen Ginsburg and Andrew Lass, March 23, 1986." *Massachusetts Review* 39, no. 2 (Summer 1998).

Loss, Christopher P. "Party School: Education and Political Ideology and the Cold War." *Journal of Political History* 16, no. 1 (2004).

Lynd, Staughton. "Oral History from Below." *Oral History Review* 21, no. 1 (Spring 1993).

Lyons, Pat. *Mass and Elite Attitudes During the Prague Spring Era: Importance and Legacy*. Prague: Institute of Sociology AV CR, 2009. Reviewed in *Sociologický časopis/Czech Sociological Review* 47, no. 6 (2011).

_____, and Bernardyová, Alžběta. "Satisfied, Sceptical or Simply Indifferent? Current Public Opinions Toward the Fall of Communism in the Czech Republic." *Europe-Asia Studies* 63, no. 9 (November 2011).

Macura, Vladimir. *The Mystifications of a Nation*. Madison: University of Wisconsin Press, 2010.

Markham, James M. "Young People in East Europe Turn Increasingly to Church." Special to the *New York Times*, January 23, 1984.

McDermott, Kevin. *Communist Czechoslovakia, 1945–89: A Political and Social History*. Basingstoke: Palgrave Macmillan, 2015.

Moree, Dana. *Učitelé na vlnách transformace. Kultura školy před rokem 1989 a po něm*. Prague: Karolinum, 2013.

Mueller, John. "What Was the Cold War About? Evidence from Its Ending." *Political Science Quarterly* (Winter 2004).

"The New Czech Dramatic Avant-Garde." Open Society Archives, Radio Free Europe Research, 2/17/65. Nižňanský, Ladislav. "A Move to Destroy the Dubček Legend." Radio Free Europe, 7/21/70.

Pool, Ithiel de Sola. "Public Opinion in Czechoslovakia." *The Public Opinion Quarterly* 31, no. 1 (Spring 1970).

Porton, Richard. "Porn Again: The People vs. Larry Flynt: An Interview with Milos Forman on Censorship and His Years in Stalinist Czechoslovakia." *Cineaste* 12, no. 4 (March 1997).

"The Problem of Excess Purchasing Power in Czechoslovakia." Open Society Archives, Radio Free Europe Research, 8/3/65.

Ramet, Sabrina. "UFOs Over Russia and Eastern Europe." *Journal of Popular Culture* 32, no. 3 (1998).

"Regime's Account of Religious Freedom in Czechoslovakia." Radio Free Europe Research, Open Society Archives, 6/21/77.

"Return to Economic 'Normalcy' in Czechoslovakia." Open Society Archives, Radio Free Europe Research, 6/22/70.

Richter, Jan. Český rozhlas 7-Radio Praha Broadcast, "Twenty-Six Years After Velvet Revolution, Czech Communists Say History's Still in Their Favor." 11/17/15.

Rogin, Michael. "Kiss Me Deadly: Communism, Motherhood and Cold War Movies." *Representations* 6 (Spring 1984).

Schendler, Revan. "Spinning Yarns." *Columbia: A Journal of Literature and Art* 29 (Winter 1997-1998).

_____. "They Made Freedom for Themselves: Popular Interpretations of Post-Communist Discourse in the Czech Republic." *Oral History* (Autumn 2001).

Selverstone, Marc Jay. *All Roads Lead to Moscow. The United States, Great Britain, and the Communist Monolith*. Dissertation, Ohio University, 2000.

Shaw, Tony. "The Politics of Cold War Culture." *Journal of Cold War Studies* 3, no. 3 (2001).

Sokolová, Vera. *A Matter of Speaking: Racism, Gender and Social Deviance in the Politics of the Gypsy Question: Czechoslovakia*. Dissertation, University of Washington, 2002.

_____. "Planned Parenthood Behind the Curtain: Population Policy and Sterilization of Romani Women in Communist Czechoslovakia, 1972–1989." *The Anthropology of East Europe Review* (2005).

Spiritus-Temporis. "The Cold War Historiography." http://www.spiritus-temporis.com/ cold-war/historiography.html.

Stroscheim, Sherrill. "Strategies for Roma and Hungarian Minorities in Central Europe." *Voluntas: International Journal of Voluntary and Nonprofit Organizations* 13, no. 1 (2002).

Szostkiewicz, Adam. "Religion After Communism." *Commonweal* 126, no. 16 (September 24, 1999).

Ulc, Otto. "Communist National Minority Policy: The Case of Gypsies in Czechoslovakia." *Soviet Studies* 20, no. 4 (May 1969).

Vaněk, Miroslav. *Velvet Revolutions: An Oral History of Czech Society*. Oxford: Oxford University Press, 2016.

Vigil. Special issue, 1992, St. Michael's Garbandal Center for Our Lady of Carmel.

Walaszek, Zdzislawa. "Religion and the State: The Struggle for Legitimacy and Power." *Annals of the American Academy of Political and Social Science* 483 (January 1986).

Winter, S.A. "The Sovietization of Czechoslovakia: 1968–1983." Open Society Archives, Radio Free Europe Research, 8/16/83.

Zeiss, Laura McKenzie. *Cold War Fictions of Behaviorism: Theories of Psychological Influence in American Cold War Literature.* Dissertation. University of California-Irvine, 2008.

Zivotni Prostredi, # 6, November–December 1982.

Index